Primary teaching skills

Primary teachers have always been required to master a wealth of knowledge and professional skills, and recent debate has lead to pressure for ever higher levels of competence. *Primary Teaching Skills* reports on the findings of the three-year Leverhulme Primary Project, one of the largest studies of teaching skills ever undertaken in English primary shcools. Ted Wragg reports this research and provides a comprehensive guide to many of the skills needed by today's primary teachers. Separate chapters cover such central aspects of the job as explaining new topics, asking stimulating questions and settling down with a new class, as well as the more general demands of class management and subject knowledge; and one chapter is devoted to the particular problems of supply teachers. This is a book that will enlighten and inform experienced and novice teachers, advisers and inspectors, researchers and anyone interested in the workings of the primary classroom.

E.C. Wragg is Director of the School of Education at the University of Exeter and Co-director (with Neville Bennett) of the Leverhulme Primary Project. His publications include *Classroom Teaching Skills* (Routledge 1989) and three workbooks for the Leverhulme Primary Project *Classroom Skills* series: *Class Management, Explaining* and *Questioning* (Routledge 1993).

Primary teaching skills

E. C. Wragg

London and New York

First published 1993
by Routledge
11 New Fetter Lane, London EC4P 4EE

Simultaneously published in the USA and Canada
by Routledge
29 West 35th Street, New York, NY 10001

© 1993 E. C. Wragg

Typeset in Linotron Times by
Ponting–Green Publishing Services, Chesham, Bucks

Printed and bound in Great Britain by
Biddles Ltd, Guildford and Kings Lynn

British Library cataloguing in publication data

A catalogue record for this book is available from the British Library.

ISBN 0–415–08351–6
ISBN 0–415–08352–4 (pbk)

Library of Congress cataloging in publication data has been applied for

ISBN 0–415–08351–6
ISBN 0–415–08352–4 (pbk)

Contents

Figures

Tables

Preface

This book describes some of the research undertaken during the Leverhulme Primary Project, a three-year research and development project funded by the Leverhulme Trust. There were two strands to the research, and this book describes the studies of class management and related matters which I directed. The findings of the other strand of the project, directed by my colleague, Neville Bennett, are described in the companion book to this one, *Learning to Teach* (Bennett and Carré, 1993).

During the project we observed over a thousand lessons, conducted more than a thousand interviews with teachers, students and pupils, gave tests to over a thousand pupils and teachers, and analysed over two thousand questionnaire responses. A variety of research procedures was used, and these are described in the text. Much as I should like to have included all the observation schedules, test papers, interview pro-formas and questionnaires in appendices, this would have added well over fifty pages to the book, and publishing economics rule it out, so the instruments are described in the text instead.

There have been several significant studies of primary classrooms, including those by Bennett (1976) and the ORACLE Project (Galton *et al.* 1980). It is to be hoped that the Leverhulme Primary Project will add to our knowledge of classroom processes in the primary school. The chapters in this book describe some of the empirical work undertaken in what became one of the largest studies of teaching skill ever undertaken in English primary schools. Even so, I am only able to scratch the surface of the vast and complex matter of studying and nurturing skilful teaching, and much remains to be done.

E.C.W.

Acknowledgements

In a complex research and development project like the Leverhulme Primary Project each member of the team is dependent on the others. I should like to thank in particular my co-director, Neville Bennett, and the project co-ordinator Clive Carré; the principal research assistants in this part of the project, Allyson Trotter, Caroline Wragg, Barbara Janssen, Sarah Crowhurst and Jill Christie; Tricia Bisley and Jo Small, who typed the manuscript; the numerous part-time research assistants who observed lessons, interviewed teachers, scored tests, or analysed transcripts; and the numerous teachers and heads of primary schools who allowed us to observe their lessons. I should also like to express my gratitude to the Leverhulme Trust for their support of the project.

E.C.W.

Chapter 1

Skilful teaching

The need for skilful teaching

Primary teachers have always needed a wide range of subject knowledge and a large repertoire of professional skills. Teaching young children to read and write, to understand the world around them, to grasp and be able to apply fundamental mathematical and scientific principles, to use their developing intelligence and imagination, to live and work harmoniously with others, all these require that an effective teacher should possess knowledge and understanding of the content of the subjects and topics being taught, as well as the ability to manage a class, explain clearly, ask intelligent and appropriate questions, and monitor and assess learning.

There are many factors which have combined, during the last few years of the twentieth century, to demand from teachers even higher levels of professional competence. They include the rapid growth in the acquisition of knowledge, the changing nature not only of adult employment, but also of recreation and leisure, the increased public pressure for accountability, the development of new forms of educational and information technology, and the broadening role of the primary teacher. Any single one of these individual issues would require a radical review of the teacher's professional role, and of the nature of professional competence required to accommodate change and improve practice. In combination they represent an overwhelming pressure for improvement by all practitioners, even the many who already manifest a high degree of skill in the classroom.

In the nineteenth century teacher training institutions were known as 'normal schools', on the grounds that there was some single 'norm' endorsed by society. The function of a training establishment was to perpetuate this stereotype, and a 'Master of Method' was employed in the model school to ensure that each new generation of teachers was poured into the same approved mould (Rich 1933). Today the factors mentioned above combine to require levels of skill, understanding, imagination, and resilience from teachers which go infinitely beyond the rudimentary common sense and mechanical competence fostered by the normal schools of the last century.

The massive explosion of knowledge gathering during the last fifty years has produced banks of data in such profusion that no human being is now capable of grasping more than the tiniest fraction of their contents. There are examples of computer-stored research data, such as the Lockheed Dialog system, which contain research reports in hundreds of fields, and the largest files in subjects like chemistry and biology can disgorge millions of abstracts.

It is not only in the pure and applied sciences that knowledge has burgeoned, but also in several other areas of human endeavour, including the humanities, with thousands of new books and articles in many fields being published each year. In addition to this formidable advance in the discovery of new information there has been a considerable development of new skills. Transplant and bypass surgery, for example, unknown only a few years ago, have become a standard part of many surgeons' professional armoury.

The implications for teachers of this knowledge explosion are clear. If you cannot know everything, you must know something. Hence the many efforts made either at regional or national level to determine the *content* of education – what children of a particular age or level of ability ought to learn, or by teachers themselves at local level to shape and implement a coherent curriculum. Secondly, if you cannot know or learn everything, you must be able to find out for yourself, and this is why the *process* of learning has become important, as well as, though not instead of, the content. Thirdly, since their pupils can acquire only a tiny fraction of the knowledge and skills currently available to humanity, teachers must develop teaching strategies which not only transmit information, but also encourage children to learn independently and as a member of a group. Although no committee would ever have composed Beethoven's Fifth Symphony, it is also unlikely that any individual could have sent a rocket to the moon. A great deal of human achievement will in future be the result of *teamwork*.

Alongside the demands placed on teachers by the expansion of knowledge and skills are those caused by the significant social changes in recent years which are taking place on a scale unparalleled in any period other than wartime. During the 1970s one million jobs disappeared from manufacturing industry in Britain, and millions more were obliterated during the following two decades. Most were unskilled and semi-skilled forms of employment which will probably never return.

Faced with youth unemployment on a large scale, many teachers, especially in inner-city schools, found during the 1980s and 1990s that traditional forms of motivation, such as urging pupils to work hard at school so that they would obtain a good job, no longer had the appeal they once enjoyed. Disaffection over the apparent futility of learning can even be experienced by quite young primary pupils. It offers another formidable challenge to the professional ingenuity of the teacher.

Employers, meanwhile, able to erect artificial barriers when applicants for jobs vastly exceed the actual vacancies, may require high GCSE grades for posts previously taken by the less well qualified, A levels where GCSE was once sufficient, and a degree in what was formerly a non-graduate profession. This spiralling demand for qualifications puts yet more pressure on teachers to use their skills effectively during the compulsory years of schooling, especially in the early years when firm foundations should be laid. In our increasingly technological and bureaucratic society those who leave school under-educated, for whatever reason, are at risk, likely to be unemployed, or fall victim to loan sharks and the other predators in society.

The more optimistic scenario, that labour will shift out of the factory and into the leisure industry, that people will have more free time in future and be relieved of the tedium of monotonous jobs, that early retirement will give a boost to community and lifelong education, is no less demanding on teachers' skills. To enjoy leisure, adults must have learned how to use it fruitfully. Citizens in the twenty-first century are more likely to be willing to learn throughout their lives if they have been fired and enthused, rather than rebuffed and demoralised, in school. The quality of personal relationships between teacher and taught, therefore, is a direct result of the interpersonal skill of the teacher, who usually sets the tone in a class, or has to take the initiative to improve relationships should they go awry. A notion of teaching skill that embraced only the transmission of knowledge would be a poor one in such a context.

Furthermore in the twenty-first century many people will work in service industries, and others will run small businesses. This shift out of the factory and into closer contact with people, rather than machinery, requires a high degree of imagination, inventiveness, drive and interpersonal skills. Again a sound basis for those qualities can be established in good primary schools, and teachers who nurture them should be greatly valued.

Public pressure for accountability has increased throughout the 1980s and 1990s, and it is an international phenomenon. Uncertainty over employment, scarcity of resources and demands for proper scrutiny of any enterprise receiving funding, public or private, have combined to provide a widespread call for a high degree of competence in the teaching profession, with particular focus on the primary phase, from parents, politicians, and the press. This has been mirrored in Britain in the various Acts of Parliament which have introduced requirements on schools to publish information about themselves, carry out the appraisal of teachers and heads, teach a national curriculum, and apply national tests to children aged 7 and 11, the scores from which can then be published and compared with those of other schools. This is not the place to go into the pros and cons of the measures taken by British governments during the 1980s and 1990s, as I have done that elsewhere (Wragg 1988, 1990, 1991). It is cited here as an example of a further external pressure on schools for highly skilled teaching.

The development of new technology such as the micro-computer, forms of teletext, the interactive video disc, direct broadcasting by satellite and cable television offer a further challenge to primary teachers. One important feature of some of the more recent forms of technological development is that the micro-computer and the interactive video disc in particular, offer an interactive facility on a scale not previously available, changing the position of the teacher as the single authoritative initiator of, or respondent to, enquiry. In 1985 and 1986 the BBC Domesday Project involved 14,000 schools using modern technology to survey the whole of the United Kingdom, in celebration of the 900th anniversary of the original Domesday book. Pupils who took part were mainly aged 9 to 13, and two significant interactive video discs were produced as a result.

Such developments test the flexibility and adaptability of teachers, who need to be able to modify their teaching styles to accommodate some at least of the many new developments which have a potential to improve learning. Indeed, broadcasting technology itself has made teachers more vulnerable than ever before. The teacher attempting to teach the topic 'Insects' to a primary class fifty years ago would not have been compared with anyone other than another teacher. Today she will be compared with the finest television presenters in the world, whose programmes on insects enjoy multi-million-pound budgets and access to the very best of wildlife film available.

Even if primary teachers were able to concentrate entirely on their classroom role as transmitters of knowledge, skills and values to the next generation, the assignment would be a formidable one. However, the role of the teacher has broadened during the last decades of the century. The real or imagined ills of society are often attributed, rightly or wrongly, to schooling. Teachers can find themselves playing many roles, such as social worker (dealing with children whose families experience economic and social deprivation), jailer (coping with children reluctant to come to school), administrator (handling the increasing bureaucracy surrounding curriculum and assessment), public relations officer (meeting parents, members of the community, dealing with local meetings), and numerous others. Teaching is certainly not a job for the faint-hearted.

In many countries changes in birth rates have led to concomitant changes in school size and in the age distribution of the teaching profession. The roller-coaster graph of annual birth cohorts is followed by a related graph of teacher recruitment. In Britain and other industrialised countries like Germany, the birth rate fell dramatically for over a decade and then rose again. A British peak of nearly a million births in 1964 was followed by a thirteen-year decline of a third. The consequence of this was that primary school populations fell by over a quarter during the first few years of the 1980s, leading to numerous primary school closures and mergers.

A rapid expansion in the recruitment of teachers during the 1960s and early 1970s was followed by a decline in the 1980s, when many primary trained teachers failed to find a job at all until the later years of the decade as schools expanded once again. By 1990 three out of every five primary teachers were aged over 40, leading to reduced promotion prospects and falling morale. On the positive side, there was a great deal of professional experience available, which certainly helped considerably when the national curriculum was introduced in 1989. The negative aspect, however, is that after years of repeats of favoured teaching strategies, it is not always easy to make changes when they become necessary.

One way to reduce, if not avoid, falling morale when promotion prospects are less in evidence than they were formerly is for teachers to take pride in honing their professional skills, and a number of in-service courses, especially certain school-based ones, have attempted to facilitate professional development and self-appraisal for experienced teachers. This theme will be taken up again in chapter 12.

It was not possible in the Leverhulme Primary Project at Exeter University to investigate and analyse all the vast complexity of skills mentioned above as necessary for teaching the present and future generations of young children. It was decided, therefore, in the strand of the project which I directed, to concentrate in particular on class management, but also to investigate such key skills as explaining and questioning, as well as teachers' subject knowledge and the strategies teachers employ when they are on new or unfamiliar ground. The matters of subject knowledge and student teachers are also taken up in more detail in the other major strand of the Leverhulme Primary Project, directed by Professor Neville Bennett, and reported in the companion volume to this one, *Learning to Teach* (Bennett and Carré 1993).

Identifying and defining teaching skills

The Leverhulme Primary Project took place at Exeter University during a period from the 1988 Education Act to the General Election of 1992 when debates about educational standards were commonplace and sometimes acrimonious. For the reasons cited earlier in this chapter there is understandable concern that the levels of attainment of children should rise to help them meet the increasing demands of life in the late twentieth and early twenty-first centuries. Even if the quality of teaching improves, it may not improve far or fast enough to match the escalating demands on teachers.

Unfortunately the accompanying debate about teaching competence has too often been oversimplified and caricatured as 'traditional' versus 'progressive', 'formal' versus 'informal', 'phonics' versus 'real books', when the reality of classroom life is that many teachers prefer to use a mixture of methods rather than fill out a single stereotype. The Leverhulme Primary Project was based on the premise that all teachers have to manage a class of children, however differently conceived their styles of class management may be, and that such professional communication skills as questioning and explaining are witnessed in every primary classroom.

There was, therefore, no conscious favouring of any single style of teaching. Individual researchers do, of course, have personal preferences and prejudices like other people, but wherever possible we tried to push these to the periphery and concentrate on interpretations of what we saw and then both report these as research findings as well as develop teaching materials and ideas, an empirical approach in the main. Our intention, however, was that teachers should be able to read, in the books on research findings, about what we had discovered, and that, in the accompanying workbooks on professional skills, such as *Class Management* (Wragg 1993), *Questioning* (Brown and Wragg 1993) and *Explaining* (Wragg and Brown 1993), trainee and experienced teachers would be encouraged to analyse and determine their own teaching strategies, rather than merely copy someone else's preferences. In the various strands of the project we observed over a thousand lessons, conducted more than a thousand interviews with teachers, students and pupils, gave tests to over a thousand teachers and pupils, and analysed over two thousand questionnaire responses. Some of the samples were carefully selected national ones with balanced numbers of teachers from large and small, urban and rural, northern and southern schools, others were more rough-and-ready, opportunity samples of teachers willing to be observed, or agreeable to being interviewed at length.

There is less dissent about what constitutes effective teaching in dis-cussion between people outside the profession than there is in the research and evaluation literature. Good teachers, it is commonly held, are keen and enthusiastic, well organised, firm but fair, stimulating, know their stuff, and are interested in the welfare of their pupils. Few would attempt to defend the converse: that good teachers are unenthusiastic, boring, unfair, ignorant, and do not care about their pupils.

Once the scrutiny of teaching is translated into the more precise terms demanded by the tenets of rigorous systematic enquiry, the easy agreement of casual conversation evaporates. Biddle and Ellena (1964), reporting the Kansas City role studies, found that there was not even clear agreement amongst teachers, parents and administrators about the role teachers should play.

In the 1970s and 1980s some of the attempts to see consensus in the research literature were criticised. For example, Gage (1978), summarising research studies which had attempted to relate teaching style to children's learning, concluded that in the early years of schooling certain kinds of teacher behaviour did show some consistent relationship to children learning reading and arithmetic. From this he derived a set of prescriptive 'Teacher should' statements like 'Teachers should call on a child by name before asking the question,' 'Teachers should keep to a minimum such activities as giving directions and organising the class for instruction' or 'During reading-group instruction, teachers should give a maximal amount of brief feedback and provide fast-paced activities of the "drill" type'.

Among the criticism of prescriptions based on summaries of recent findings is the proposition that much American work in particular is based on short-term tests of memory; that formal didactic styles of teaching often show up better on short-term measures and could, therefore, easily be perpetuated; that the 'gains' of method A compared with method B are often slight. This last argument is skilfully countered by Gage (1985) in his book *Hard Gains in the Soft Sciences*. He shows how significant policy decisions, in fields such as medicine and public health, are often made on a degree of statistical 'superiority' that would receive little attention in educational research. He quotes examples of trials of beta blockers and low-cholesterol diets to reduce the incidence of heart attacks, which showed only 2.5 and 1.7 per cent differences respectively between experimental and control groups' mortality rates, but which nonetheless led to significant changes in public health policy and practice.

Doyle (1978) observed that reviewers of research into teacher effectiveness 'have concluded, with remarkable regularity, that few consistent relationships between teacher variables and effectiveness can be established'. Even reviewers of the same studies have sometimes reached different conclusions about them (Giaconia and Hedges 1985). Some investigations have used meta-analysis (Glass 1978) to aggregate studies and identify trends and effects, but the conclusions are often mixed, and sometimes, especially when pioneers of some new approach conduct research into their own practice, a noticeable Hawthorne Effect occurs. That Kulik *et al.* (1979) found consistently higher learning gains in classes using the Keller Plan (a form of teaching which involves pupils completing individual assignments) compared with control groups is not an argument for saying that all teachers should copy the approach. Teachers often aspire to achieve a mixture of shorter-term (complete a worksheet, learn a principle) and longer-term (develop a sustained interest in music, lead a healthy lifestyle) objectives.

The difficulty of identifying and evaluating teaching skills and their effectiveness is neatly illustrated by an interesting experiment at the University of Michigan. Guetzkow *et al.* (1954) divided first-year students on a general psychology course into three groups. The first group was given a formal lecture course with regular tests, the second and third groups took part in tutorials and discussions. At the end of the course the lecture group not only outperformed the tutorial discussion groups on the final examination, but was also more favourably rated by the students. So far this represents a victory for lecturing and testing on two commonly used criteria: test performance and student appraisal.

The investigators discovered, however, that the students in the discussion groups scored significantly higher than the lecture groups on a measure of interest in psychology, the subject being studied. They hypothesised that though the lecture-group students gave a favourable rating of the teaching they had received, this may have been because they had less anxiety about grades for the course through their weekly feedback from test scores. It was decided to monitor the subsequent progress of all the groups. Three years later not one student in the lecture group had opted to study the subject further, but fourteen members of the two discussion and tutorial groups had chosen to major in psychology. Thus on short term criteria the lecture method was superior, but taking a longer perspective the discussion method appeared to motivate students more powerfully, and ultimately some must have learned a great deal more (McKeachie 1963).

Defining teaching skill in such a way that all would agree, therefore, is not a simple matter. If we were to say that teaching skills are whatever strategies teachers use to enable children to learn, then most people would want to rule out intimidation, humiliation, the use of corporal punishment or other forms of teacher behaviour of which they personally happen to disapprove. It is perhaps easier when seeking a definition of teaching skill to describe some of the characteristics of skilful teaching which might win some degree of consensus, though not universal agreement.

The first might be that the behaviour concerned 'facilitates pupils' learning of something worthwhile', such as facts, skills, values, concepts, how to live harmoniously with one's fellows, attitudes, or some other outcome thought to be desirable. The notion of something being 'worthwhile' brings together both content and values in teaching. Skill is not a uni-dimensional concept. Teaching someone to steal might in one sense be skilfully done but it would attract professional odium rather than admiration. A second quality therefore could be that it is acknowledged to be a skill by those competent to judge, and these might include teachers, teacher trainers, inspectors, advisers and learners themselves. We shall see in chapter 7 that pupils can be shrewd in their appraisal of the teacher's craft, and that the ability to explain is often highly rated by them.

For it to be a recognised part of a teacher's professional competence the skill should also be capable of being repeated, not perhaps in exactly the same form, but as a fairly frequent rather than a single chance occurrence. A chimpanzee might randomly produce an attractive colourful shape once in a while, given a brush and some paint, but an artist would produce a skilfully conceived painting on a more regular basis. Teachers who possess professional skills, therefore, should be capable of manifesting these consistently, not on a hit-or-miss basis.

One frequently cited observation on skills is that of the philosopher Gilbert Ryle (1949), who distinguished, in his book *The Concept of Mind*, between being able to state a factual proposition and being able to perform a skilful operation. The difference between 'knowing that' and 'knowing how' is the difference between inert knowledge and intelligent action. Unfortunately, some competent teachers are not especially articulate about their skill, and it would be wrong to assert that skill may only be recognised as such if the person manifesting it is capable of explaining and analysing it in textbook language. The intelligence of an action may perfectly well be explained by another, and the behaviour is not necessarily unintelligent or shallow if its perpetrator is tongue-tied about it.

One problem encountered in defining teaching skills is that though in some contexts the term 'skill' has good connotations, attracts adulation, is a gift of the few, the result of years of practice or the mark of an expert, in other circumstances it is looked down upon, regarded as mechanical, the sign of a rude technician rather than an artist. We tend, for instance, to admire a surgeon's skill or that of a tennis player. Both may have had the same years of dedicated practice, but the intellectual nature of the knowledge and understanding required by the surgeon is vastly more exacting than that required by a sportsman.

Where the imagination is involved, even more fine distinctions exist. A sculptor would probably be disappointed to read a report that described his latest masterpiece as an example of skill. He would expect eulogies to contain words like 'artistic' and 'creative'. For those who liken teachers more to expressive artists than to surgeons, the very term 'skill' may be seen as belittling, reducing creative endeavour to mechanical crudity. It is difficult to dry-clean the term of these emotional associations with other kinds of human enterprise.

This uncertainty about the proper standing of the notion of skill when applied to teaching is partly explained by the varied nature of the teacher's job. Pressing the right button on a tape recorder, or writing legibly on the blackboard, require but modest competence, and are things most people could learn with only a little practice. Responding to a disruptive 10 year old, or knowing how to explain a difficult concept to children of different ages and abilities by choosing the right language register, appropriate examples and analogies, and reading the many cues which signal understanding or bewilderment, require years of practice as well as considerable intelligence and insight. Although the term 'interpersonal skills' is now quite widespread, there is still some reluctance to classify human relationships in this way.

When children learn something there is often a magical quality about the excitement of discovery, the warmth of regard between teacher and taught, or the novelty to the learner of what is taking place, and the romanticism seems to be destroyed if teaching is seen as too deliberate, calculated, manipulated or over-analysed. Hence the debate, to which I shall return in chapter 12, about learning to teach and whether the act of teaching should be seen as a whole, or is at all capable of being separated into discrete, if interrelated, sub-skills.

My own view is that the extreme optimism of the supporters of the so-called Performance- or Competency-based Teacher Education programmes fashionable in the United States during the 1970s was misplaced. It was assumed that teaching could be broken down into hundreds and indeed thousand of particles, that trainees could learn each of these, and that they could be certificated on the basis of their proven ability to manifest whatever set of competencies had been prescribed. Lists of approved competencies were produced such as the 1,276 compiled by Dodl (1973) under the heading *The Florida Catalog of Teacher Competencies* and hierarchies were assembled with the skills required given a level. Thus an operation by the teacher like 'form reading groups and give a good rationale for the grouping' was seen as being at a lower level than 'implement managerial procedures for efficient group operation'. There was an arbitrary quality to some of these hierarchies, and competency-based teacher education was criticised by writers such as Heath and Nielson (1974) for not being founded on any sound empirical evidence. The survey of teaching competence in initial training courses in parts of Britain by Her Majesty's Inspectorate (DES 1991) rejected the notion of such narrowly conceived notions of competency. Houston (1985) concluded his survey of competency-based teacher education by observing:

> Amid the worldwide actions in competency-based teacher education, it must be remembered that while the concept is sound and fundamental, the implementation is still primitive in terms of its inherent promise.

In the Leverhulme Primary Project we decided to concentrate on more general broadly based skills, with particular emphasis on class management. We also decided to focus on crucial skills, such as questioning and explaining, and to study aspects of teachers' subject knowledge, a particular problem for generalist class teachers, who, in a world where knowledge is being gathered at a phenomenal rate, are expected to grasp several academic disciplines. These areas of skill tend, according to the tenets described above, to represent activities which require professional competence, intelligent action and sensitivity from teachers. They were not so vague as to defy analysis, nor so minute and piddling (like 'smiling' or 'ability to hold chalk') as to attract ridicule, nor were they likely to be dismissed by practitioners as unimportant. They were all valuable aspects of teaching for beginners and experienced teachers alike. They do not, however, represent a complete list of teaching skills, as we inevitably left unstudied many other areas of professional competence. Even though we have observed and analysed large numbers of lessons in many primary classrooms, we recognised that we could hope to make only a modest contribution to the understanding and nurturing of the teachers' professional art and craft.

Classroom observation

Up to the late 1950s there were very few examples of research on teaching which had used direct observation of lessons. Many inferences about classroom life were drawn from interviews, questionnaires or from folklore, anecdotes and hearsay. During the 1960s and 1970s this situation changed rapidly, and hundreds of reports were published ranging from case studies of a single classroom to large-scale observations of practice in hundreds of lessons. Throughout the 1980s and 1990s classroom observation became a regular feature of evaluation projects and research into classroom competency of various kinds. The legal requirement for teacher appraisal in many countries often includes an obligation for teachers to be seen at work in their own classroom, so evidence from classroom observation is used not only in research projects but in formal assessments of competence.

There is not the space here to document the many forms of enquiry which have been undertaken nor the thousands of 'findings' reported in the literature around the world. These are in any case to be found in several standard reference books such as those by Dunkin and Biddle (1974), Delamont (1976), Wragg (1976), Cohen and Manion (1981), Stallings and Mohlman (1985), and many others.

There are considerable advantages and a few disadvantages to studying classrooms by observing what happens at first hand. The major disadvantage is that the presence of an observer invariably has an effect on what takes place, however slight, and there is no foolproof way of knowing what might have transpired had no outsider been there. Samph (1976) planted microphones in classrooms and then sent observers either announced or unexpected some weeks later. He found that teachers made more use of questions and of praise and were more likely to accept pupils' ideas when someone was present. Teachers and indeed pupils may attempt to provide what they think the visitor expects, and this will vary according to the impression or stereotype they form of the observer concerned. Teachers may be irritated by a visitor and behave differently from normal, hence the need for observers, where possible, to study a series of lessons rather than a single one.

Several traditions of observing classrooms have developed. In the United States the great majority of published classroom studies have been based on a degree of quantification, often using some kind of category system. This tradition dates back to the attention studies of the 1920s and 1930s reported by Jackson (1968), and even earlier. It gained in popularity during the 1950s and 1960s, especially after the seminal article by Medley and Mitzel (1963) describing how to construct category systems. Some of the work is closely related to behaviourist learning theory; other studies attempt to relate measurements of the frequency of certain kinds of behaviour to tests of pupil learning or other estimates of outcome.

Since the hope of this kind of research was to establish a body of knowledge which would show some consistency about what successful teachers do, several writers have attempted to establish theories of teaching and learning based on systematic empirical enquiry. Techniques such as meta-analysis (Glass 1978) have been developed which aggregate quantitative studies based on correlation coefficients, chi-squares, or analysis of variance, and determine an overall effect size. Thus, it is possible to calculate from several studies the average relationship between, say, the teacher's use of praise and pupils' learning. Although the apparent neatness of such an aggregation may appeal to some administrators looking for guidance from research, the proposition that fairly exact relationships can be discovered between what teachers do or are and what pupils learn has been criticised by several writers. Jackson (1962) described the findings of half a century of study on the relationship between teachers' personalities and pupil learning as 'so low in intellectual food value that it is almost embarrassing to discuss them'. Typically, small but significant correlations of around 0.2 or 0.3 have been commonplace, leaving a great deal still unexplained.

The more carefully conducted quantitative analyses of teaching have nevertheless yielded some useful and interesting information, even though much less has been delivered than was once hoped. For example, the extremely busy nature of the teacher's job is now well documented. Teachers may have up to 200 days a year with their classes, and an early survey by Jackson showed over 1,000 interpersonal exchanges in a day (Jackson 1962); teachers' use of praise seemed relatively infrequent and haphazard (Brophy 1981); some teachers in inner-city schools spent up to 75 per cent of their time trying to keep order (Deutsch 1960); or teachers allowed on average one second between a pupil answer and their own statement (Rowe 1972). It is quite clear that in the course of the millions of exchanges in which teachers may engage during a quite short phase of their career they can find little time for a leisurely scrutiny of classroom processes. Kerry (1984) found that the classroom transactions of teachers in his sample consisted of 54 per cent to do with management, 42 per cent informing and only 4 per cent which he labelled as 'stimulating', that is, provoking higher levels of thought.

Many teachers develop fairly fixed patterns of teaching which may well be laid down at the training stage. When new curricula, school reorganisation or other changes in circumstances come along, it is difficult to unlearn habits and strategies which have been rehearsed millions of times, even if they are no longer appropriate. Hence the criticism in some of Her Majesty's Inspectors' reports of teachers who have not looked critically at their own teaching styles, or the difficulties experienced by teachers trying to use a fresh curriculum with old teaching methods. Alexander et al. (1992) repeated the assertion that proper scrutiny of classroom processes was necessary, in a report on primary teaching commissioned by the Secretary of State.

Alongside these many quantitative studies has been a different style of enquiry based more on the pencil and notebook tradition used by anthropologists seeking to analyse human behaviour by recording phenomena in detail, and then inviting participants to explain them. Sometimes the investigator is also a participant, as in the case study by Hamilton (1975) of the introduction of integrated science teaching in two Scottish schools, sometimes a non-participant, like King (1978), who documented practice in three infant schools and deliberately avoided becoming enmeshed in the life of the classrooms in which he spent many hours.

Incisive ethnographic accounts of classrooms often give intimate case details and interpretations which some of the quantitative accounts might have missed. The observations made in lessons by Ball (1981), who recorded how a ten-form-entry comprehensive school changed from a system of broad banding to one of mixed-ability classes, are quite close in tenor to those reported in the 1978 HMI paper on the same topic, which was based on evidence from the classrooms of several schools. The strategies employed by teachers of different subjects, the arguments underlying their behaviour and the reaction of pupils, however, are all described in much greater detail through the single case study.

Lacey (1970) taught twelve lessons a week himself, and spent another twelve lessons a week observing teachers and their classes in his study of Hightown Grammar. The result is an analysis of teaching and a description of individual pupils and teachers that set classroom processes in the wider context of the school in its social environment. A similar depth and breadth of insight was offered by Hargreaves (1967) in his study of Lumley Secondary Modern School.

In addition to the two major styles of enquiry there has been other research into teaching based on different procedures and traditions. Blurton Jones (1972) brought together a collection of research reports based on the ethological techniques used by students of the behaviour of animals, and Barnes (1971), Stubbs (1976), Edwards and Furlong (1978), and Feagans and Farran (1981), are among several investigators who have reported linguistic analysis of classroom transactions. Though verbal aspects of teaching and learning have commanded attention from researchers, increasing interest has been shown in non-verbal aspects of classroom communication by, among others, Argyle (1967), Knapp (1980), and Wilkinson (1975), the last of whom combined a variety of techniques for the analysis of both verbal and non-verbal behaviour.

Studying teachers and pupils by direct observation of what they do and say provides valuable information on which to base judgements about skilful teaching and intelligent action. There are many observation procedures from which to choose, each with its supporters and practitioners. It is a pity that the debate between proponents of various schools has occasionally been acrimonious. Attempting to decide whether, for example, quantitative studies are better than qualitative ones is about as fruitful as trying to determine whether a black-and-white photo of the front of the building gives a truer representation of reality than a painting of the rear, a scale drawing or an aerial photograph, or whether bacon and eggs are tastier than fish and chips. I have written a fuller account of classroom observation in the book *An Introduction to Classroom Observation* (Wragg 1993), also published by Routledge.

The Leverhulme Primary Project

We decided in the Leverhulme Primary Project to use a variety of methods, but to put classroom observation right at the centre of our research. The research was conceived as two major linked strands. This book describes the classroom management strand which the present writer directed. The other major strand concentrated on the development aspect of teacher competence by exploring the relationship of subject matter and pedagogical knowledge to the emergence of teaching competence during an initial training programme. That strand was directed by Professor Neville Bennett and its findings are reported in the parallel book to this one, *Learning to Teach* (Bennett and Carré 1993).

Our intention was to study classroom management across a broad front, looking at the management of pupil behaviour, of knowledge, the teachers' management of very first encounters, when roles and relationships are established, and of professional skills such as questioning and explaining. During the period of the project from 1988 to 1992 there was a great deal of debate about and scrutiny of teachers' professional competence. The Elton Report (1989) looked specifically at class management; numerous reports, some official, some quasi-official, some based on research, others on polemic or political beliefs, gave accounts of different aspects of classroom practice in the primary school. The discussion paper by Alexander *et al.* (1992), which was produced in response to an enquiry set up by the then Secretary of State, Kenneth Clarke, concluded that amongst the most pressing needs were:

– extending teachers' skills in the main organisational strategies we have discussed, giving particular attention to whole class teaching and properly focused on organised group work;
– extending teachers' skills in the key classroom techniques of explaining and questioning

(Alexander *et al.*, 1992, paragraph 178)

Several other reports addressed matters such as reading standards, whether teacher training should be more school-based, the place of the specialist teacher in primary schools, teacher appraisal, and teachers' subject knowledge. In most of these there was an explicit or implicit reference to teachers' classroom skills and new ability to adapt and develop them.

In order to study this range of class management demands on primary teachers, we embarked on nine sub-projects. These were:

1 *Effective/ineffective classroom management* – a study of how student and experienced teachers handle disruptive incidents.
2 *Intervention programme* – experiments with training materials during teacher training programmes.
3 *Pupils' views of class management* – the perceptions of primary school children of different ages of what constitutes effective class management.
4 *First encounters* – what happens when beginners and experienced teachers meet a new class for the first time.
5 *Attitude change* – how student teachers' attitudes to class management change during teaching practice.

6 *Explaining* – how primary teachers explain concepts to children.

7 *Questioning* – the use of different kinds of questions by teachers.

8 *Teachers' knowledge* – particularly of unfamiliar subject matter and what strategies they use to cope with teaching a fresh topic.

9 *Supply teachers* – how they manage classes, given that they must meet new groups on a far more regular basis than teachers in permanent posts.

Having identified important topics for scrutiny, we decided on the following strategies:

Involve the profession

Some teacher training procedures have excluded classroom practitioners. We decided it was most important to involve heads and teachers: to solicit their views in interviews and questionnaires, to obtain descriptions of practice, to do research into classroom behaviour, to use teachers to field-test training procedures with students on teaching practice, and to ask them to give a professional evaluation of our materials. It was equally important to involve the teacher training profession, and we decided that all the above should apply to them too.

Teachers should seek their own styles

Although one can learn a great deal from intelligent current practice, any training materials based purely on what teachers are seen to do would be ultra-conservative. Had such a procedure prevailed in the medical profession, doctors would still be using leeches. Teachers exercise skill and make their decisions in different contexts. In the absence of any single consensus about effective teaching, therefore, practitioners need to learn to use their senses to appraise situations and their intelligence and imagination to respond. The notion of teachers being researchers in their own classrooms, or engaging in regular reflection in order to improve practice, has been developed by, among others, Stenhouse (1975) and Schoen (1983). In order to reflect, however, teachers need information about their own and others' classrooms on which they can then exercise judgement. Practitioners can learn a great deal from their fellow human beings, and so the training materials we produced were devised in such a way that teachers could work either alone or together to analyse each other's teaching. Historically, teaching has been a far more isolated job than it needed to be. In chapter 12 there will be a further consideration of learning from and with a professional partner.

Research and development

Some curriculum development projects have no research base at all, and may be none the worse for it, depending more on the professional and creative wisdom of team members than on some kind of systematic enquiry. We decided to combine research and development in the Leverhulme Primary Project.

There are a number of difficulties involved in a research and development project. The first is that it is rarely possible to complete a thorough enquiry first and then produce the programme afterwards. A research project takes about three years, by the time the design has been worked out, the fieldwork has been completed and analysed, and the implications have been identified. If one starts development only at that stage, then circumstances may already have changed compared with when the research phase was first undertaken. On the other hand, if one starts with development, then research can consist only of *post hoc* evaluations, and it may be difficult to incorporate findings once well tested materials are already in existence.

Within these limitations different lines of research were necessary. Some were relatively short-lived, others ran for a full three years. Different kinds of methodology were used, including classroom observation, interviews, tests of learning or attitude, photographs (to elicit the reaction of pupils and teachers to classroom events) and diaries. The advantage of a research and development project, if it works well, is that it both provides research data for teachers, teacher trainers and fellow researchers in the same field, and also offers directly training materials and ideas based on the research. It would be foolish to try to base a curriculum development project entirely on one's own or even other people's research. Perhaps the best example of the slavish application of research findings was programmed learning, which dwindled in popularity after the 1960s, partly because of the tedium experienced by those working through endless sequences of mind-corroding frames containing the classic ingredients of active responding, small steps, immediate confirmation and high correct response rates. We decided that our own and other researchers' findings would inform training materials, not dominate them.

The research in this project adopted a variety of standard research practices and one or two less common ones, like the use of photographs. Whenever quantitative methods were used, two or more observers were trained in classrooms or by using videotapes, until a high level of agreement was achieved in the use of whatever category or sign system was being employed. In qualitative research two or more members of the team analysed data, such as transcripts or interviews, until there was agreement about the salient features or the selection of illustrative quotations or examples.

In writing an account of research findings which we hope will be read by experienced heads and teachers, student teachers, researchers, lay people interested in primary education, administrators, and policy workers, we are caught in the usual dilemma facing those addressing different audiences. Sometimes the text does contain tables based on one of the commonly used statistical techniques, like correlations, chi-squares, t tests, analysis of variance, or multivariate analysis such as factor or cluster analysis. I have tried to use natural language wherever possible, and readers who are not interested in the detail of the research findings should not feel guilty if they skip over some of the statistical tables and concentrate more on the case material and summaries of research results.

Chapter 2

The management of teaching

In his classic text *The Theory of Social and Economic Organisation* (1964) Max Weber observed that power in any social relationship is reflected in the probability that one person will be in a position to carry out his own will despite resistance. In theory, teachers have the power to control the behaviour of children in their charge. Since society has given them the 'duty of care', as it is known in legal parlance, because they are acting as a parent substitute, *in loco parentis*, they must be given power to administer fair punishments, for example, so that they can carry out their duties.

This neat view of life in the classroom does not always translate easily into actuality. A major survey of over 500 primary schools by Her Majesty's Inspectorate (DES 1978) concluded that 'a quiet working atmosphere was established in nine out of ten of the classes wherever it was needed'. But behind this general orderliness lies an intricate complexity which involves far more than just the socially acceptable behaviour of pupils. Teachers have to manage the learning of their pupils as well as their classroom behaviour. They must constantly make selections from their repertoire of personal and professional skills, deciding what children shall study and by what means; the extent to which pupils should themselves be encouraged to make decisions; when, to whom, and what sort of questions to ask and what explanations to give; whether pupils shall work in groups, as individuals, as a whole class or in some other combination; how time and space should be deployed – where, for example, to place tables and chairs, and where to stand when addressing individuals or groups; how best to husband and deploy resources – like books, materials, equipment or cash; what rules will operate in their classroom; what sort of relationships they would like with children, fellow teachers and the wider community, parents, ancillary staff, governors; how to manage tensions and crises, of individuals or groups; what range of professional roles to play, when, for example, to act as a substitute parent or social worker to a despairing child from an unhappy home, or to stand back from this; how to manage the monitoring and assessment of children's progress.

Within school, teachers are, inescapably, members of a social and management structure, and, in their study of inner London schools, Rutter *et al.*

(1979) concluded that, in those schools judged to be 'better' on various criteria, such as test scores and attendance rates, teachers felt more involved in decision-making. They were also part of a wider community with, in turn, its values and practices. Managing children is usually thought to be harder in schools located in areas with high crime rates. Johnson and Brooks (1979) have produced a useful model (see figure 2.1) of this intricate nexus of relationships between tasks which society expects teachers to perform, such as planning and organising lessons, the many kinds of setting in which teaching and learning may take place, the values that teachers and learners may hold, and the tensions between people and amongst roles.

Class management is a topic which is frequently mentioned in professional debate about primary schools. The Plowden Report (1967) posited a non-authoritarian but nevertheless planned regime based on consideration for others and industry:

> For all the appearances of free-and-easiness, for all the absence of the traditional forms of discipline, there is, behind it all, not only a deep understanding of children, but careful planning. The two basic assumptions are that children respond in kind to courteous and considerate treatment by adults, and that they will work with concentration and diligence at tasks which are suited to their abilities. Neither assumption is true for all children, or for any child all the time, but both are true enough to make them a workable basis for many primary schools.

The large-scale survey of over 500 primary schools by Her Majesty's Inspectorate (DES 1978) spoke of two general approaches to teaching and the styles of management that went with them, one 'mainly didactic', the other 'mainly exploratory'. The report warned, however, of the misleading nature of such oversimplification, and stated:

> It is clear from the evidence that a variety of types of organisation was used in arranging the work of the classes. Generally, the organisation was designed to provide satisfactorily for children of different attainments and abilities, to accommodate various types of work, including practical work, and to take advantage of the resources and teaching strengths available within a particular school.

The question of class management was referred to in the survey by HMI (DES 1987) of new teachers in schools. Here the precepts informing HMI's judgement were spelled out explicitly:

> Good management of classes containing children up to the age of seven was characterised by planning which provided opportunities for groups and individuals to work on tasks of intrinsic interest, allied to the ability to maintain an overview of the activities of all the children and to intervene as necessary. Good management of junior age classes was typified by detailed

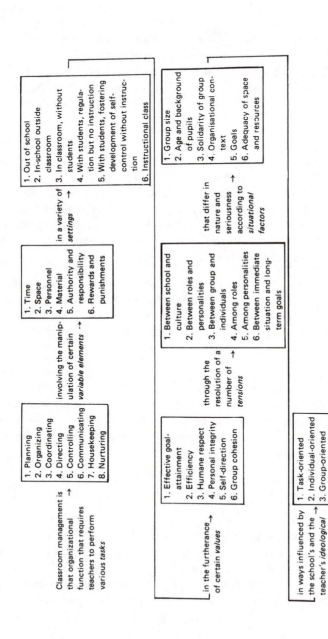

Classroom management is that organizational function that requires teachers to perform various *tasks*

1. Planning
2. Organizing
3. Coordinating
4. Directing
5. Controlling
6. Communicating
7. Housekeeping
8. Nurturing

involving the manipulation of certain *variable elements* →

1. Time
2. Space
3. Personnel
4. Material
5. Authority and responsibility
6. Rewards and punishments

in a variety of *settings* →

1. Out of school
2. In-school outside classroom
3. In classroom, without students
4. With students, regulation but no instruction
5. With students, fostering development of self-control without instruction
6. Instructional class

in the furtherance of certain *values*

1. Effective goal-attainment
2. Efficiency
3. Humane respect
4. Personal integrity
5. Self-direction
6. Group cohesion

through the resolution of a number of *tensions* →

1. Between school and culture
2. Between roles and personalities
3. Between group and individuals
4. Among roles
5. Among personalities
6. Between immediate situation and long-term goals

that differ in nature and seriousness according to *situational factors*

1. Group size
2. Age and background of pupils
3. Solidarity of group
4. Organisational context
5. Goals
6. Adequacy of space and resources

in ways influenced by the school's and the teacher's *ideological stances*.

1. Task-oriented
2. Individual-oriented
3. Group-oriented

Figure 2.1 A conceptual model of classroom management (from Johnson and Brooks 1979)

planning, effective organisation of resources, the provision of interesting learning-experiences, high expectations on the part of the teacher, and a clear understanding by the pupils of what they were expected to do.

Often the principal focus in considering or discussing class management is on discipline and pupil behaviour, even though this is but one, albeit very important, aspect of it. The Elton Report (1989) emphasises the 'whole school' aspect of management: that it should be seen as planned, not accidental, conscious and not *ad hoc*, and a shared responsibility, not an isolated one:

> We recommend that headteachers and their senior management teams should take the lead in developing school plans for promoting good behaviour. Such plans should ensure that the school's code of conduct and the values represented in its formal and informal curricula reinforce one another; promote the highest possible degree of consensus about standards of behaviour among staff, pupils and parents; provide clear guidance to all three groups about these standards and their practical application; and encourage staff to recognise and praise good behaviour as well as dealing with bad behaviour.

Another report commissioned by the Secretary of State on primary classroom practice (Alexander *et al.* 1992) also considered such organisational aspects as the use of whole-class, group and individual teaching, concluding that many teachers used all three, as they were not mutually exclusive. It cautioned that doctrine should not override educational judgements on such organisational matters:

> teachers need the skills and judgment to be able to select and apply whichever organisational strategy – class, group or individual – is appropriate for the task at hand. The judgment, it must be stressed, should be educational and organisational, rather than, as it so often is, doctrinal.

Class management is a central notion in classroom research, in teacher education, both at initial and post-experience level, in teacher appraisal, and in the public mind. It is neither simple nor uni-dimensional. There are numerous views about its nature, and the research literature, which cannot be fully covered in the limited confines of this book, abounds with studies of class management using a variety of approaches, interpretations and data-gathering strategies. It not only contains an important set of interrelated skills in its own right, but is also intricately bound up with other professional skills, for without competence in class management teachers cannot display to full advantage the other skills they may possess. In this context, it can be regarded as a 'threshold variable', as teachers need to have sufficient skills in organisation, control and co-ordination to allow the rest of their professional competence to flourish.

Studies of class management

It is not possible to describe at this point more than a small amount of the research done in class management, and more references to research are included in later chapters, but the field has been surveyed by several writers such as Dunkin and Biddle (1974), Docking (1980) and Emmer (1985). There is no shortage of 'how to handle classes' books for student teachers, often written by practitioners such as Francis (1975) and Marland (1975), or teacher trainers (Robertson 1981). Some of the books and pamphlets on class management for teachers try to incorporate research findings, like *Maintaining Discipline in Classroom Instruction* (Gnagey 1975), the workbook *Class Management and Control*, which was field-tested as part of the Teacher Education Project by Wragg (1981), and the workbook on primary class management (Wragg 1993) which grew out of the Leverhulme Primary Project. Others concentrate on a particular set of research findings and precepts, such as the 'behavioural interactionist' perspective (Wheldall and Glynn 1989), which combines the analysis of behaviour and behaviourist learning theory with the view that learning is interactive and children need to initiate as well as respond.

Although a great deal of the research in the field has been undertaken in the last twenty-five years, American studies by Wickman (1928), who enquired into teachers' definitions of behaviour problems, and the so-called 'attention studies' of the 1920s and 1930s, when an observer sat at the front of the class scanning faces to assemble a simple measure of attentiveness (Jackson 1968), show that interest in the topic is not entirely recent.

In Britain, Highfield and Pinsent (1952) obtained estimates of what were perceived as pupil misdemeanours from a sample of 724 teachers. Restlessness and fidgeting, laziness and boisterous, noisy behaviour were seen as the most common forms of misconduct. Several surveys, some by local authorities or teacher associations, have addressed the problem of more serious misbehaviour. Lowenstein (1975) intended to show trends in 'violent and obtrusive behaviour', but failed to do so because, he claimed, there was a lack of objectivity and accuracy on the part of teachers filling in report forms and describing incidents.

A number of investigators, some through scrutiny of several teachers, others by in-depth case studies of individual classrooms or schools, have tried to map out the strategies which teachers use to control the behaviour of groups or individual pupils. One of the best-known and most influential series of research programmes was undertaken by Jacob Kounin and his associates from the late 1950s to the early 1970s. Kounin concentrated on, among other events, the teacher's reaction to pupil deviance, and studied the clarity, firmness and roughness of what he called 'desists', that is, teachers' attempts to terminate behaviour of which they disapproved.

In a study of forty-nine teachers of children aged 5 to 8, of grades 1 and 2,

Kounin (1970) observed each for one whole day, and concentrated in his analysis of videotapes and transcripts on the techniques of group management teachers employed. He coined a set of somewhat off-beat terms to describe various kinds of teacher behaviour that seemed to be positively related to the involvement of pupils in their work or to freedom from deviance in the classroom. These included the following:

1 *With-itness* Having eyes in the back of your head and thus picking up misbehaviour early.
2 *Overlapping* Being able to do more than one thing at once – for example, deal with someone misbehaving whilst at the same time keeping the children you are with occupied.
3 *Smoothness* Keeping children at work by not:

   (a) Intruding suddenly when they are busy (thrusts).
   (b) Starting one activity and then leaving it abruptly to engage in another (dangles).
   (c) Ending an activity and then returning to it unexpectedly (flip-flops).

4 *Overdwelling* Avoiding staying on an issue for longer than necessary.
5 *Momentum* Freedom from slow-downs.

Kounin found strongest relationships between 'with-itness', the ability to scan the class, and pupil involvement and lack of deviance, with correlations of from 0.307 to 0.615, depending whether children were working individually at their desks or engaged in whole-class activity, when the correlations were higher.

In an earlier set of studies Kounin and Gump (1958), looking at twenty-six kindergarten teachers, identified the 'ripple effect', that is, the impact of something the teacher does on pupils other than the target child, for example, when a teacher says, 'Haven't you started yet, John?' and other pupils near by begin work because they read the signal that the teacher expects pupils to have commenced work. The findings were not entirely conclusive, though a later study suggested that the ripple effect made most impact on the highly motivated pupils, and that liking or disliking the teacher also influenced the degree of effect. Reviewing Kounin's work, Dunkin and Biddle (1974) concluded that it held considerable promise for the eventual improvement of classroom teaching, and it has certainly been influential on much that followed it.

Emmer (1985), in his overview of class management research, divided the field up into a number of domains. Criteria for effective management included such matters as pupil engagement, absence of conflict and deviant behaviour, time management, fulfilment of goals and pupil learning. He also highlighted theoretical perspectives, such as a behaviour modification or a humanist–interactionist orientation; specific management tasks, like beginning the school day, whole-class and group teaching, end-of-day routines and transitions from one activity to another; the early part of the school year; maintaining the classroom management system, and the place of rewards and punishments; and contextual features, such as the organisation of the school and pupil achievement level.

Whereas some investigators have concentrated on studies of several classrooms, other researchers have conducted intensive case studies of a smaller number. Woods (1979) described what he called 'mortification techniques' used by some teachers which strip the personality of certain pupils, as well as forms of fraternisation and negotiation which are often employed when first-line approaches fail. Other investigators have catalogued various 'coping strategies' witnessed during observation, including D. Hargreaves (1975), A. Hargreaves (1978), and Stebbins (1981). These include not only those described by Woods (1979), but also the use of promises, and keeping pupils busy so there is little time for deviance.

Freiberg (1983), writing about the notion of consistency in classroom management, cites a number of models of class management, including those that focus on psychological roles, methods of communication, the behaviour of the individual, pupil responsibility or rule-based models. A comprehensive summary of these has been produced by Charles (1981). Several of the models, notably those based on Skinnerian behaviourist theory using behaviour modification techniques, have a sizeable and, in some cases, controversial research literature attached to them. Others, like Rogers's (1970) influential writing on interpersonal relationships, or the proposals of Glasser (1969) for what he calls 'reality therapy', that is, the involvement of pupils in decisions about rules and procedures, have produced some empirical research but tend to be less positivistic in style.

The management of time on the task

Some investigators have chosen to study one particular dimension of class management, like the time pupils appear to spend on the task they are supposed to be doing, on the grounds that the more time pupils spend on academic activities the more they may learn. Brophy and Evertson (1976) in a correlational study of 7–9 year-olds, found that Kounin's categories of withitness, overlapping and smoothness were related not only to good behaviour, but also to greater pupil learning. Their conclusion was that the amount of time the pupil was engaged on the task was 'the key to successful classroom management'. The notion of 'time on the task' or 'academic engaged time' attracted considerable research interest, and the California Beginning Teacher Evaluation Study (Denham and Lieberman 1980) devoted much of its enquiry to the nature and amount of time spent by pupils on the task in hand.

This issue was taken up by Gage (1978), who summarised several studies of academic learning time, and concluded that time was in itself 'a psychologically empty quantitative concept'. What was needed, he argued, was a more refined analysis of the notion of time. In the California Beginning Teacher Evaluation Study, such factors as allocated time and success rate were taken into account, but more value- and problem-laden concepts, such as the degree to which the tasks set were worthwhile, were not fully scrutinised.

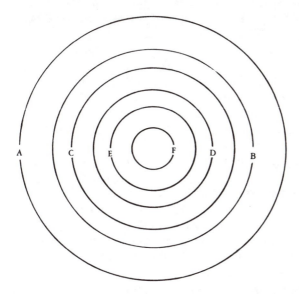

Figure 2.2   Time circles: a model of time management (not to scale)
Circle A, all time   Circle B, time spent in school
Circle C, time assigned to a subject   Circle D, time actually spent on the task
Circle E, time on a worthwhile task   Circle F, with some degree of success

One way of conceptualising effective time management would be to see it as a 'bullseye' model (Wragg 1984), that is, a set of concentric circles (figure 2.2, not to scale): the largest, circle A, would be 168 hours per week, that is, the total time available during seven days and nights. Inscribed within it, the next circle, B, would be quite small by comparison, only some twenty-four hours, being roughly the amount of time spent in school averaged over the year. This ranks in scale with some studies of children watching television which have shown an average of twenty-five hours per week (Balding 1990). Circle C would show the amount of time assigned to the area under scrutiny, for example, number work in the infant school or science for 10 year-olds. This would vary from school to school. It could be two hours in one school and four hours in another.

So far, none of the circles is a direct reflection of the class management skill of the individual teacher, since allocations are usually fixed by governors, heads and teachers. The size of the smaller circles, however, is indeed affected by the individual teacher's skill. Circle D would be the amount of time pupils actually spend on the tasks in hand. If the school had assigned three hours to science, then teachers with ineffective class management, or very adverse circumstances, might find pupils engaged in learning for less than an hour. Other classes might spend over two hours. Totals for individual pupils, rather than class means, will show an even wider spread. Some of the studies in the Leverhulme Primary Project considered this aspect, and they are reported in later chapters of this book.

Circle E brings in the domain of 'worthwhile tasks'. Engaged time in a certain classroom might be high, but the task set might involve the equivalent of copying out telephone directories, so the concept of what is worthwhile, a major philosophical issue discussed by, among others, Peters (1966), is important but highly subjective and contentious. It must, however, logically be a subset of engaged time. Again, it will be a function of the skill of the teacher how much time is spent on worthwhile activities.

Finally, the concept of success at the task must be incorporated. If children spend time learning erroneous concepts in science, their experience is less profitable than it would have been if they had learned correct ones. Thus, the final circle F encompasses that portion of circle E which is done with some degree of success. This circle is closely related to the matter of primary teachers' subject knowledge, which we also investigated in the present project. One operational definition of skilful classroom management, there-fore, would be the extent to which teachers are capable of maximising circle F for each child, that is, the amount of time spent on something worthwhile with some degree of success, in other words, 'hitting the bullseye'. The model is certainly not the only way of conceptualising time management: one could add such important aspects as enjoyment, but it is offered as a way of depicting some of the factors frequently mentioned when the matter is discussed.

McNamara (1981) has criticised the emphasis on time management, in some studies, arguing that, taken too far, it can become an end in itself. It can also become a recipe for over-directive teaching. In the Leverhulme Primary Project research described in the following chapters, time on task does constitute one aspect of some of our studies, but we concentrated also on other constituents, such as rules and relationships, the handling of disruption, the management of pupil behaviour and of the teachers' own professional skills.

Schools of thought

It has already been stated above that, in a pluralist society, there will be more than one perspective on a subject like class management. Sometimes public debate is reduced right down to two contending factions, 'traditional' and 'progressive', though evidence from surveys cited above shows that this is an oversimplification of a much more complex situation. Below are but seven conceptions out of a potentially much larger set of viewpoints. They are neither rigid nor permanent classifications, in that teachers may, for example, behave in an authoritarian manner in one context, but in a different way in another. Similarly the use of behaviour modification can be handled in an authoritarian way, with the teacher specifying all the conditions, or be negotiated by teacher and pupil. Thus some of these notions can be laid over others in a two or three-dimensional model of class management, but, equally, some can be seen as mutually exclusive. They are, therefore, general orientations and beliefs, not permanent conditions. Teachers have to react rapidly to, perhaps, 1,000 or more interpersonal transactions in a single day (Jackson 1968), so their responses may be varied and subject to more than one single influence.

Authoritarian

The principal belief here is that teachers are paid to establish and maintain order within a school. They probably, therefore, know best, and should expect to be obeyed. Authoritarianism is sometimes stereotyped as 'hard' or 'unkind', but this need not be the case at all. There are many teachers who are firmly in charge, and exercise authority, whom one could not describe as lacking kindliness, understanding or concern for the child as an individual. In Victorian times great stress was laid on the authority of the teacher, and classes frequently chanted in unison learned answers to standard questions. Teachers were expected to exercise firm social control over behaviour and also over the knowledge children acquired, and corporal punishment was used extensively. In more recent times, corporal punishment has been abandoned and the role of the teacher has come under close scrutiny, with vigorous debate about whether what is taught should be determined by the class teacher, fashioned by children themselves or laid down centrally in a national curriculum by statute.

Geoffrey Bantock asserts what for him is the inescapable 'authority' of the teacher in his book *Freedom and Authority in Education* (1965):

> The teacher, however much he may attempt to disguise the fact, must, if only because he is not appointed or dismissed by pupils, represent an authority. He must do so, also, because he is inescapably 'other' than the children. For one thing, he is older; he has inevitably undergone experiences which give him a different background of assumption from that of his charges. He is, that is to say, psychically different. He has, too, certain legal responsibilities and is answerable to the community at large for aspects of his behaviour. There is therefore unavoidably, 'mechanically', as it were, a gulf which no attempt at disguise can hide, because it is endemic in the situation, 'given'. Nor do I think that it should be disguised. Power is an inescapable element in adult life, with which we all at some time or other have to come to terms; and I deprecate a great deal of the current insincerity which strives to hide the true situation and thus prepares

the child for a fictitious world, not one of reality, even when the circumstance is blanketed under some such grandiose title as 'training in the self-responsibilities of citizenship'. It is to be deprecated for a number of reasons, not least of which is the need to learn respect for the idea of authority as such, as a necessary element in the proper functioning of the community.

Teachers operating in an authoritarian mode would expect to make many of the decisions about content and procedure, with perhaps fewer explanations or justification of the reasons for such decisions. There might be less permitted movement or talking to other pupils. More directions would be given with the intention that they should be carried out. Hand raising before speaking would probably be insisted upon. Supporters of this mode of management argue that chaos ensues unless a teacher is clearly 'in charge', that children themselves expect teachers to be strict (see chapter 7), that teachers have the experience to know what children should be doing. Critics argue that authoritarian teaching can easily become repressive, that children need to learn to manage and determine their own behaviour if our rapidly changing society is to be truly democratic.

Early work in classroom interaction, occurring as it did before and after the Second World War, took a negative view of authoritarian teaching. Anderson (1939) observed the contacts between nursery children and teachers who were categorised as either 'dominative' or 'integrative' and found more dominative contacts (snatching toys, striking playmates, giving commands to others) between children in the classes of teachers who were themselves labelled 'dominative'. In the classes of teachers classified as 'integrative' there were reported to be more integrative acts (sharing toys, offering help, playing harmoniously). Lewin *et al.* (1939) carried out their well known study of the effects of adults role playing 'authoritarian', 'democratic' and 'laissez-faire' styles of leadership on small groups of boys in boys' clubs. They reported more acts of aggression during the absence of the 'authoritarian' style leader, whereas the 'democratic' group appeared to work equally well whether the leader was present or not. This research was not only based on very small samples, however, but was also undertaken at a time when, because of the rise of fascism, there was a strong belief that authoritarian fathers and teachers had produced a compliant citizenry, easily taken over by a dictator. It was this concern that, for many years, gave authoritarian teaching a largely negative association.

Permissive

This is usually regarded as the polar opposite of authoritarian teaching. Children's freedom to develop autonomy, it is argued, will be inhibited by undue interference from the teacher. The following extract from A. S. Neill's

Summerhill (1961) illustrated this concept in a form which has been influential on some schools, but rarely copied in its original form:

> Summerhill is a self-governing school, democratic in form. Everything connected with social, or group, life, including punishment for social offences, is settled by vote at the Saturday night General School Meeting.
>
> Each member of the teaching staff and each child, regardless of his age, has one vote. My vote carries the same weight as that of a seven-year-old.
>
> One may smile and say, 'But your voice has more value, hasn't it?' Well, let's see. Once I got up at a meeting and proposed that no child under sixteen should be allowed to smoke. I argued my case: a drug, poisonous, not a real appetite in children, but mostly an attempt to be grown up. Counter-arguments were thrown across the floor. The vote was taken. I was beaten by a large majority.
>
> The sequel is worth recording. After my defeat, a boy of sixteen proposed that no one under twelve should be allowed to smoke. He carried his motion. However, at the following weekly meeting a boy of twelve proposed the repeal of the new smoking rule, saying, 'We are all sitting in the toilets smoking on the sly just like kids do in a strict school, and I say it is against the whole idea of Summerhill'. His speech was cheered, and that meeting repealed the law. I hope I have made it clear that my voice is not always more powerful than that of a child.

'Permissive' is but one term which may be used here. Others include 'informal', 'progressive' and 'democratic'. Each of these terms carries with it associations, either of approval or of opprobrium, and there is no real clarity about distinctions between them, though some writers would prefer 'democratic' on the grounds that it is a term more likely to gain approval than 'permissive', with its 'anything goes' associations, or 'progressive', which may bring on an attack from the political right. Teachers operating in this less didactic mode are not so likely to issue commands, use reprimands or punishment. Freedom of movement is more likely to be permitted and the buzz of conversation amongst pupils may be louder. Emphasis will be more on pupils taking responsibility for their own behaviour. Supporters argue that management in Victorian times was repressive, producing too many un-inventive and compliant adults, that children are capable of sensible behaviour, provided they are trusted. Critics claim that permissiveness too frequently degenerates into a laissez-faire *ad hoc* classroom where too little time is spent on learning, where social chit-chat can consume much of the time in school, at the expense of what the children are supposed to be studying.

Whereas the work of those who investigated authoritarianism induced a negative association in the years following the Second World War, a set of research studies in the 1960s and 1970s, summarised by Gage (1978), tended to establish a similar image for less directive approaches. Bringing together studies by several investigators, as well as comparing syntheses of research findings by Rosenshine (1976), Medley (1977), Crawford and Gage (1977) and Glass *et al.* (1977), he contrasted what he called 'direct' and 'open' teaching. 'Direct' is largely didactic, information-giving teaching, the term often derived from studies using the Flanders (1960) ten-category system of interaction analysis. This codes 'direct' teaching as lecture, command or criticism, as opposed to questioning, praise and acceptance of ideas and feelings, which are deemed to be more 'indirect' or 'open'. Gage concluded that, so far as teaching basic skills in the early years of primary education was concerned, there might be a slight superiority of 'direct' over 'open' approaches, but that this difference would need to be tested experimentally before it could be said to constitute a causal relationship.

Behaviour modification

This approach is based on the learning theories developed by B. F. Skinner (1954) and his associates. We learn best, it is believed, when positive behaviour is *reinforced*, often by reward or recognition. Thus children who seek attention and are 'told off' are actually being encouraged to misbehave further to attract more attention. The role of the teacher is to help children to learn socially desirable behaviour. The conventions of behaviour modification require teachers to ignore anti-social behaviour, on the grounds that failure to reinforce it by giving it attention will lead to its extinction, and reward or publicly recognise approved behaviour, sometimes by giving out tokens, in the belief that this reinforces it and makes it more likely to occur.

This form of class management has been criticised, partly because in early work in the United States drugs were used on hyperactive children. Critics argue that the treatment is mechanistic, seeing people as machines, not humans, that formal reward systems are merely a form of bribery, and that it is too overt a manipulation of young people. They also say that ignoring misbehaviour does not necessarily improve it and that, in the case of children who use swear words, for example, 'reinforcement' may come from other pupils. Supporters counter this by saying that most teachers, and indeed most human beings in their relationships generally, use reinforcement techniques, and it is dishonest to pretend otherwise, that many children have learned to behave badly and want to behave well if only someone will show them how, and that 'contract' systems, whereby children specify what they themselves would like to achieve, have removed the 'teacher manipulation' objection.

Certainly the early use of behaviour modification in the 1950s and 1960s was often undertaken in a mechanical way. Reinforcers were seen as consisting of two kinds, *primary*, that is, basic life-sustaining, non-learned items or conditions like nourishment, warmth, and *conditioned* reinforcers, rewards we learn to understand and appreciate, like money or praise. Children who behaved in a manner of which the teacher approved were given tokens or praise on a consistent basis. More recently behavioural approaches to class management have become the subject of negotiation rather than imposition. Nowadays it is more likely that proponents will begin with the observable, and assemble baseline data on whether a child appears to pay attention to the task in hand, for example, and there will usually be a deliberate attempt to change behaviour. However, it is also likely that a much more determined attempt will be made to involve the child in independent learning and autonomy, rather than dependence (Wheldall and Glynn, 1989).

Interpersonal relationships

The belief here is that learning takes place where positive relationships exist between a teacher and the class and amongst pupils. The teacher's role is to develop a healthy classroom climate within which learning will automatically thrive. Often much influenced by the views of Carl Rogers (1970) and his followers. Teachers put a premium on personal relationships both between themselves and pupils, and amongst pupils. There may, therefore, be more involvement of pupils in, say, the negotiation of rules, with discussion and suggestions about why these make sense. When problems occur, the teacher may employ what Glasser (1969) called 'reality therapy', whereby an interview takes place between the pupil and the teacher with whom he has the strongest rapport, to establish why things are going wrong, what are the consequences of the pupil's attitudes and actions, and how he might proceed in future. Supporters of this point of view regard personal relationships as of crucial importance to all human beings and argue that children must learn how to establish positive relationships with their peers and with adults from an early age. They point out that frequently, in schools, situations which would be difficult in other contexts are easily managed in classrooms where relationships are good. Critics counter that this can easily be overstated, that the pursuit of good relationships can begin to override the acquisition of skills and knowledge, and that there are classrooms where relationships are sound but where little is learned.

Whereas the research literature on a topic like behaviour modification is huge, there is far less systematic enquiry, though a great deal of analytical writing, on such matters as the precepts of Carl Rogers or 'reality therapy'. Some studies have been conducted into the nature of classroom relationships (Hargreaves *et al.* 1975), the kinds of people who enjoy good relationships with others, some of it inspired by Maslow's theory of self-actualisation (Maslow, 1970) and the field has been summarised by Brammer (1985). Those who work in this mode, however, are often averse to and suspicious of the 'findings' of research conducted in the sort of quantitative tradition which earns citations in the literature.

Scientific

Professor Nate Gage, of Stanford University, in his books *The Scientific Basis of the Art of Teaching* (1978) and *Hard Gains in the Soft Sciences* (1985) has put forward the proposition that teaching is a science as well as an art, and that teaching can be systematically studied and analysed. Once we know enough, behaviour can be predicted and 'successful' strategies identified. An example of this approach would be the work by Jacob Kounin (1970), described earlier in this chapter, who, in his book *Discipline and Group Management in Classrooms*, used systematic observation of video-tapes of primary classrooms to identify what he called 'desist' techniques, that is, action by teachers which seemed to be particularly effective when children misbehaved. He did not identify one single 'desist' as supremely effective, but rather described a series of strategies which were used by teachers who appeared to be successful at managing misbehaviour.

Gage argues that careful analysis of the relationship between classroom process data and various measures of outcome, whether these are changes in behaviour, knowledge or attitude, is an important first step in the establishment of a scientific basis for the art of teaching. Rosenshine and Furst (1973) described this as a *descriptive–correlational–experimental loop*. For example, suppose an investigator decided to study class management in the primary school and to consider in particular which pupils were called upon by the teacher to answer questions during whole-class teaching. Watching lessons and noting which pupils answered questions would be the first stage of this loop, the *descriptive* phase. Let us assume that, when the researcher gave tests of what the pupils had learned, he found a significant correlation between answering questions in class and learning the subject matter of the lesson. This would constitute the second, or *correlational* phase of the loop. It may be the case, however, that quicker learners answer more questions in class, so there might be a correlation but no causal link between process and outcome. In the third phase of the loop, therefore, the teacher would deliberately call on some pupils who had not volunteered to answer to see if, under *experimental* conditions, frequency of answering was related to actual learning.

The difficulty of this approach is, of course, that many 'findings' are based on short-term tests of memory, and that true experiments are notoriously difficult to conduct. It is not possible to 'script' a lesson. One may be able to script the teacher's questions, but then not be able to control the nature and direction of pupils' answers. Nor are curriculum materials, even self-instructional ones, entirely teacher-proof. Nonetheless it is worth teachers experimenting in their own classrooms, and research findings can be a stimulus for further enquiry at individual classroom level. An infant teacher who had read about Kounin's notion of 'with-itness', for example, might try splitting her attention between the pupil she was hearing read and the rest of the class from time to time, to see if she felt intuitively that this improved her class management. Or she might make a quick tour of the class, once children had begun work, making comments publicly on the work of one or two children, to see if the 'ripple effect' seemed to have a positive influence on others.

Critics argue that teaching is an art and cannot be analysed or taught in any systematic way, that there is not, as yet, sufficient research evidence to constitute a science of teaching, and that teachers are more influenced by their own personal experience than by what they read in research reports. Supporters point out that medieval doctors defended the use of leeches on similar grounds, that research evidence is necessary if teaching is to move forward, and that rather than replace a teacher's artistry, carefully collected evidence forms what Gage called a 'scientific basis' to enhance it.

Social systems

Some researchers and writers have considered aspects of management that extend beyond the walls of a single classroom. People in school are believed to belong to a sub-system of a wider social organisation in which many influences are at work on the group's behaviour. These may be academic, political, social, financial or emotional. Failure to understand these processes, it is said, will inhibit the teacher's ability to work effectively in a school, although learning itself is seen as an individual process. It is difficult to translate this belief into behavioural terms, but the teacher would probably be interested in the wider aspects of education, be knowledgeable about the school's catchment area, the family background, religious beliefs and community traditions and values.

Many school problems, argue adherents of this viewpoint, cannot be dealt with in isolation. Poor housing, financial hardship, family circumstances, parents' employment or lack of it, their education, aspirations and attitudes, all these may exert more powerful influences over pupils' behaviour than anything that happens in school. Teachers need to know about the religious beliefs of the children in their classes, for instance, so that they understand why a child might be away from school celebrating a particular festival, or why the pupil might hold a certain view of diet, physical education and dance, or family life. Critics counter by saying that teachers have little or no control over these external factors, and, whilst able to be understanding, must of necessity act within the framework of the school. Hence the complaint sometimes heard from teachers at conferences, 'I am a teacher, not a social worker.'

Numerous writers have analysed and described these wider background issues. Such matters as the effects of home background on children's learning were considered in the research undertaken for the Plowden Report (1967) which underlined the importance of parental attitudes. Rutter *et al.* (1979)

and Mortimore (1988) have studied different primary and secondary schools to understand the relationship between such factors as leadership and management within the school and pupil achievement and attitudes. Schools in similar social environments were found to have different levels of achievement, and the authors attributed this to such matters as management style within the school, leading to the argument that 'schools can make a difference', a matter of some dispute amongst researchers (King 1980). Duke (1979) established a link between good pupil behaviour and a consistent school policy on discipline.

Folklore

There is a belief amongst many practitioners that experienced teachers already possess intuitive professional expertise which may often be articulated in unpretentious terms, and I am not here disparaging that view. It is held by some that most teachers, over the years, have built up a stock of 'tricks of the trade'. These can be learned, it is said, and the young teacher will be equipped with an omni-purpose set of recipes which will be useful in most situations. Among the most common tips reported by teachers and students we interviewed during the Leverhulme Project were: 'Prepare and plan carefully,' 'Be well organised and anticipate problems,' 'Develop different strategies for different ages of children,' 'Establish good personal relationships,' 'Be firm in your guidelines, and let children know the limits,' 'Keep children busy.' How this manifests itself in the classroom depends on the kind of folklore which has been purveyed, but someone offered the common tip 'Start strict and ease off later' may well attempt to be more severe than she might otherwise have been in the early stages of teaching practice or when starting a new post in a primary school.

Those who believe in tips claim that considerable accumulated professional wisdom lies behind them, that such tips are fairly universal in many schools and cultures, and that generations of trainees have gratefully acknowledged their value. Critics argue that tips are lacking in any theoretical basis, are random and unrelated to each other, and may suit the person who proffers them but not the recipient.

The present study of management issues

It was not possible during the Leverhulme Primary Project to investigate every aspect of this vast field, and so we had to select certain key aspects for special study, as described in chapter 1. The remaining chapters of this book describe some of our findings. It seemed logical to begin with a study of the genesis of class management at the beginning of the school year, and chapter 3 describes our interviews with, and observations of, a sample of experienced teachers starting their new school year in September, as well as of student teachers commencing teaching practice. The literature suggests that these first few days are an important phase, when ground rules and personal relationships are established, and there are few studies of this establishing period, so we gave it a high priority.

One significant focus in the project was on teaching styles, and chapter 4 brings together observations of several hundred lessons given by student and experienced teachers to see what principal strategies of class management they employed. Chapter 5 focuses specifically on the handling of disruptive and deviant behaviour. The data here come from the analysis of hundreds of 'critical events' observed in classrooms, as well as from teachers' comments on a set of photographs showing children misbehaving. Chapter 6 describes a special set of twenty case studies of supply teachers. These teachers have to manage a variety of classes, often at short notice, so we felt a great deal could be learned from them. Interviews and photographs of disruptive classroom scenes were used to elicit responses.

One of the most consistent areas of educational research is that of pupil perceptions of teaching. No study of class management would be complete without the pupil perspective, and chapter 7 describes the findings from several hundred interviews with primary pupils, in which we used the same photographs of disruptive incidents as we had employed with teachers. Chapters 8 and 9, on the other hand, focus specifically on teachers' management of two important professional classroom skills: explaining, often reported as the one most valued by children, and questioning. Chapter 8 reports a study of 128 explanations to children aged 8 and 9, and chapter 9 describes an analysis of over 1,000 questions asked by primary teachers.

Another significant area of interest was how teachers manage the subject matter of their lessons, especially in fields where they do not feel especially competent. As was mentioned in chapter 1 there is an enormous range of subject matter to be mastered during the compulsory years of schooling. Many primary teachers have found problems coping with the subject knowledge required in fields like science and technology. Chapter 10 describes two large-scale national surveys we conducted of over a thousand teachers in which we asked them how competent they felt to teach the different subjects and also the extent to which they could teach specific topics in subjects like English, mathematics and science with their existing subject knowledge. There is also a study of teachers teaching what to them was unfamiliar subject matter, like 'electricity' or 'floating and sinking', to see what coping strategies they employed and what problems they encountered.

Finally we focused specifically on student teachers learning this array of management skills. During the project we observed and interviewed numerous student teachers and chapter 11 brings together the work we did on teaching strategies, attitude change during teaching practice, and views on disruption, in the strand of the project which I directed. There is also a great deal of relevant information about trainees in *Learning to Teach*, the parallel book of research findings to this one written by Neville Bennett and Clive Carré (Bennett and Carré, 1993). Chapter 12 gives an overview, in the light of the Leverhulme Primary Project research, of the skills primary teachers need for the present and the future, and the sort of training that might be necessary for both beginners and experienced teachers.

Chapter 3

First encounters with a class

Every September a traditional set of rituals is repeated in thousands of primary schools: 5 year olds commence school for the first time; 6 year olds return to find they are no longer the novices of their school; 7 year olds move on to the junior school, or to a higher class in their present school; other classes meet their new teachers; parents wonder whether their children will settle in; teachers establish themselves with their new class, meet new pupils, renew acquaintance with others they have taught before. Not surprisingly, these first encounters have been less well documented and analysed than later phases in the year. It is common for researchers seeking to visit and observe classes early in the year to be asked to come back in late September or early October 'when things have settled down'. First encounters can be private affairs, even in schools which are normally open to observation and scrutiny.

Yet patterns can be laid down in these first few days, rules and relation-ships established, which, for good or ill, will affect both children and teachers, possibly throughout the year, so we felt it was very important to undertake case studies of a number of student and experienced teachers to see first of all what their aspirations and intentions were and, secondly, what actually transpired when teachers and pupils met for the first time. Such research is much more labour-intensive in the primary school than in the secondary school. When we analysed several hundred lessons in secondary schools as part of a first-encounters' study (Wragg and Wood 1984), it was feasible for one observer to watch the lessons of three or four different teachers. Secondary teachers may take five or six different classes each day, sometimes even more, so it is possible for an investigator to see several different teachers, each meeting a new class for the first or second time. In primary schools it is much more likely that each teacher will only have one class, so a separate observer is required for every teacher studied.

A number of social psychologists have looked at first encounters between human beings in a variety of social settings. Goffman (1971) has described the process of impression management which commences at first meetings and continues through subsequent encounters:

The individual's initial projection commits him to what he is proposing to be and requires him to drop all pretences of being other things. As the interaction among the participants progresses, additions and modifications in this informational state will of course occur, but it is essential that these later developments be related without contradiction to, and even built up from, the initial positions taken by the several participants.

Argyle (1967) has described the rapidity with which people reach conclusions about those they meet, the difference in sensitivity of acute observers, like Sherlock Holmes, and the mental patients whose perceptions appear distorted, and the growth of relationships in the early period of acquaintance:

A will categorize B in terms of social class, race, age, intelligence or whatever dimensions of people are most important to him, and this will activate the appropriate set of social techniques on the part of A. It is found that people vary widely in what they look for first in others.

It is not merely the individual personalities which are important when people meet. The social setting is also a powerful influence on events: whether one person meets another as a colleague, employer, supplicant, whether someone holds a certain rank or status, wears a uniform, whether the encounter is in private or in public, between two people or several, takes place informally on the street, in a home, or formally at a gathering, in an institution or workplace.

When teachers meet a new class of pupils, a variety of social, environmental and institutional factors are at work in addition to the effects of the several individual personalities involved. Teachers, whatever their individual style, are known to be legally *in loco parentis*. They are inescapably part of a national, local and professional culture, even if they personally reject a number of aspects of it.

When teachers have been in a school for some time their reputation will precede them, and pupil folklore will have told their new classes a great deal about what to expect. Experienced teachers who have moved to another school frequently express surprise during their first few weeks about the difficulty of establishing their identity in a new location after their previous school in which so much could be taken for granted. Supply teachers in particular have to become adept at managing first encounters in new and varying locations because they have so many of them, and our case studies of twenty supply teachers are not included in this chapter, but are described in chapter 6.

Evertson and Anderson (1978) studied twenty-seven teachers of third-grade classes in eight American elementary schools for the first three weeks of the school year, followed by occasional visits later in the school year. They used a mixture of interviews and observations of lessons, concentrating largely on pupils' engagement in their task. Those teachers who secured highest pupil involvement as measured by their schedule showed more evidence of having thought in advance about rules and procedures, gave more time to clarifying rules and procedures, and introduced their pupils gradually to independent work. This kind of study is of considerable interest, but is sometimes criticised for being self-fulfilling, that is, by setting a premium on task involvement, finding that formal and carefully structured teaching is 'effective'.

Eltis (1978), in an Australian study, concentrated on the extent to which impressions formed in early lessons influenced subsequent events. He found that both experienced and student teachers' perceptions of pupils were influenced by speech, appearance, voice and written work. Pupils' accents were thought to be particularly influential on teachers' early and subsequent judgements. He also found that both beginning and experienced teachers were reluctant to discuss pupils' progress and attributes during this early phase.

Eisenhart (1977) concentrated on teachers' methods of establishing control in her two-year study of fifth- and sixth-grade classes in a city in the southern United States. Most teachers assigned seats to pupils rather than let them choose, and several developed their own distinct style of control from the beginning. One teacher capitalised on the impending arrival of autumn by writing each pupil's name on a leaf which was pinned to a large picture of a tree. Children were exhorted to keep their leaf from falling, and miscreants found their personal leaf removed from sight.

Soar (1973) followed the progress of a cohort of children in 289 kindergarten, first- and second-grade classes for three years. In a smaller-scale study of twenty teachers who were especially high or low in class control, he found that teachers with a high degree of control had started by permitting little pupil freedom and then increasing it, and teachers with a low degree of control had begun with high pupil freedom which they then attempted to decrease.

Some investigators have concentrated on the establishment of classroom rules. Buckley (1977), in an ethnographic study of one classroom, identified thirty-two rules, of which twenty-two had been spoken of in some form by the teacher within the first six days of the school year. Of these thirty-two rules some fifteen came from outside the classroom, mainly from the principal. A number of rules emerged after the initial period, such as when a pupil in the third week played in a certain courtyard during break and was told by the teacher on duty that this was not allowed, even though no formal announcements had ever been made. Some rules were established indirectly and by euphemism. The teacher, rather than state that cheating was not permitted, proclaimed that some pupils 'had big eyes'.

In a study of forty-one secondary teachers and trainees Wragg and Wood (1984) analysed over 300 lessons given at the beginning of the school year or of teaching practice. It was found that many experienced teachers established a big public presence in the very first lesson, making extensive use of their eyes to sweep the class or engage individuals. The most common classroom rule noted was 'no talking when the teacher is talking' (in public situations), followed by 'no disruptive noises', and rules about entering and leaving the classroom and not interfering with the work of others. Student teachers concentrated on the subject matter of their first lesson, on 'making an impact', and were less likely to use their eyes to sweep the class. Experienced teachers tended to focus more on establishing a climate, and stressed rules that had a moral dimension, like the 'proper' way to set out work, or respect for property. They were also much clearer than students, in interview, about what they expected and how they would conduct their lessons, whereas some students said that rules would be established as the need arose, rather than predetermined.

Several investigators into aspects of teacher or pupil expectancy and the way people typify each other have also identified factors which can be of concern during initial meetings. King (1978) observed infant teachers in three schools, and described how they typified children mainly from their own perceptions in the classroom rather than from written reports of other teachers, and how their typification changed as the school year proceeded. Nash (1973) used personal construct theory to study what constructs eight junior school teachers had assembled about the children they taught. He found that teachers based their perception of the children they taught largely in terms of personality and behaviour rather than ability. Hargreaves (1977) identified three models of teacher typification from the literature, an ideal-matching model whereby pupils are set against some imaginary paragon, a characteristic model which is like an identikit, and a dynamic interactionist model, favoured by symbolic interactionists, which tries to reflect the effects of context and the changes in perception which occur over time as a result of events. Anderson *et al.* (1980) and Emmer (1985) have also summarised some of the findings on the first part of the school year.

The study of experienced teachers

We decided to undertake a study of twenty experienced teachers and both to interview them in July about their intentions in the following September, and then to observe them for the first three days of the school year. In order to recruit sufficient observers primary specialist student teachers in the final stages of their course were trained as interviewers and classroom observers, using specially devised interview and observation schedules. Contact was made with schools in different parts of the country near to the students' homes, so that travel was minimised. A choice was made in each case from the local list of schools and in all cases the first or second randomly selected school agreed to participate. The twenty teachers were interviewed extensively in July and then observed for the first three days of the school year in the following September. Field workers used three schedules altogether, an interview schedule, a first lesson observation schedule and a subsequent lessons observation schedule. Several group and individual training sessions were held, using videotapes to train the twenty field workers. The schedules concentrated on qualitative data, and so every item was discussed in detail and a high level of agreement on principles and conventions was reached before observations and interviews began. Observers were given considerable help with the nature of field notes that would be needed, with numerous specific exemplars.

Of the twenty case studies six teachers were male and fourteen female. All were very experienced, with from eleven to thirty years of teaching with a mean of 19.3 years. Half had originally qualified exclusively as primary teachers and half as secondary only or primary and secondary. Nine were deputy heads with full teaching programmes. Preliminary interviews showed that most were satisfied with their job, were appreciative of the quality of relationships, the facilities available, but were more critical where facilities were poor, as they were in several schools. Twelve were critical of the quality of accommodation and felt that this hindered them in their work. Sixteen operated in traditional closed classrooms, two in open-plan and two in what they described as 'semi-open-plan'. Much concern about the beginning of the year concerned the poor layout of the school, lack of space for storage and display, lack of sinks, hot water, bookcases, poor decoration and other features which they felt made a bad impression on incoming children. Expressions like 'diabolical', 'barely adequate' and primary schools being 'the Cinderella of the education system' confirmed this concern and shame over the working environment. Few teachers had extra help, though fourteen made use of parent helpers in the classroom. Class sizes observed ranged from fifteen to thirty-nine with a mean of twenty-nine, and most classes had roughly equal numbers of boys and girls.

Preparation and planning intentions

Only seven teachers said they knew all or most of their new pupils, but most claimed they would not know their new pupils other than from playground duty or perhaps from occasional first aid or deputy head duties. When asked whether there was anything they wanted to know about their new class which would help them teach well or hinder them, fifteen mentioned features such as the reputation of the class, whether they worked well or badly together, what able or special-needs children they would be teaching and who might have behavioural difficulties. One teacher said she was really looking forward to taking her new class simply because it was known to be a difficult one: 'Every school has one class no teacher would like to teach. This is one of them.'

When asked about differences in style between their approach and that of the previous class teacher, thirteen thought there would be a significant difference, two a slight difference and five said no difference at all. Amongst features mentioned most frequently were being more formal, more structured, more organised and more strict, with higher standards and a closer check on children's work. Eight of the twelve who commented mainly on these features stressed their intention to be deliberately more firm and structured than their predecessor. It is difficult to say whether this tendency might be widespread, but it is noteworthy that, at the intention stage at least, there is such a conscious emphasis on greater firmness and less tolerance of low standards. It is one of the shortcomings of the present study that we were not able to monitor these particular classes throughout the year to see if stated intentions were implemented.

We also asked teachers about their preparation for their very first lessons, what they would prepare, what they would do and think about an hour before and five minutes before meeting the children. A diversity of responses was noted. An hour before the first meeting many would be concentrating on actual preparation, checking and actually rehearsing in their minds what they would be doing, down to going through their intended opening words mentally in some cases. Questions in teachers' minds varied from immediate ones like 'Will all the children expected actually turn up?' and, from a teacher of younger children, 'How many children will cry?' to the longer-term 'How will this class develop during the year?'. Some of the deputy heads also had to consider general school issues like 'Have the steps been repaired?' About half expressed general feelings of hope or excitement. In the last five minutes before the children entered the class most said they would have completed their preparations and would try to relax, one with deep breathing exercises, another with a cup of coffee. Some of the deputies were aware that they would probably have general duties, like seeing all the children in from the playground and then meeting their own class. Other likely activities mentioned were talking to parents, wondering how the children would be feeling, and dealing with problems. Four of the teachers taught infant age classes and the other sixteen juniors. Twelve of the teachers taught children in the 9–11 age group.

Very first encounter

A separate schedule A was devised for the very first encounter. Most of it was the same as schedule B, which was used for all subsequent lessons, but there were additional sections in which to record whether teachers introduced themselves, showed or talked about different areas of the room, or talked about school or classroom rules. The first session observed occupied typically ninety to 100 minutes and included an assembly. All teachers were well prepared for the children's arrival, and in sixteen cases there were specific worksheets or assignment cards for children to do in the first session. In only four cases did pupils enter the classroom before the teacher. Of the others, eight were already there waiting for the class to arrive and eight accompanied the pupils into the room. Both the formality of the actual entry into the room and the subsequent degree of 'chaos' were coded by the research team on a 1–5 point scale, with 1 being the most formal room entry and 5 representing a very unorganised arrival, and similarly for 'chaos', with 1 representing none and 5 a great deal. The word 'chaos' here should be dry-cleaned of its usual pejorative overtone. That a particular classroom was in some disarray during the first few minutes of the school year, as parents and children arrived, did not necessarily mean that no effective learning would take place during the rest of the day, as the account in this chapter shows.

It is possible for the two scales to differ, in that an entry may be informal but not necessarily followed by chaos. Two extracts from observers' logs reveal the range:

Formal entry (scoring 1 for formality and 1 for lack of chaos) The class (of 10–11 year olds) were assembled outside (the room) and told to get their dinner money ready and line up. The class were then told to lead in, wait across the front of the room and await further instructions as to where they should sit. A reminder was given not to talk. The class did as they were told.

Informal entry (scoring 5 for informality and 5 for chaos) The (5–6 year old) pupils came into the room informally along with some parents. The teacher was in the room trying to converse with a worried parent. The children were told to sit on the mat, but few obeyed the instruction. There was a lot of excited chatter and confusion – a state which continued until the bell went and parents left.

Table 3.1 shows the very mixed pattern of entry for the twenty teachers.

Once children had entered the classroom and been seated the degree of orderliness tended to remain steady or increase. In only three classes did observers record greater disorder. Teachers used various devices for

Table 3.1 Degree of formality and chaos on 1–5 point scales during opening session of the year (1=highest degree of formality, 1=least amount of chaos)

Formality score	Chaos score	Number of teachers
1	1	1
1	2	2
2	2	3
3	2	3
3	3	2
3	4	1
4	3	1
4	4	2
4	5	1
5	2	2
5	4	1
5	5	1

establishing or maintaining order. One teacher of 7–8 year olds calmed down noisy children who were sitting on the carpet by saying they were to be quiet so that they would be 'the best class in the school'. An older class of 10–11 year olds became more aggressive post-entry, fighting over where to sit, confused in some cases, walking around wearing coats and carrying bags, as the teacher had not arrived and chairs were on tables, so no one could sit down.

Observers noted down what happened when teachers first sought to gain the attention of their class. Only three made a formal attempt to greet their class, saying, 'Good morning class 7,' 'Good morning, everyone. I hope you had a nice holiday,' and 'Good morning, everyone. Did you have a good holiday?' respectively. However, observers' notes show that few actually needed to introduce themselves as they were known to the pupils, having taught them previously or met them in a previous term's induction session. One teacher said to the class, 'Everybody knows me. I don't know you all yet, but by the end of the day I will.' Some teachers used non-verbal signals, a male teacher of 11 year olds, for example, being described as standing hands on hips until pupils fell silent. Most common attention-gaining words were 'Right' and variants of 'Could you all please listen.' This was usually followed by instructions about seating, register calling and talk about lunchtime arrangements. In the majority of cases children became immediately attentive, but observers recorded non-attentive behaviour in seven classrooms: that pupils carried on whispering excitedly, continued conversations begun in the playground or fiddled with artefacts like pencil cases or bags. Usually this non-attention was picked up, except in two cases, by the teacher naming the child, asking for silence or directing questions specifically at those not attending. In half the classes there was some introduction to the classroom and its resources – the reading corner, for example.

One feature of the first session of the first day, usually with older pupils, was a strong moral exhortation. This confirmed to some extent what teachers had said in interview the previous July about wanting higher standards than the previous teacher. Instances recorded by observers included a statement by one teacher of top primary pupils that they were 'VIPs' who should set an example, 'image setters' for the whole school. Other teachers made similar appeals and assertions. Some schools were to take a selective 11+ test later in the year to determine which secondary school they should attend, and success in this was sometimes linked to a responsibility to 'have a good year and reap the rewards'.

This moral exhortation was often reinforced in the first school assembly, which frequently took place on the first morning. In addition to the hymns and prayers there were examples of several explicit or implicit purposes, such as establishing control, inspiring, informing, laying down of rules, outlining of expectations, establishment or reinforcement of the school ethos, 'making a fresh start', assertion of community values, as the following recorded incidents reveal:

1   The head praised pupils on how smart they looked and asked them to keep it up.
2   'When you come into assembly, imagine a zip across your mouth. It is your responsibility to keep it closed.'
3   Class 7 (the oldest pupils) had had a poor reputation the year before. The head told them they would be expected to behave well and show a high degree of responsibility now they were the top class.
4   A theme, 'the importance of friendship', was introduced.
5   The children were told the story of Robert the Bruce, and the moral message it contained, to keep on trying, was emphasised.
6   The head said that the school rules were based on 'common sense, such as taking care of people'.
7   Children were told not to come to school before nine o'clock as they would not be allowed into the building.
8   The head asked pupils to look at her during assembly when she was talking. One small group of pupils did not do this, so she stared at them until they did.

What characterises this very first encounter at the beginning of the school year is the very multiplicity of purposes it must fulfil. A significant part of this is children's socialisation into a new yet, in most cases, familiar environment. There are conventions to learn – how the register is called, what happens about school dinners, where one sits, hangs clothes, puts bags. In addition, there are rules specific to the new teacher – where free movement is permitted, how to set out work, what noise level is tolerated, what happens when pupils misbehave and, indeed, what constitutes misbehaviour, a topic which will be dealt with again in chapters 4, 5 and 7. An interesting aspect of this initial socialisation occurred when choice of seating was analysed. The continuum was from high teacher direction to completely free choice. Three teachers simply assigned each pupil to a seat, there was no choice; eight offered a partial choice, some permitted pupils to select a seat, others told them where to sit because of specific circumstances or known bad behaviour; three teachers offered free choice, but warned that it was a privilege dependent on good behaviour and that miscreants would be reseated at the teacher's behest; finally, six teachers offered a completely free choice of seat with no conditions attached, though in some cases this was for the first session only, while other matters were sorted out.

Teachers' reasons for their seating policies were sometimes stated explicitly and sometimes concealed. One teacher of 10–11 year olds began in a highly directive manner:

Now, I have decided on places for you this half-term. This is based on maths groups. There is no point in sitting next to children on different books. I change places regularly. The set places I have decided on are . . . [naming each child and indicating assigned seat].

The surface reason here seems to be an ability grouping, but the teacher explained that this was a class which had acquired a bad reputation and she was determined not to let it continue. In practice each group consisted of similar numbers of boys and girls. A number of teachers in the 'semi-directive' category specified a gender mix, as in the case of the teacher who began, 'Sit where you like, but I want a mixture of boys and girls on each table.' The general convention, with these exceptions, appeared to be conditional freedom of choice, contingent on what the teacher regarded as responsible exercising of that freedom.

With so much attention to socialisation and administrative routines, the academic content of the very first session of the year took second place. Some kind of reading or writing activity was the most common focus noted by observers, a handwriting exercise, writing about what children had done on holiday, silent reading being noted in half the cases. Three examples of maths (one as assessment test), two of art and one of music (hymn practice) were also recorded. The tasks were generally common to the whole class, though a small number of teachers began immediately with group work. The majority of classes settled down to the task in hand immediately, and only in four cases was more than two minutes needed before children commenced their work. The longest recorded settling-down and starting point was four to five minutes for a group given a writing assignment. Early signs of classroom rule establishment often occurred at this stage and teachers usually commented on noise if it occurred, saying, 'I want no talking when I'm talking,' or 'Only the occasional chat with your neighbour. No more.' In nineteen out of twenty classrooms there was no recorded comment about excessive noise. In the remaining class the observer noted that the level of noise did appear to be distracting, especially when the teacher left the room.

In order to take stock of this very first session, observers were asked to make a 'dipstick' report at roughly the half-way stage, recording what was happening some forty-five or fifty minutes into the first day. By this point in the day, fourteen out of twenty classes were expected by the teacher to be engaged on some specific task. Of the remaining six, three were sorting out resources, one was engaged in registration and dinner money collection, one was mid-way in transition between two assignments, and the other was returning from assembly. Many of the teachers were walking round the room monitoring work, checking progress, collecting dinner money, talking to individuals, or engaging in several of these activities. Only two remained seated at their desk and another two stood at the front of the class.

Observers frequently commented on the nature of individual interactions.

These often reflected the 'firm but friendly' manner that teachers had described in their interviews the previous July, with emphasis on personal understanding:

> the teacher knew something about every child. In some cases she had taught other members of their family, even some parents . . . [she took] time to chat about each family and check whether they [the children] liked a shortened or full version of their names . . .

A teacher of 6–7 year olds was described as 'very friendly towards children, although she expects what is said to be done. [She is] well prepared, both with activities and resources. No need for much checking from the teacher, as the children are very quiet and apprehensive.'

There was only one exception to this generally businesslike first session, when one teacher did not leave enough time for children to carry out an activity involving their new trays – 'disorganisation and chaos set in, with a resulting increase in the amount of noise and too many children moving about in a narrow area'. Although observers were asked specifically to record behaviour judged to be 'inappropriate', there was very little of it in this first session, after the occasional chaos of the first few minutes. Some classes were excited and had to be quietened, but it was more likely that, as one observer described it, 'the children were playing safe and responding with care'. Such mildly deviant behaviour as was recorded tended to occur towards the end of the first session or when the teacher left the room or was occupied with some administrative task.

At the end of these first sessions, usually at playtime, or going to assembly followed by playtime, few instructions were given, as most pupils were familiar with the school's routines for assemblies and morning break. Six classes were given a five or ten-minute warning. Actual dismissal of the class was, however, quite tightly organised in sixteen of the classes, though four classes simply left the room informally. Nine of the classes were lined up at the door, six were dismissed group by group, and the dismissal of the remaining class was not recorded by the observer.

General comments were made by observers at the end of this first session on aspects of class management that seemed worthy of note. Many of these reinforced and restated the generally businesslike nature of what had been a mixture of administration, familiarisation and a certain amount of writing or reading work, mostly done in a friendly manner. One teacher's use of both voice and non-verbal communication was described, showing her use of eye contact for control, something identified by other observers as a notable feature:

> She regains attention by raising the tone of her voice. Her basic attitude is a very friendly one. She uses her eyes a lot and smiles. She talks a lot but tolerates orderly interruption. The situation is controlled by her looking at

the child she wishes to speak to. The others stop talking and everyone is given a fair chance.

This predominant image of the very first session in the primary school year is in marked contrast to the study we conducted of secondary teachers' first encounters (Wragg and Wood 1984). Whereas a friendly smile, businesslike manner and benign firmness characterised the presentation of self by the twenty primary teachers in this present study, the twenty secondary teachers in the earlier study were more aggressively assertive. Most of them stressed in interview the need to project a larger-than-life image in order to establish social control over potentially disruptive adolescents, summed up by one teacher as 'I'm very stern and very hard. I am consciously being a little harder than I am.' Observation of secondary teachers' lessons showed a similar use of eyes to sweep the whole class or engage in eye contact, but the use of a harsh voice, a higher degree of public reprimanding and a very territorial manner (*my* classroom, *my* lab) were much more in evidence. Primary teachers used a much gentler manner, orientated towards the individual pupil, with little angularity and no example of public shaming in these first sessions. Social control was certainly established in almost every case, but with none of the overt dominance and aggression noted in the earlier study of secondary teachers.

Establishing and maintaining rules

A significant feature of the first three days of the school year which were observed in this study was the establishment, maintenance or reaffirmation of rules. Many human activities are governed by rules of conduct, and learning what these formal rules or informal conventions are, when to follow and when, perhaps more occasionally, to break them, and about the consequences of conformity or dissension, are commonplace both in childhood and in adult life. In school there are the *national rules*, many incorporated in Acts of Parliament, which govern attendance, parental rights and duties, or the use of punishment; there are *local authority rules*, perhaps a code of conduct in physical education lessons or on field trips; there are *school rules*, concerning dress, behaviour in classroom and playground; and finally there are *individual teacher rules* about talking, moving and setting out work or behaviour.

Interviews with teachers in July showed that about three-quarters said they expected to introduce rules from the first session and one said the first session would be devoted largely to rule setting. Others were less explicit, feeling that rules would emerge more as the need arose, and one saying that there was little point in giving too many at any one time as 'they wouldn't remember anyway'. Analysis of interview responses showed that rules could be grouped under several headings, such as movement, talking or work-related. The following nine categories of teacher rules were identified:

1   *Movement*

Walk quietly.
No running.
Ask first if you want to go to the toilet.
Don't just wander around the room unless you're getting something.
Stick to chosen seat.

2   *Talking*

Don't talk when I'm talking to you.
You should only be talking to each other if it's about your work.
Don't talk when someone is answering a question.
Only one person talking at a time.
No shouting out.
Put your hands up if you want to ask a question.
Silence during registration.
Silence in the library area.
Listen to the teacher and other pupils.

3   *Work-related*

Being able to work independently on your own.
Being able to work harmoniously in a group.
Working quietly even if the teacher is out of the room.
Getting out your own tray at the beginning of the day, after lunch or after
    playtime, and then starting work without having to be told.
Not distracting or spoiling the concentration of others when they are
    working.

4   *Presentation*

Knowing how to set out work and when to hand it in.
Taking care with content.

5   *Safety*

Care with cupboards, sinks.
Care with scissors, rulers, pencils.
No swinging on chairs.
No playing on slippery banks in wet weather.

6   *Space*

Not allowed in classroom at break.
During wet weather being allowed in school or classroom to read, play
    games or sit quietly.
This classroom is a work area, not a play area.

7   *Materials*

Equipment to be handled carefully and kept in its proper place.
Keep library books tidy.
Know the correct place for returning equipment or unused materials.
Put things away properly at the end of the day.
Clothing and PE equipment to be kept on pegs.
No writing on desks or book covers.
Return borrowed items to their owner.
Stack chairs on or under tables or desks at the end of the day.

8   *Social behaviour*

Show consideration for others.
Be willing to share things and co-operate.
Don't go into someone else's tray unless you've been told to.
Be polite and thoughtful: treat others as you would like to be treated
    yourself.
Show good manners.

9   *Clothing*

Clothing to be neat and clean.
Wear uniform properly (i.e. school tie).
All clothing to be labelled.
During hot weather sleeves may be rolled up and cardigans, jackets,
    pullovers and tie removed.

It is one thing to be able to express a set of rule expectations in a quiet
interview in July, but quite another to implement these aspirations amid the
rapid-moving novelties of the first session of the school year. Analysis of first
sessions showed that sixteen teachers did talk explicitly about classroom
rules and that the others also made children aware of rules without describing
them in detail, saying, for example, 'You know what we expect of you,' or
'You know what to do.' This taken-for-granted approach to rule establishment or maintenance was particularly noticeable with older pupils. Most of
the rules noted in classroom time were teacher rules, sometimes specific to
the particular teacher's preferred way of working, whereas in assembly the
heads tended to mention school rules about entry and departure or playground behaviour. There was general consistency between what teachers had
said in interview and what happened in the classroom, but not exact
congruence. For example, one teacher who had expressed in interview a 'no
writing on desks' rule did not react when a pupil did write on a desk, as she
appeared preoccupied. The numerous demands on a teacher's attention can
act as a constraint in rule enforcement.

During the first classroom sessions observed there were fifty examples
noted by observers of rule establishment or maintenance. A third of these

were related to equipment, materials and resources and involved pens, pencils, notebooks, trays or chairs. A further quarter involved general classroom procedures and sixteen per cent concerned noise levels. Between them, these three aspects covered over three-quarters of all rule-making observed. The remainder dealt with dinner money, parental access before school, dress and appearance, movement and personal property.

There were different strategies for the introduction and reiteration of rules. Most frequently, teachers used direct commands, often expressed in precise terms: 'Always bring a book to class,' 'Don't eat pencils,' 'Always underline your work with a ruler – it looks neater.' This last instance is an example of a command plus an explanation, like 'Bring exact change for dinner money, to make life easier.' Some commands were accompanied by a warning: 'Don't talk when I'm talking, or by the end of term we won't like each other.' Table 3.2 shows the distribution of the fifty rule-setting examples over different categories of strategy:

Rule making is only a first step in the establishment of classroom order and effective working relationships. The first test of teachers' rules comes when they are broken. The major strategy in rule making, as table 3.2 shows, was direct command, the do's and don'ts of classroom life. Observers were asked to made notes about teachers' responses to breaches of their rules, what happened, whether the teacher responded and what the outcome was.

Only one serious incident occurred, when a newly arrived 5 year old, who was in a highly emotional state, kicked a supply teacher on the shin. The worst incident, apart from that, was when a girl slammed a book on the desk while answering a fellow pupil's question, and scattered some crayons. Chapter 5 deals with pupil disruption in more detail, so, at this stage, the analysis of 223 incidents of what is usually minor misbehaviour during first

Table 3.2 Analysis of fifty examples of rule establishment or maintenance in the very first session of the year in all twenty classrooms observed

Strategy	No. of examples
Direct command	23
Explanation	5
Statement with expectation	4
Command with warning	3
Command with explanation	3
Expectation	2
Statement	2
Question	2
Statement with command	2
Unspecified	2
Expectation with warning	1
Explanation with question	1
Total	50

lessons will be considered. Of these, sixty-five were described and analysed in greater detail by observers and analysts as being particularly illustrative of misbehaviour occurring. The largest category involved talking either too noisily, out of turn, or failing to listen. The other two most common categories were fiddling with items such as rulers, pencil cases or bags, and being out of seat and/or distracting other pupils. There was no physical aggression between pupils, other than two instances of pushing each other. Most of the illicit talk was between pairs of pupils rather than larger groups. Fidgeting and fiddling with artefacts was mostly associated, in the comments of observers, with children losing interest when passive for too long. In about two-thirds of cases teachers checked, by comment, reprimand or statement of a rule, the noisy chatter, usually reacting before it had escalated. Eye contact, moving over to the pupils concerned, touching lightly and moving pupils to another seat, were also recorded as response strategies. The assertions of authority were firm but not as hard and aggressive as had been noted in earlier studies of both male and female secondary teachers: 'Hands, please. Let us have manners at all times,' 'For the moment, I'm the boss. No talking when the teacher is talking.' Reprimands were administered slightly more to individuals than to small groups or the whole class. In 90 per cent of cases the misbehaviour ceased immediately. Only rarely did it not stop at all. This picture confirmed that teachers appeared to follow the rule-making and rule-enforcing behaviour they had described in interview, though demands on their attention, and pressure of objectives to be achieved, sometimes acted as a constraint.

Later encounters

The patterns of the first week of the school year in the twenty schools we studied were very varied. Even the school day varied in length by fifty minutes, or four hours ten minutes per week. The longest school day recorded was 415 minutes, the shortest 365 minutes. Time spent in the classroom, as opposed to the playground or dining room, also varied by fifty minutes, from 315 minutes down to 265 minutes. Both extremes were witnessed in older junior classes. All except one school operated two morning sessions, the remaining school had just one with a flexible break. A quarter of schools had a single continuous session in the afternoon, the others ran two sessions. Observers commented on the loss of concentration during the late afternoon in schools that had no break.

After the first day teachers' patterns of behaviour did change. The entry routine at the beginning of the day would obviously be different when there was no need to seat pupils, but registration followed whatever the teacher regarded as her standard pattern. Entry to class at other times did change, however, and it became less likely that the teacher and pupils would enter the room together. More commonly pupils arrived first, often because their teacher had lunchtime or break duties in the playground or elsewhere. Some teachers who had stated in interview their desire to be more formal or not allow misbehaviour were amongst the ones more likely to be in the classroom when the class arrived. Table 3.3 shows a summary of entry behaviour over the three days observed. The later entries were also generally much less formal than on the first morning, with few classes lining up outside. In several cases girls were seen to enter the room first. Although entry was informal it was rarely described as disorderly.

On the first day most teachers had had all necessary materials to hand for the beginning of the session and there were few instances during the day of these not having been prepared by the beginning of the session or of teachers still assembling the necessary equipment or materials as the class arrived. This general pattern of preparedness continued almost unaltered, apart from a very slight tendency for more examples to be recorded of preparation going on as pupils arrived, an increase from two instances on the first day (out of seventy-seven sessions) to five on the third day (out of seventy-one sessions).

Analysis of the first few minutes of each session showed that in most cases work began quickly. Occasional boisterous entrances were recorded, but these were usually followed by orderly work. There was just one exception, a teacher whose lessons always began in an unruly way, and the observer recorded on the first day, 'Entrance noisy . . . fighting over desks and when putting school bags and jumpers into classroom'; on the second day, 'Turbulent pushing and shoving'; on the third day, 'Half the class in by 8.50. Remainder enter in various ways. Much movement between 8.50 and 9.00, one group looking at a book, one group fighting, two children helping teacher. When bell rings pupils sit down noisily . . . talking, pushing, bickering over a ball.' The children did then get on with some work, but interventions from the teacher were not noted, and no task demand was recorded. A much more typical first few minutes, however, would show pupils entering in an orderly manner but talking to other pupils, sitting down after hanging up coats and beginning to work fairly promptly, usually without the need to be directed, as teachers had made it clear that this was what was expected. In one classroom parents (of 7–8 year olds) came in with

Table 3.3 Number of occasions when various patterns of entry into the classroom were observed during first three days of year (total sessions observed = 222)

Type of entry	Day 1	Day 2	Day 3	Total
Teacher in room first	29	31	24	84
Pupils in room first	29	37	35	101
Simultaneous entry	15	4	6	25
Not recorded or unknown	4	2	6	12
Total number of sessions	77	74	71	222

the children each morning and the teacher encouraged this. There could be delays as a result, one parent, for example, explaining to the teacher about a child's medicine, but on another occasion the day began with a parent showing the class how to make a French plait. Application of the 1–5 'chaos' scale, described earlier, at the outset of the session and after children had taken their seats, showed that usually there was no change or the classroom had become less chaotic. Table 3.4 shows the analysis of these early minutes of each session. There is very little difference in the three daily patterns. Individual teachers' patterns were also quite consistent. Fourteen teachers' lessons showed a predominant pattern of no change or less chaos, two teachers a pattern of no change or more chaos, and four had mixed patterns.

A further example of rapid socialisation of pupils was shown by the decline in the number of acts of inappropriate behaviour observed during the three days. The following findings must, however, be interpreted with some caution. Although every effort was made during training, through videos, discussion and analysis of lessons, to ensure consistency in what was regarded as 'inappropriate' – for example, distracting others, talking illicitly, fiddling with pencil case instead of working – there were twenty different observers, and it is never possible, with such numbers, to guarantee absolute consistency. With this caveat, it does seem that instances of inappropriate behaviour declined after the first day. Almost all inappropriate behaviour observed was trivial. There was one incident, referred to above, of a distraught 5 year old kicking a supply teacher on the very first morning, and there were examples of pupils fighting for desks or chairs, but most other inappropriate behaviour was noisy chatter and this was almost always reprimanded by the teacher, whereupon, in most cases, it ceased. Table 3.5 summarises some of the inappropriate behaviour data.

There were fifteen teachers whose patterns showed less inappropriate behaviour on day 3 compared with day 1, and five whose sessions showed more, but the general trend was down. Given that the average length of a session was seventy to seventy-five minutes, and some classes were over thirty pupils, the overall mean of fifteen instances per session seems relatively low, and observers' field notes constantly confirm the orderly nature of the classrooms they observed.

Table 3.4 Degree of chaos post-entry compared with actual entry in 222 sessions observed during first three days

Nature of change	Day 1	Day 2	Day 3	Total
More chaos	15	12	12	39
Less chaos	34	37	33	104
No change	24	18	19	61
Not recorded or unknown	4	7	7	18
Total	77	74	71	222

Table 3.5   Number of instances of inappropriate behaviour per session

Overall mean number of instances of inappropriate behaviour per session	15.0
Mean number of instances of inappropriate behaviour per session, day 1	16.3
Mean number of instances of inappropriate behaviour per session, days 2 and 3	14.3
Teacher with highest mean number of instances per session	27.4
Teacher with lowest mean number of instances per session	3.8

Relationships continued to be friendly, with most teachers fine-tuning classroom rules by restating them or by commenting on an event. On one occasion, on the third day, for example, several children who had finished rushed towards the teacher's desk, something which had not happened on the first or second day. She told them there was no need to rush once they had completed a piece of work and no further instance was noted. Though the formality of the first morning was reduced in most cases on the second and third days, it was noticeable that those teachers who, in interview, had said they would be more strict than the previous teacher were usually quickest to react to inappropriate behaviour, except for one teacher who made no such efforts.

There will be further comment on these first encounters in chapter 11 when our research into student teachers is described, as they were also studied for the first few days of their block teaching practice, and some interesting comparisons can be made. It is a pity there have been so few studies of first encounters, as it is a fascinating area of classroom research. Skilful teachers observed in this study were able to receive as many as thirty-nine children, in the case of the largest class observed, a group of 9–10 year olds, and, despite the boisterous excitement, apprehension and noisy chatter of the first arrival, set them to work in an orderly manner within a short time. This was almost always done in a friendly but firm manner, with rules made explicit, in most cases, from the beginning. There was much exhortation in assembly, as well as in class, about the need for higher horizons, good behaviour, good standards of work, but there was very little of the harsher-voiced authoritarian stance taken by secondary teachers in a similar study (Wragg and Wood, 1984) by the present writer. The rapidity with which even children with difficult behaviour problems or anxieties became absorbed in activity is illustrated by these extracts from a researcher's notes of a reception class on the first day of the year.

The school is a large nursery and first school for 3–8 year olds in the middle of a huge working-class estate. From 8.30 onwards children arrive, some alone, some in twos and threes, sometimes with, sometimes without their parents. Whole families appear – mother, Grandma, Granddad, the child starting school, often a younger brother or sister, maybe two, with one in a pushchair, even the family dog. It is a big family occasion. By nine o'clock most children are in school and the street outside is deserted apart from the occasional passer-by or late arrival. Mrs A. has about two-thirds of her class present. She sits in a chair with the children around her feet. They talk about dinners, classroom rituals, who knows who in the class and where children might sit. Every five minutes or so a parent appears at the door with a child. An extra teacher, brought in for the first week, is on hand to feed in the latecomers. By 9.30 the class appears to be complete and children are assigned to tables where they choose an activity from several possibilities . . .

. . . at 10.20 there is an ear-splitting yell from down the corridor. The last arrival has appeared. She is clearly not enamoured of the idea of coming to school and her cries of 'No, Mummy, I don't want to go,' are joined in counterpoint by her mother's audible threats, bribes and oaths, 'I'll come and fetch you at teatime,' 'You've *got* to go to school or I'll get into trouble.' Outside Mrs A.'s classroom the extra supply teacher attempts to soothe parent and child. 'What's her name? Tina, is it? Well, come with me, Tina, and I'll take you into Mrs A.'s room.' Tina kicks her violently on the shin.

The supply teacher brings Tina and her mother into the classroom. She sits Tina down at a table and starts to do a jigsaw with her. 'I'm just going to have a word with Mrs A., I'll be back in a second.' Meanwhile, Tina's mother slips gratefully out of the room. A brief ten-second conversation between the supply teacher and Mrs A. follows, in which the supply teacher says she will leave Tina to get on with the jigsaw. She returns to the table and crouches alongside Tina. 'Oh, well done. You're good at jigsaws, aren't you, Tina?' With that she mutters a vague 'I'll be back soon' and leaves the room. A couple of minutes later Mrs A. goes over to Tina. 'You've nearly finished that, Tina, well done. Here's a box of building bricks. When you've finished see if you can build something nice and then I'll come and have a look at it . . .

For the whole of the day Tina worked assiduously alongside the rest of the class, slightly reserved, but indistinguishable from the others, doing the activities, eating her lunch, playing in the playground during breaks.

The supply teacher made a brief return visit to see how she was, but by then she was immersed in constructing an elaborate arrangement of building bricks and barely looked up. At 3.15 she listened attentively as the teacher read the class a story, congratulated the children on their good behaviour and said she was looking forward to seeing them all the following day. At 3.30 the bell rang for the end of school and parents clustered outside the classroom to collect their children. Tina's mother appeared, pale-faced and anxiously asking how she had got on. 'Fine,' replied Mrs A. 'See you tomorrow, Tina,' whereupon Tina burst into tears. Her mother may well have been convinced that she had spent the day on the rack. The following day, however, Tina came to school on time, was calm in appearance and manifested no outward signs of distress about school.

Chapter 4

Systematic studies of class management

Managing the very first encounters with a new class is an important aspect of teaching, but sustaining and enhancing rules, relationships, application to the task in hand, preparation and planning must go on throughout the time that teachers and pupils are together. In order to monitor what happened in these more mature phases of the school year or term, once daily routines had been established, we decided to study the classrooms of a sample of experienced and novice teachers in different kinds of schools. Schools in ten local authorities were approached as being representative of a variety of large and small urban and rural schools. Thirty schools agreed to participate, and between one and nine teachers were observed in each school, giving a total of sixty teachers and students, of whom fifty-one were female and nine were male. Each was observed for four sessions, except for one teacher who was ill for several weeks and so was only observed for three sessions. The distribution of teachers and lessons is shown in table 4.1. This chapter concentrates on the quantitative data from these observations. The qualitative data are reported in chapter 5.

Table 4.1 Number of teachers and lessons observed in present sample

Region	Teachers	Lessons
North-west	25	100
London East End	9	35
South-west	14	56
Student teachers in South-west	12	48
Total	60	239

A mixture of observation methods was used, some structured and quantified, others semi-structured, yet others freehand. There were interviews with the teachers as well as observations of their 'lessons'. For this purpose a session, which usually lasted between half an hour and an hour, was termed a 'lesson', though it may have consisted of more than a single type of activity. The observer used first of all a version of the Nottingham Class Management

Observation Schedule (Wragg 1984). This is a category system in which the researcher ticks any of seventy activities which occur in each observation period: what teachers do, what pupils do, what the outcome is, as well as the degree of deviance. This is done for five separate lesson segments lasting ninety seconds each, once the session has begun. Thus 1,195 lesson segments were analysed from the 239 lessons observed. Most of the categories in the Nottingham Class Management Observation Schedule were used, but several were dropped, as primary classrooms are more complex to observe than secondary, so, for example, the three pupil movement categories of the original 'at wrong time', 'at wrong speed', 'to wrong place' were put together as 'inappropriate movement'. The principal focus in the schedule is on the teacher's handling of misbehaviour.

The definition of 'deviance' in classroom observation is not an easy matter. To some extent it is defined by the teacher. One teacher may permit free movement, another forbid pupils to leave their seat without permission. However, observers do have to make a number of personal decisions about what constitutes deviant behaviour, for a teacher may ignore, albeit rarely, one pupil hitting another, and though this may appear to legitimate such behaviour in one classroom, it would not constitute acceptable behaviour in most. Observers took what were perceived as the teacher's rules of conduct as a starting point, but had to exercise judgement about misbehaviour that would have been perceived as deviant in most other classrooms. It is a judgement between the individual and the norm which is by no means perfect, but observers did reach a high degree of agreement about interpretations before the research began, and maintained it through the duration of the study, as described below.

The second part of the schedule involves a sweep of every pupil in the class. The observer studies each pupil in turn for twenty seconds and then makes two decisions about on-task behaviour and deviance. The on-task behaviour category involves a decision as to whether the child being observed spends roughly 0–6 seconds, 7–13 seconds or 14–20 seconds on the task in hand. 'Mild' deviance is defined as misbehaviour like noisy or illicit talk, distraction of others, or wrong movement, whereas 'more serious' deviance includes violence to another pupil or to the teacher, insulting behaviour to the teacher, or damage to property. An involvement and a deviance index are then calculated by the following formula:

$$\text{Involvement or deviance index} = \frac{\text{Factor A} \times 100}{\text{Number of pupils} \times 2}$$

In each case, factor A is calculated by weighting each of the three observation categories 0, 1 or 2 and multiplying by the number of pupils in each category. Thus if, out of twenty-eight pupils, two were 'low' on task, ten were 'medium' and sixteen were 'high', then factor A would be $(2 \times 0) + (10 \times 1) + (16 \times 2) = 42$. Inserted into the involvement equation, this would give an index score of 75, that is, 42 divided by 56 (twice the number of pupils) times 100. The deviance index score is calculated in a similar manner. The possible range, therefore, is from 0 to 100, a score of 0 being obtained if all pupils were low on-task and not deviant, and a maximum score of 100 achieved if all were on task and behaving in a more seriously deviant manner. This is inevitably a rough-and-ready estimate, as the categories could be weighted in different ways, or not weighted at all, but it was used consistently in each lesson, so despite its limitations it is of some interest.

Two trained observers carried out the observations and, in order to check the extent to which they agreed or disagreed with others, two inter-observer agreement measures were taken, before and after the fieldwork. A percentage agreement figure was used, that is, the percentage of times the two observers agreed with each other on all the categories for five lesson observation segments. Observations were done on videotapes so that observers' ratings could be compared before and after the fieldwork. The use of percentages would be open to criticism if there were many unlikely categories like 'teacher flies through window' or events that never occurred, but the schedule consists of categories of behaviour all of which have been observed in classrooms. Agreement between observers was very high. Inter-observer agreement (comparing one observer with another) was 95.2 per cent before the fieldwork and 88.6 per cent after completion of all observation. Intra-observer agreement (the extent to which observers agree with themselves on two different ratings of the same videotaped lesson) was also very high, with observer A scoring 87.6 per cent, and observer B 88.1 per cent. The observation schedule does, therefore, seem to have been applied with a high degree of consistency.

Qualitative data were collected using two different approaches. The first involved the collection of 'critical events', that is, instances of classroom behaviour which the observer judged to be illustrative of some aspect of the teacher's class management, perhaps a rule being established, observed or broken, an aspect of interpersonal relationships or some other indicative event. The 'critical events' approach is based on the 'critical incidents' technique developed by Flanagan (1949). The observer wrote down what led up to the event, what happened and what the outcome was. After the lesson, teachers were interviewed and asked for their perception of what happened. The interviewer used neutral language like 'Can you tell me about . . .?' rather than loaded or leading questions, such as 'Why didn't you . . . ?'.

The second source of qualitative data was through the use of three photographs in the interviews with teachers. These were employed in other parts of the Leverhulme Primary Project to interview student teachers, class teachers, supply teachers, and pupils – so chapters 5, 6, 7 and 11 all contain descriptions of responses. Photograph 1 shows two pupils pushing each other, photograph 2 is of a class bursting into a room after break, and photograph 3 shows a girl, who has been told off for scribbling on a pupil's book, standing at the front of the class and muttering, 'Old cow,' under her breath. These photographs (figure 4.1) were selected from a larger sample of pictures which had been piloted as being illustrative of different types of deviance: a common piece of group misbehaviour (rushing into the room), a quarrel between a small group, with minor aggressive physical contact, and a more serious piece of misbehaviour involving damage to property and audible insult to the teacher. Teachers are asked how they would react were these events to happen in their own classroom.

We obtained, therefore, a considerable amount of data from the sixty teachers in the sample: structured lesson observations, critical events and interview statements. These responses are reported in this and the following chapter, and also in chapter 11, which deals specifically with student teachers and their class teacher supervisors.

Strategies observed

A wide range of lesson settings was covered for the whole sample. Most of the lesson segments, 58 per cent in all, covered mixed subject matter. Of the rest, 13 per cent were exclusively maths, 13 per cent English, 8 per cent humanities, 5 per cent science, and one per cent art, physical education and technology. None was exclusively music. The ages of classes ranged from 4 up to 12, with 18 per cent in reception or year 1 classes, 28 per cent in years 2 and 3, 28 per cent in years 4 and 5, and 26 per cent in years 6 and 7. In each lesson segment, the predominant type of activity was recorded, and table 4.2 shows the breakdown according to whether the teacher was acting solo, for example addressing the whole class, whether there was teacher–pupil inter-action, if the pupils working with or without the teacher monitoring, or if there was a transition from one activity to another. In each case, the one predominant activity during the period of observation was noted.

The principal choice of working strategy by primary teachers in this sample, therefore, is for a two-thirds to one-third split between individual or group work and whole-class teaching. Of the larger category – that is, pupils

Table 4.2 Predominant type of activity in each of 1,195 lesson segments observed for the whole sample (forty-eight teachers and twelve student teachers)

Activity	Percentage of occurrences
Teacher solo	9.7
Teacher–pupil interaction	20.6
Pupils working, teacher monitoring	63.4
Pupils working, teacher not monitoring	2.3
Transition with movement	1.5
Transition without movement	2.5
Total	100.00

Figure 4.1   The three photographs used in the interviews

working singly or in groups – almost all of it was being monitored by the teacher. In the case of whole-class teaching, about two-thirds involved teacher–pupil interaction and the remaining third usually the teacher addressing the class, often explaining the topic, telling a story or presenting information.

When we looked at misbehaviour, we found that very little of what was observed was serious, only 2 per cent deviant behaviour being coded in that category, the other 98 per cent being coded as 'mild'. What tended to happen was that in just over half the lesson segments analysed there was some minor misbehaviour. Coding was done quite strictly, so if, out of thirty pupils, one distracted another, that would have been registered under the 'one pupil' category. Table 4.3 shows the number of pupils involved when misbehaviour was noted.

Table 4.3 Number of pupils involved in misbehaviour during lesson segments (whole sample = forty-eight teachers and twelve student teachers)

Number of pupils involved	Percentage of occasions
No misbehaviour	44.6
One pupil	16.5
Two to four pupils	19.5
Five or more pupils	19.4
Total	100.00

In about a fifth of cases, two to four pupils were involved, and in another fifth of cases it was five pupils or more. Very often this would be a single group: frequently, though not always, boys sitting round the same table. The most common form of misbehaviour was noisy or illicit talk, which was noted in just under a third of lesson segments. Inappropriate movement, like leaving the seat without permission, when it should have been requested, or running, was the second most frequent form of misbehaviour, occurring in just over a quarter of lesson segments. Inappropriate use of materials – for example, twanging a ruler – occurred in 10 per cent of lesson segments. Defiance of the teacher, in fourth place, was observed in 8 per cent. Table 4.4 shows these and some minor categories of misbehaviour.

Almost always when misbehaviour did take place the teacher responded, usually before the deviance had escalated. Only in 9 per cent of cases was there no response. The most common responses were an order to cease or a reprimand, sometimes both, usually involving one or more pupils being named. Table 4.5 shows the distribution of teachers' responses and the most common as well as some less frequently occurring categories. A1 to A3 figures show the targets of the response, B1 and B2 the times, C1 to C12 actual strategies, and D1 and D2 the length of the response.

Reprimanding the pupils who were misbehaving, often to re-involve them in their work, was a common strategy, as were other non-verbal forms of behaviour like gesture and facial expression. Touching was usually to steer pupils away, tap them on the shoulder or turn them round, not physical punishment, which was not observed once. Confiscation of objects, ridicule, detention and the involvement of other teachers, including the head, were all rare, occurring on one per cent or less of occasions. The involvement of another teacher was only seen seven times in the whole set of observations. The outcome of these interactions can be seen in table 4.6, in which A1 to

Table 4.4 Percentage of lesson segments in which various kinds of misbehaviour occurred (total sample = 1,195 lesson segments)

Types of misbehaviour	Percentage of occurrences
1 Noisy or illicit talk	32.9
2 Inappropriate movement	26.4
3 Inappropriate use of materials	10.3
4 Defiance of teacher	8.3
5 Taking something without permission	1.8
6 Physical aggression towards another pupil	1.4
7 Illicit copying	0.6
8 Damage to materials/equipment	0.3
9 Insult to teacher	0.3
10 Illicit eating or drinking	0.3
11 Refusal to move	0.1

Table 4.5 Teachers' responses to misbehaviour (total sample = 1,195 lesson segments)

	Teachers' responses to misbehaviour	Percentage of occurrences
A1	To whole class	26
A2	To group	38
A3	To individuals	36
B1	Before escalation of misbehaviour	94
B2	After escalation of misbehaviour	6
C1	Order to cease	72
C2	Pupil named	68
C3	Reprimand	45
C4	Involve pupils in work	26
C5	Proximity (going over to pupil)	22
C6	Touch	16
C7	Facial expression	15
C8	Gesture	13
C9	Pause	7
C10	Pupil moved	5
C11	Praise/encouragement	4
C12	Humour	4
D1	Teacher response brief	78
D2	Teacher response sustained	22

Table 4.6 Outcomes of teachers' interactions, shown as a percentage of all responses (total sample = 1,195 lesson segments)

	Outcome of teacher interaction	Percentage of occurrences
A1	Pupil(s) silent	90
A2	Pupil(s) accept(s) teacher's action	6
A3	Pupil(s) altercate(s) or protest(s)	4
B1	Misbehaviour ends	79
B2	Misbehaviour lessens	15
B3	Misbehaviour is sustained	5
B4	Misbehaviour increases	1
C1	Teacher calm	90
C2	Teacher agitated	8
C3	Teacher angry	2

A3 give pupils' reactions, B1 to B4 reveal whether the misbehaviour increased, decreased, remained the same or not, and C1 to C3 show whether the teacher appeared calm, agitated or angry.

The summary of outcomes confirms the general orderliness. Mostly teachers dealt calmly with the minor deviance which occurred, like noisy talk or unauthorised movement. In most cases the immediate outcome was that misbehaviour ended or lessened, though other acts of minor deviance might recur later. Relatively few pupils challenged the teacher, only 4 per cent occurrences of altercating or protesting were observed. In about 7 per cent of lesson segments, the level of deviant behaviour was labelled 'high', which was interpreted as five or more witnessed acts of misbehaviour. The overall picture of primary classrooms observed in this particular study, therefore, is one of several minor irritations that affect harmonious working, rather than large insurrections or mayhem.

Classrooms in different contexts

Lessons were observed in a variety of contexts, some with older pupils, others with younger, some in city schools, others in more rural areas. It is worth considering what, if any, differences were found in these various circumstances, though it must be stressed that any descriptions in this chapter are of the present sample only. It would not be wise to generalise what is reported here to all classrooms in the regions or according to age groups. This is strictly a report of one study. The classrooms of student teachers, compared with those same classrooms when the regular class teacher was in charge, will be considered in chapter 11, so all tables and discussion in the remainder of this chapter refer to the sample of forty-eight experienced teachers only.

As shown in table 4.1, there were 100 lessons observed in the North-west, fifty-six in the South-west and thirty-five in the East End of London. Table 4.7 shows the distribution obtained in each of those three locations on some of the major categories from the classroom observation schedule. The overall patterns in the three regions are more notable for their similarities than their differences. Categories of misbehaviour such as 'defiance of teacher' and

Table 4.7 Percentages of different categories of teacher and pupil behaviour of experienced teachers in three regions (experienced teachers only, students excluded)

Category	North-west	South-west	London
Teacher solo	12	5	5
Teacher–pupil interaction	13	20	30
Pupils working, teachers monitoring	69	66	59
No misbehaviour	43	50	50
Noisy or illicit talk	29	25	36
Inappropriate movement	33	24	15
Inappropriate use of materials	9	9	10
Defiance of teacher	9	8	7
Order to cease	69	68	66
Pupil named	67	67	71
Reprimand	44	36	56
Involve pupils in work	29	44	10
Pupil(s) silent	94	84	85
Pupil(s) altercate(s) or protest(s)	2	3	12
Misbehaviour ends	86	78	84
Misbehaviour sustained	4	8	0
Teacher calm	89	94	93

'inappropriate use of materials' occur on a virtually identical scale in each of the three locations. Teachers' strategies such as 'order to cease' and 'pupil moved' are also similar in distribution. The results have not been subjected to analysis of variance or any other statistical procedure for determining whether the differences between groups are statistically significant, as this would make them look more precise than they are. In the London schools there is a tendency for slightly more teacher–pupil interaction and a lower frequency of pupils working alone or in groups, with the teacher monitoring, than in the others. Noisy or illicit talk is slightly higher in London, but inappropriate movement is lower, the North-west showing highest incidence of this. South-west teachers were less likely to use reprimand and most likely to re-involve pupils in their work, a strategy more rarely used by the London teachers. London children were more likely to altercate or protest at the teacher's action than pupils in the other two places. However, it is worth repeating that these tentative findings refer only to the present sample and should not be generalised to whole regions, until significant numbers or other research projects report similar trends, and regional comparisons are very rare in classroom observation research.

Another aspect of context worth exploring is the similarities and differ-

Table 4.8 Percentages of different categories of teacher and pupil behaviour with three age groups: reception class, year 1, year 2 (4–7 year olds), years 3 and 4 (7–9 year olds), years 5, 6 and 7 (9–12 year olds)

	Age group		
Category	*4–7*	*7–9*	*9–12*
Teacher solo	7	9	14
Teacher–pupil interaction	22	22	18
Pupils working, teacher monitoring	65	65	61
No misbehaviour	46	32	54
Noisy or illicit talk	32	46	25
Inappropriate movement	27	36	18
Inappropriate use of materials	8	15	8
Defiance of teacher	6	12	5
Order to cease	70	76	69
Pupil named	62	69	61
Reprimand	43	51	39
Involve pupils in work	34	26	20
Proximity (going over to pupil)	23	23	19
Touch	30	15	7
Facial expression	13	19	11
Pupil(s) silent	95	90	85
Pupil(s) altercate(s) or protest(s)	4	5	4
Misbehaviour ends	87	69	85
Misbehaviour lessens	10	22	11
Misbehaviour sustained	2	9	4
Teacher calm	96	84	94

ences in patterns across age groups. Table 4.8 shows the sample split into three different age groups, infant age, covering the reception class, and years 1 and 2, that is, children aged 4 to 7; lower juniors, which consisted of years 3 and 4 with children aged from 7 to 9; and upper juniors, which was classes 5, 6 and 7, children aged from 9 to 12, as there were some older middle-school groups in the sample. The three groups made up 28, 32 and 40 per cent of the sample respectively. Some very interesting trends and differences can be seen when different age groups are compared. The first striking feature is that there is more misbehaviour in the classes of younger junior pupils aged 7–9 than there is amongst infants or older primary pupils.

Whereas misbehaviour occurred in about half the lesson segments we analysed for infant and older juniors, in year 3 and 4 classes of younger juniors it was observed in about two-thirds. Consequently, table 4.8 shows a noticeably higher incidence of noisy or illicit talk, inappropriate movement or use of materials, defiance of the teacher, as well as more reprimands, orders to cease and naming of pupils. Misbehaviour is less likely to end, though more likely to lessen, and also more likely to be sustained at the same level as before the teacher's intervention, and teachers are less calm. In order to check whether a degree of distortion may have occurred because of one or two especially badly behaved classes in a particular year group, we compared the separate profiles for 7–8 year olds and 8–9 year olds. They were virtually identical, noisy or illicit talk being 46 per cent for both year groups, no misbehaviour 32 per cent for both, defiance of the teacher 12 per cent for both, and reprimand being 51 and 49 per cent respectively.

Least misbehaviour was recorded with the oldest pupils and there were certain interesting trends across age groups. The most obvious difference in teachers' responses to misbehaviour is the sharply diminishing occurrence of touch from 30 to 15 to 7 in the three groups. Touch is not always a hostile act, like pushing someone into place or tapping them sharply on the shoulder. With younger children it was sometimes an affectionate hug or an arm around the shoulder. Touch and proximity were often observed together in infant classes. The teacher would go over to a misbehaving pupil and steer the pupil gently back to the task in hand, hence the higher incidence of the category 'involve pupils in work' with younger children. With older pupils there is much more of a touch taboo. Specific examples of these aspects are given in chapter 5 when the qualitative data are described.

Another feature we decided to investigate was whether there were differences between morning and afternoon activities. Some primary schools prefer a 'drills' and 'frills' approach, with more structured work or basic activities in core subjects like English and mathematics in the morning, and more project work and choosing in the afternoons. Others make no such distinctions. Inevitably we observed more morning lessons than afternoon sessions, about three-quarters of the observations being before lunch, as in all the schools we studied the morning half-day was longer, often much more so, than the afternoon period. We were also interested to see, as teachers sometimes said in interview that children were more tired in the afternoon and more likely to misbehave, whether this really was the case. Table 4.9 shows some morning and afternoon comparisons.

Table 4.9 Percentages of different categories of teacher and pupil behaviour in morning and afternoon sessions

Category	Morning	Afternoon
Teacher solo	9	12
Teacher–pupil interaction	19	27
Pupils working, teacher monitoring	66	53
No misbehaviour	46	39
Noisy or illicit talk	31	40
Inappropriate movement	26	27
Inappropriate use of materials	9	13
Defiance of teacher	7	12
Order to cease	71	76
Pupil named	67	69
Reprimand	42	55
Involve pupils in work	29	16
Pupil(s) silent	90	90
Pupil(s) altercate(s) or protest(s)	4	6
Misbehaviour ends	81	74
Misbehaviour sustained	5	5
Teacher calm	92	86

The profiles of morning and afternoon sessions are quite similar. There is slightly more teacher solo or teacher–pupil interaction in the afternoons and slightly less misbehaviour, though the incidence of noisy or illicit talk, inappropriate use of materials and defiance of teacher are all a little higher. Teachers tended to use more reprimands and were less likely to re-involve the pupils in their work, and misbehaviour was less likely to end after a teacher intervention, but these differences were all relatively small rather than dramatic. Nonetheless, the evidence here does corroborate, to a moderate degree, some teachers' belief that afternoon sessions contain more misbehaviour.

The evidence we obtained from the individual pupil studies, which allowed the calculation of task involvement and deviance levels, largely confirmed what has already been described in this chapter. Involvement and deviance index scores can, in theory, range from 0 to 100, but in practice the range is much smaller. During each observation period, every pupil in the class was observed in turn for twenty seconds. The average scores for the whole sample were 71 for involvement and 5 for deviance. What this means in practice is that if, during the lesson observed, there were thirty children in the class, average scores would be obtained for involvement and deviance as follows: the average involvement score of 71 would mean that about sixteen of the of the class would be engaged in the task in hand, whatever that might be – working individually, listening to the teacher, answering a question – but about three or four pupils, often in the same group, might be not working on their task, or be engaged in mild misbehaviour, most frequently talking to their neighbours instead of working, or moving round the room when they should have been at their place. The range of involvement and deviance scores is shown in table 4.10. This reveals that individual lesson scores would range from as low as 0 up to 26 for deviance, and from 28 to 100 for involvement.

Table 4.10 Range of involvement and deviance scores obtained for total sample

Measure	Involvement score	Deviance score
Average of whole group	71	5
Lowest average for individual teacher (four lessons)	38	0
Lowest score for individual lesson	28	0
Highest average for individual teacher (four lessons)	92	20
Highest score for individual lesson	100	26

At the extremes a score of 0 for deviance means no one misbehaved at all during the period of observation and 100 for involvement meant that every child observed was fully devoted to the task in hand. A score of 26 for deviance would be obtained in a class of thirty if sixteen pupils were misbehaving in a mildly deviant fashion and the other fourteen were behaving well, and an involvement score of 28 would result if, for example, five pupils were seen to be highly involved in the task, seven were medium involved, and the other eighteen were not involved in what they were supposed to be doing. Involvement and deviance scores alone are not, it must be stressed, measures of effective teaching and learning. After all, it would be possible to obtain a deviance score of 0 and an involvement score of 100 by terrorising children into copying out telephone directories. They are rough-and-ready estimates of attentiveness to the task and pupil behaviour. As will be shown in the next chapter, some teachers teach in very difficult inner-city schools with large classes of unruly pupils, and others are in smaller orderly communities. These figures may well be related to the quality of teaching, but they are not absolute measures of it. One would expect there to be a high inverse correlation between attentiveness and deviance, the more of the one the less of the other, and indeed the highly significant correlation obtained was -0.56***.

Teachers' decision-making

Teachers were asked in interview to say how they would react to the situations seen in the three photographs shown to them, as described earlier in this chapter. The most common replies, in descending order of frequency of mention, are given below. Some teachers gave more than one response to a situation.

Picture A (Two children seen pushing each other)

Introduction 'You're sitting with your back to this group when you hear a noise. You turn round and see two children messing about. You have told them off once that day for not getting on with their work. What if anything do you do?'

1 Separate the two children.
2 Find out what has happened (many of these also included movement, either by the teacher or the teacher calling the pupils over).
3 It would depend on the children/their expectations/children's response/ school sanctions.
4 Look at the task the children are supposed to be doing and reassess it, check it or discuss it.
5 Tell them off/comment on the behaviour.
6 See it as time-wasting and so get them back to work.
7 Punish (this usually meant keeping the children in if they hadn't finished the work or because they had already been told off).
8 Threaten punishment or warn the children.

Other mentions Shout or express emotion, send to the head, seat them next to the teacher, keep an eye on them, ask the class to reflect, throw them a glance/stare.

By far the most popular response, with almost two-thirds of teachers choosing this strategy, was to separate the children in some way. A number of these mentioned that this course of action would be taken because the children had already been warned:

I'd separate them immediately, because if they'd already been warned, they'd had their opportunity to behave . . . I would just separate them, one at one end of the room and one at the other end of the room.

If I'd already told them off once, I'd probably separate them straight away, either take one off the table . . . move them to the front of the class, whatever the system is. . . . I might be tempted to say, 'Look, what's going on?' but if I'd already told them off once that day I don't think I'd question them, I'd just separate them . . . to stop the distraction.

Picture B (*class rushing into the room after break*)

Introduction 'This class has just been out for break. They come running back into the room, pushing each other, squealing and laughing. What, if anything, do you do?'

1 Send them outside and make them come in again.
2 Stop them as they come in.
3 Talk about their behaviour, which included pointing out the dangers of rushing into the room.
4 Seat the children.
5 It depends on the circumstances.
6 Tell off/pass comment on behaviour.

Other mentions Get them to return to work, ignore it, keep them in, reassess the room's layout, shout at them.

The overwhelming response, given by nearly 80 per cent of respondents, was to send the children out. Many teachers gave reasons for their reaction, explaining that they wanted to calm pupils down or that they felt the class ought to know better:

> I would probably get them all to sit down in an area like this [pointing to one part of the classroom], an area where they can all sit down, and tell them that they are going to calm down and that break time is over, and if that isn't effective, I'd probably read a story to them to get them calmed down. . . .

Others merely saw their action as punitive in a self-explanatory way:

> I'd make them all sit down and be quiet and then I'd say, 'Right! We're going back into the playground, and when I blow the whistle, line up at the door and walk in quietly.' And we'd just keep doing it over and over again, really, just wasting time, until they managed to come in quietly and sit down.

Picture C (*girl scribbles on books and calls teacher 'old cow'*)

Introduction 'You have caught this girl scribbling on someone else's book. You have told her off in front of the class and you hear her mutter "old cow" under her breath. The children near by snigger. What, if anything, do you do?'

1 Speak to her on her own, now or later, to discuss her behaviour.
2 Show emotion – anger, sarcasm, upset, humour.
3 It would depend on the child.
4 Send to the head.
5 Involve the whole class in some way.

6   Punish the girl.
7   Ask her to repeat it.
8   Tell her off.
9   Ignore the behaviour.

Other mentions   Withdraw her, make a joke of it, be seen to deal with it, get her to rub out the scribbling.

About half the teachers gave the most common response, which was to avoid public confrontation by seeing the girl on her own:

> I would certainly take her somewhere and speak to her quietly. I wouldn't want to have a confrontation with her in front of the other children. I would deal with it (myself) . . . I would either take her aside, or take her to a quiet part of the classroom, where I could speak to her softly and sort it out from there.

About a quarter of respondents described how they would give some emotional reaction to signal to the girl and the class how they felt:

> I'd put her in a withdrawal situation. It would all depend on how I was feeling at the time. If I was level-headed and taking it very calmly . . . I'd say, 'You go over there and I'll talk to you later on. At the moment if I talk to you I'll get too angry' and I'll explain to the others there may be reasons behind why she's doing this. . . . The group make themselves an audience and could send her up to be more of an actress than she need be . . . (I'd) talk about being more understanding (to the class). . . . I might know what the child's like . . . there's certainly a lot of investigative work can be done there.

Most teachers responded quickly and without hesitation to each of the pictures, and this confirmed not only the conclusions in the research literature described in chapter 2 on speed of decision-making but also the findings of our own research, that teachers usually responded before the escalation of deviance. Teachers make thousands of decisions every week, often with only a second or so in which to sum up a vast amount of visual information, past histories, precedents, consequences, context factors and individual differences, so it is not surprising that most responded fairly quickly. Many of the popular strategies involved some degree of confrontation rather than evasion, though the exact opposite was the case in the third picture when personal insult to the teacher was involved.

The most common inclination in the first two pictures was to engage in a mild to medium confrontation of the situation, with immediate countermeasures: separate quarrelling pupils, send the class outside. In the case of the personal insult, it is a delaying strategy, a private conversation rather than a public harangue, possibly held later when the emotions on both sides have subsided. Occasionally, the suggestion was to ignore what had happened, but this was relatively rare. Telling off is the most common reaction predicted by pupils, as will be shown in chapter 7, but it is lower down the list in teachers' minds.

Another strategy proposed with the pictures, but not always observed so frequently in the classrooms of the teachers who advocated it, as described in this chapter and the following one, was that of reasoning and negotiation. Looking for explanations, asking children why they did something, was indeed a feature of some teachers' lessons, but the immediate pressure to respond to misbehaviour sometimes meant that such intentions evaporated in the heat of real classroom aggravation. On the other hand, the events in the photographs are a little more dramatic than the illicit chatter and movement which make up most classroom misbehaviour, so one cannot expect complete congruence. Many teachers did show, in their responses to these photo-graphs, glimpses into their behaviour which mirrored their actual classroom practice. In a small number of cases there was a large gulf between armchair decision-making and the real thing. The responses to the photographs by experienced teachers, supply teachers, pupils and student teachers will be discussed again in more detail in chapters 5, 6, 7 and 11 respectively.

Chapter 5

Managing children's behaviour and work

It is 8.20 a.m. in the downtown area of a large Northern city. As the bleak morning light flickers across the broken tiles and the for years unpointed brickwork of the grim terraced houses round about, the first few pupils and teachers are arriving at school. In the playground lies a dead rat. How had it perished? There is speculation among pupils and staff. Perhaps someone had shot it with an air rifle, or maybe it had just finally breathed its last in the grimy environment in which it had spent its brief existence. It lay there, another symbol of decay and neglect in a crumbling inner city. Meanwhile the head greeted our project researcher with the news that this was a tough school in a tough area. There had been thirteen break-ins in the last thirteen months – even the few plants in front of the school had been dug up and removed. In a nearby school we visited, a pupil proudly told his teacher that his father had been on television. Pleased at this mark of recognition of an otherwise ignored sector of society, she enquired what programme he had appeared in. The answer was BBC national news. He had been shown throwing slates from the roof of a prison during a jail riot.

In a pretty town in another part of the country it is also 8.20 a.m. This is no wealthy commuter belt community, just a small market town in the south of England with a low crime rate and a more rural aspect. An abundance of green surrounds the local school, with small gardens, mainly well tended, a patch of grass and several trees. The children arriving are certainly not from rich families, quite the reverse, nor do they look sedated as they walk or jog into the playground, but the contrast with the city environment described above is a sharp one. The head greets our project researcher with a friendly welcome. She has a big problem today, she tells him, as the caretaker is away and he normally carries the heavy television equipment across to the temporary classroom in the playground. It seems a million miles away from the inner-city school charged with educating children in some of the most desperate circumstances found in our society.

Yet just as some classrooms fill out the stereotypes, others belie them. During the Leverhulme Primary Project we occasionally observed badly behaved classes in what looked to be idyllic surroundings and orderly classes in the most unpromising environments. As will be described below we sometimes saw two teachers in the same school, one with a high degree of task involvement and orderliness, the other with lower pupil application and more misbehaviour. Social conditions certainly do affect class management, but they are not the sole determinants of it. This chapter will give some further detail to flesh out the quantitative data described in the previous chapter.

Maintaining classroom rules

Classroom rules and conventions establish the framework within which learning takes place, and chapter 3 described how teachers assert, establish or negotiate these in their first few lessons. Once the school year is under way many rules are so firmly established they need no further reiteration. Others demand constant fine-tuning, especially those to do with noisy or illicit pupil talk, which was shown to be the most frequent form of deviant behaviour in chapter 4. What constitutes 'noise' rather than normal conversation is a variable rather than a fixed concept. Some teachers' tolerance is quite high, whereas that of other teachers may be low. Young children in particular, partly because their voices are at a higher pitch, partly because they are not always fully socialised in whatever passes for 'acceptable' levels of excited conversation, were reminded frequently about the issue, sometimes with a dramatic display, as in the case of a reception class taught by an experienced teacher in a London school where we observed:

> *Teacher* (in a loud public voice, sounding shocked)   Stop! (The class falls quiet. Pause.) All the children in the home corner come out! (Children playing in the far corner of the classroom come forward sheepishly.) Why do you think I've asked you to come out?
> *Pupil*   Because we're shouting.
> *Teacher*   That's right. Now please go back and work quietly. (Children return to their corner and the noise level remains lower.)

In this particular instance the teacher chose a minor public shaming. She could have gone over to the children concerned and spoken directly to the small group involved, but she felt a rule was being broken that children were expected to know, as they revealed when they answered her question correctly. The minor public shaming was a demonstration and reaffirmation of the rule, and the likely consequences of breaking it, to others in the class. It illustrates a common sequence of events well understood by pupils, as will be described in chapter 7: talk too loud = get told off in public. As a strategy it was in this instance, 'effective', if the chief criterion is whether it led to more tolerable levels of noise enabling others to work unimpaired, 'skilful' if the criteria are first of all exercising the vigilance necessary to pick up possible disruption before it escalates, and secondly to deal with it in a way that is understood and complied with by the pupils, and 'acceptable' if one takes as indicative of that term the pupils' apparent lack of resentment or hostility to the teacher's action.

Some rules have been made explicit, but children do not subsequently generalise them to every situation, so the teacher may then make the specific instance public. In a London class of 6–7 year olds there was a rule that equipment and materials must be put away. In one lesson a group of children had been painting and an apron had been left out:

> *Teacher* (calls back the children who had been working at the table concerned)   Who was wearing a red apron?
> *Pupils* (No reply.)
> *Teacher* (pause) Will you put it back, please? (Child returns apron to storage space.) If you need an apron you need to get it yourself . . . and you need to put it back in the right place. I'm not going to do it for you. (Pause.) Now, off you go. (Children return to their tasks.)

This reaffirmation of a specific instance of a rule in a specific context occurred frequently with the second most common form of perceived misbehaviour in the present study, inappropriate movement, when pupils left their seat without permission, at the wrong time, to the wrong place, or in the wrong manner. In a class of 7–8 year olds in the North-west there was a rule that children wanting to solicit the teacher's attention were to raise their hand and wait. This rule causes difficulties for pupils, as they may wait for some time if the teacher is engrossed with one pupil, so three children walk over to where the teacher is standing:

> *Teacher* (making a show of counting them)   Now why are there one, two, three, people here? (One pupil returns to his seat and raises his hand. The teacher walks past the other two.) Peter's got his hand up, so I'm going over to him. (The other two sit down and raise their hands.) How many children are out of their seats? One, two . . . (Points and counts.)

The problem with this rule is that there is a price to pay for it. If children are not to leave their seat frequently to solicit the teacher's attention, then two conditions must obtain. First of all, the teacher must be perpetually vigilant, otherwise several children can sit, arms aloft, for inordinate lengths of time. Secondly, the teacher must establish a high degree of pupil independence which minimises the number of occasions when they will need to approach her. Many of the questions we observed asked by children standing in line to see the teacher, or sitting at their table waiting, were simple to answer, like how to spell a word when there were dictionaries in the room, or what to do next, when the answer was turn the page and carry on, or check your answers.

In a different classroom with 8–9 year olds in the North-west we observed an application of this rule which revealed the need for consistency. Some children put up their hands, others went over to the teacher. From time to time the teacher would attempt to delineate and reinforce the rule by sending someone away. On one occasion she said to a pupil, 'Go and sit down and put your hand up if you want help.' After thirty seconds she went over to him and answered his question. She then told another child not to interrupt her, but answered the questions of other pupils when they interrupted. One girl sat for over five minutes with her arm aloft and remained unnoticed until she called out, 'Miss,' in frustration. The teacher then went over to her. It was easy to see what the rule was meant to be: put up your hand if you want help, and don't interrupt. It was much more difficult in practice, however, for children to see a pattern to breaches of the rule, because there did not seem to be one. The details of the rule were diffuse, ill-defined and unevenly reinforced. As a consequence the lessons were full of instances of roaming pupils punctuated by sporadic and largely ineffectual reminders of what the rule was supposed to be.

Successful maintenance of classroom rules, irrespective of how they had originally been introduced or negotiated, appeared to require clarity of purpose, understanding and assent from the pupils, fair-minded and appropriate interpretation or adaptation in the relevant context, and consistent application and reinforcement. Absence of some or all of these conditions was often accompanied by a higher incidence of misbehaviour by pupils.

Maintaining interpersonal relationships

While some teachers continued to make use of some public displays of anger or to use minor shaming, rather than outright humiliation, to keep order, as table 4.5 showed, about three-quarters of teachers' responses to misbehaviour were addressed to individuals or small groups rather than the whole class. Interactions with individual pupils can exert a powerful influence on the genesis and maintenance of personal relationships. Acts by the teacher which had positive or negative effects were noted by observers on numerous occasions. In most classrooms positive affect outweighed negative affect, but the obverse was also seen occasionally. Here are some instances, under several headings, of both positive and negative teacher behaviour which appeared to affect relationships and which was witnessed by researchers during the project:

1 *Academic*

   (a) Explaining patiently to a pupil who does not understand a new concept.
   (b) Making a sarcastic remark to someone who does not understand a new concept.

2 *Managerial*

   (a) Smiling at and thanking someone who has helped clear away.
   (b) Blaming someone for a mess, choosing wrong pupil.

3 *Social*

  (a) Talking to children as they enter the classroom about what they did at the weekend.
  (b) Belittling someone's hobby.

4 *Expectation*

  (a) Looking for positive qualities and achievements in children.
  (b) Having low expectations or always focusing on the negative side of pupils' work or behaviour.

5 *Home/school*

  (a) Talking positively with parents and members of pupils' communities.
  (b) Showing little or no interest in children's origins and values.

6 *Individual*

  (a) Taking a personal interest in a child as an individual.
  (b) Seeing the class as a group without individual identities.

There were many examples of teachers working in very difficult circumstances who made special efforts to raise the self-image of their pupils. One teacher of 5 year olds in a school in an exceptionally difficult area made numerous positive references to children. A child who arrives in tears and who has had no breakfast is first comforted and then taken to the reading corner. Shortly afterwards her tears have ceased and she is happily engaged in a piece of work. The teacher calls the class her 'smarties' ('Time for my smarties to go to assembly'), the combination of the name of a well-known sweet and the suggestion that the children are all 'smart' being well received by the class.

Some of the most striking examples of a predominantly positive climate of relationships were observed in the classroom which contained children who did not speak English as their first language. In establishing and maintaining interpersonal relationships most people rely heavily on spoken language, even though non-verbal cues and messages may play a part. Touch was noted much more frequently with younger children, especially when children cried or appeared upset, when the teacher would often put her arm round them. Stripped of language, however, the most obvious form of communication, many would find establishing good harmonious relationships very difficult. In the classrooms of all the London teachers we observed, in those of some of the North-west teachers, but very few of the South-west teachers, there were one or two, occasionally several, non-English-speakers. Most teachers made special efforts to establish positive relationships by involving pupils as well as themselves, as this event, noted in a London classroom, reveals.

There is a new pupil in the class of 11–12 year olds who has just moved to

England and who speaks very little English. Often there are fellow speakers in the case of languages like Bengali and the teacher assigns a 'translator' from amongst the pupils, but on this occasion no one else in the class speaks his language. The class is studying Europe, and the teacher is writing the names of European countries on the blackboard. Pupils are suggesting names she can add. The new boy raises his hand and says 'France', following a whispered conversation with his neighbour, Michael. The teacher praises him fulsomely, 'Well done, Stefan, good boy.' In the interview following the lesson she explains how she has assigned Michael to help Stefan. She had discussed with the class how they could all help someone who did not speak English. Michael had sat beside Stefan and looked at the map with him, whispering to him the names of countries when he had indicated them.

Even well intended teachers, however, can fall short of their own aspirations amid the sustained distractions of classroom life, and risk arousing animosity by a piece of unfairness. A 6 year old boy was seen in one classroom to tidy up voluntarily some pieces of equipment that had been left scattered across the floor. He had initiated this himself, even though he had not been using the pieces. The teacher went over to him and told him to leave them and go and do some printing instead. He did as he was asked, leaving five or six pieces still on the floor. About twenty-five minutes later the teacher came over to where he was printing, took him by the hand to where the remaining pieces still lay on the floor, told him it was untidy to have left them and he should now pick them up. Without protest or altercation he did so and then returned quietly to his printing. In over 90 per cent of cases where we saw a reprimand given to a pupil the target was judged to be fair by the observer, but in those cases where it was not, personal relationships could easily be soured. Unfairness is one of the events pupils resent most deeply, as will be shown in chapter 7.

Some teachers were so concerned about fairness in their relationships that they engaged in extended negotiation with pupils. Negotiated rules were relatively infrequent in our observations, as most were determined either explicitly by the teacher or implicitly by the pupils in terms of what they actually did. In the school in the North-west the extrinsic rewards and punishments system was built around house points and stars. Pupils doing well or badly could gain or lose points for their house team. One day the teacher gives Patricia house points for a piece of work

Pupil 1 That's not fair, she shouldn't get that many points.

Teacher All right. I'll give you one point Patricia. Are you all happy with that decision?

Pupil 2 No, it's still not fair.

Teacher Well, can anybody suggest a way we can overcome the problem?

Pupil 3   Give everybody a point.
Pupil 4   No, that's silly. Don't give Patricia a point at all.
Pupil 5   Give her a star instead. It's worth a star but not house points.
Teacher   All those that agree with Mary's suggestion put up your hands. Right, that's virtually everybody. Are you happy with that decision, Patricia?
(Patricia nods, smiles and seems to be pleased.)

Just as relationships between the teacher and pupils are regarded as important, so too are interpersonal relationships amongst the children themselves, for all are part of the same classroom culture. Whereas in the case of non-English-speaking Stefan, described above, the teacher had made special efforts to involve other pupils in his reception and accommodation within the class, there were examples when teachers appeared to be less effective at resolving problems between pupils.

In a class of 8–9 year olds three girls were sitting together at the same table. Two of them, Alice and Rachel, would from time to time torment Caroline, the third girl, by refusing to give her a rubber, throwing things at her, preventing her from working. The teacher rarely intervened. Occasionally she would look at Alice's and Rachel's work, but not refer to their behaviour, except indirectly, by saying to Caroline, 'Just ignore them, Caroline, and get on with your work.' Her explanation of this strategy in interview was:

> Alice and Rachel are just attention-seekers. Alice in particular is a very unsettled child. She does the same thing in the playground, picks an argument with somebody and runs up to whoever is on duty shouting about the offence being committed against her when in fact she's started it herself, or telling tales about somebody else doing something to somebody. It's a lot of attention-seeking behaviour.

To some extent, by ignoring what she rightly or wrongly judged to be attention seeking, the teacher was following the tenets of behaviour modification, which decree that 'bad' behaviour should be ignored so that it is extinguished by not being reinforced. However, the corollary to not reinforcing behaviour of which the teacher disapproves is that approved behaviour should be reinforced. The teacher did not appear to find out further information about why Alice sought attention, and this event highlights the dilemma faced by many teachers. Since eliciting deeper-lying causes of anti-social behaviour is not only time-consuming but requires considerable expertise, it is sometimes the case that, during lessons at any rate, misbehaviour is accommodated, contained, treated or ignored, rather than its causes diagnosed.

Disruptive behaviour

The most common source of disruption of a pupil's work was interruption by another pupil or occasionally by the teacher, for reasons other than to monitor what was being done. Occasionally there were aggressive intrusions into the work of an individual, a small group or the whole class, often by a single pupil. In one classroom the same 5 year old pupil was reprimanded three or four times each time registration was taken and his behaviour dominated the lessons. The teacher usually brought him to sit on the floor next to her during whole class sessions, and as he pulled objects out of the trolley that he wanted to use in the forthcoming activity she would gently take them from him and incorporate them into her explanation of what the children were to do. The demands of this one pupil consumed a great deal of her classroom time, and with twenty-seven or twenty-eight others it was often a matter of coping or containing strategies, rather than something which significantly altered his behaviour.

When more than one pupil disrupts, even more time can be consumed. An inexperienced student teacher was seen with a class of 7–8 year olds. Within one minute she asked for quiet seven times, stamped her foot, clapped her hands, named individual pupils, raised her voice, asked pupils to put their hands on their head, but none of these acts reduced the noise level. Once she had given out the maths worksheets, however, the noise diminished and most pupils worked assiduously at them, albeit with occasional conversations. When classes were engaged in work which seemed to them appropriate and worthwhile, such disruption as occurred tended to be caused by individual pupils or occasionally by a small group of two or three pupils.

As was shown in chapter 4 most teachers took action before disruption escalated, often revealing a high degree of vigilance, and were able to split their attention between the child or group they were with and the rest of the class by employing the split glance, demonstrating what Jacob Kounin called 'with-itness'. Frequently, noticing potential disruption and nipping it in the bud took place almost instantaneously. One reception class was reading a book together when a child began to fiddle with the laces on a pair of shoes, distracting others. Within seconds of this beginning the teacher called out, 'Sally, what are you doing? If you play with your shoelaces you won't learn the words. Put your shoes away.' The child complied, but before starting to talk about the next page the teacher glanced up and said, in a firm but friendly manner, 'Now, are you listening, Sally?' There was no further interruption.

By contrast, in another class of 5 year olds four children were playing with scales and bricks. One child hit another, unseen by the teacher, then another boy hit one of the girls, who asked him to stop punching her. He hit her again, so she left the table to work elsewhere. The aggressive boy called out the teacher's name several times. Twice she came over to check his work, but never commented on his behaviour, even though he continued to be noisily aggressive towards others throughout the lesson. Disruption caused by distracting behaviour, chatter, minor teasing and attention-seeking were, in general, easily contained by most teachers. It was the individual aggressive child who caused greatest dismay, both to fellow pupils and to the teacher, and the demands made by such individuals on the teacher's time and energy during a lesson could be considerable.

Yet many of the teachers who encountered this more aggressive style of disruption did deploy strategies which appeared successful in resolving or even eliminating anti-social aggression. Some used extrinsic rewards, like points or stars when the pupil had behaved well. Others eschewed this more formal recognition and made use of extensive praise instead. There were examples of assigning responsibility for some logistical operation, like giving out books or collecting in work, but where these are perceived as privileges, there can be some resentment from other pupils if aggression is thought to have been rewarded and good social behaviour ignored.

Touch was rarely used with older children but it was a common feature with younger pupils, as reported in chapter 4. For example, when a boy was said by others to have been kicking pupils, one teacher said, in a half joking, half serious manner, 'Would you like me to kick him?' and then seized him by the shoulders and pushed him towards a table. Other pupils laughed but the boy's face was expressionless. This is an interesting example of a strategy which was 'successful' in terminating the disruption, but about which opinion might be divided, given the possible apprehension of the boy concerned.

Another teacher, investigating why a 5 year old girl was crying, found that a boy had hit her. There followed a conversation between the teacher and the two pupils concerned which ended with the teacher telling them to be friends and give each other 'a big hug'. This done, no further aggression was noted. The strategy of looking for the positive was sometimes exemplified by the teacher holding up the disruptive pupil's work for admiration by the rest when he had done especially well.

Classroom routines

The daily repeated rituals of classroom life, arrival, registration, 'circle time' or 'carpet time', where children sit with the teacher to discuss matters of concern, lesson endings, are in many classrooms the secure framework within which transactions take place. In some classrooms these were highly formalised: lined-up supervised entry, great formality over registration, regimented departure. More frequently they were simply regular occurrences which signalled important messages and established or maintained a particular classroom climate.

Teachers showed considerable variation in their use of time. In some classrooms there was little sense of urgency, assignments were open-ended, to be done in the pupil's own time, even if that was slowly paced. Others made the issue of time more public, using group alerting to tell pupils how long there was left or reminding individuals of when they would be expected to have finished. In one class where 'time' was actually the topic of study, two 7 year old boys had not been working diligently, so the teacher went over to their table, put a clock on it and showed them how long they had to finish the task in hand. When one of the boys had finished, however, he reported to the teacher that the other boy had turned back the clock to give himself more time. The teacher smiled at him, seemed pleased that he had understood time well enough to realise how to create more of it, but then re-set the clock and gave him a fresh target.

Within the major routines there were often minor ones. One teacher of 5 year olds whose lesson endings always seemed to pass smoothly would warn children to be ready to stop, and then, when she actually said, 'Stop working,' all the pupils put their hands in the air and waved them. 'They're all supposed to waggle their arms in the air,' she explained in interview, 'so I can see they've actually stopped, because I only say "stop!" in order to say something to everybody.' She would then give the class ten seconds to sit on the carpet, which she counted out slowly, taking more than ten seconds so they would not rush, and then announced, 'Give yourself a clap,' when all had complied. Many other teachers had established a formal exit at the end of the day, one insisting on a very precise and straight line before anyone was allowed to leave: 'I've asked you to line up and I can see (points finger as she counts) one, two, three, four, five, six, seven, eight not in line.' Major and minor routines were observed on a regular basis in virtually every classroom observed, other than those of a few student teachers.

More effective and less effective management

Taking as two criteria of effectiveness the extent to which pupils were involved in the task and the amount of misbehaviour, it was sometimes possible to see two teachers in the same or a similar environment, where one obtained high task involvement and low deviance, and the other the reverse. Although the class itself can sometimes be the main determinant of such differences, especially when one group contains more disruptive pupils than another, there were occasions when it was not major differences between two classes, but noticeable distinctions between the teaching styles of their teachers, that seemed to explain differences in behaviour. Mrs Abel and Miss Baker taught third-year juniors and second-year juniors respectively in the same school. There were serious social problems in the area, so it was not an easy assignment teaching in that particular school. Yet, as these short accounts reveal, the two teachers were quite different from each other in terms of relationships, amount and quality of work from pupils and classroom climate. Even having a whole-school policy for such matters as discipline cannot always eradicate individual differences in temperament and practice.

Mrs Abel

There is a sense of benign urgency about Mrs Abel's lessons, whether she is checking scores on a maths test and discussing children's 'silly' mistakes, or whether the class is engaged in individual and small group work. There is a rule that children waiting for help must get out their reading book, not sit doing nothing. Yet when she asks questions she says, 'Don't panic,' to anyone not sure of an answer and makes extensive use of praise. She seems well prepared and sets tasks which hold and maintain pupils' attention. When there is incipient misbehaviour, she often defuses the situation with quick but pointed humour: 'Jason, it won't help if you're chopping her neck off with a ruler.'

From time to time she alerts the whole class to some matter of principle with specific reference to a particular event. On one occasion a girl has finished maths book No. 4 ahead of the rest. After checking her work she tells the whole class that this deserves a round of applause. In interview she explains that, when she took over the class, they were so far behind what she expected that she has put a high premium on successful achievement: 'We are so far behind in this class with maths . . . when I got them two were doing second-year work and the rest first-year work, and they were so far behind . . . so we've made this big thing about every time they finish a particular stage they get praise . . . they're really proud of themselves if they do it.' When she asked children to pat themselves on the back, some did it literally. Large-scale display of pupils' work around the classroom reinforced this public recognition of positive achievement.

Mrs Abel's high task involvement and low deviance scores (see below) seem to be the result of considerable thought about appropriate work for the class and individuals; extensive use of reinforcement, especially in the form of praise, some private, much public; completely consistent classroom rules, enforced in a benign but firm manner, so that calling out is not a problem and, when it threatens to be, children are reminded of the rule; and a considerable amount of good humour, both from herself and the children, which defuses potential trouble and cements positive interpersonal relationships. She also reminds pupils of the time available and regularly monitors their work, especially those with difficulties. When her pupils were interviewed, for the research on pupil perceptions described in chapter 7, many named her as 'the best teacher in the world'.

Miss Baker

At the beginning of lessons Miss Baker quickly announces what pupils will do, but there is a long settling down period and children seem to move around the room, often on what seems to be a purposeless perambulation, before commencing work. Task involvement levels are comparatively low and deviance is higher than average (see below). This can be partly explained by two very noticeable elements. The first is that the rules of behaviour are not always clear or consistently applied, and this relates to the second factor, which is that relationships between pupils and teacher are more negative than in Mrs Abel's classroom.

Some of the instances of misbehaviour exemplify these differences. On one occasion a boy donned a baseball cap. 'Get that hat off. I'm not going to tell you again, young man,' the teacher called across the room. He hurled his hat into the centre of the table. The teacher did not comment, though she clearly saw his response. Afterwards the teacher said she had ignored it because 'he was just being silly'. In another lesson she asked children to put their hands up before speaking. Few did. She also requested them not to walk around the room, but several ignored her. She then shouted at six pupils not in their seats and told one to go out into the corridor. He stayed in the room and she made no comment.

In interview she says, 'They're wasting their time and they're wasting the other children's time. In the last few weeks what I've actually been doing is saying they can't get out of their seats without permission. They've got to put their hands up to tell me why they want to (move) and ask me if they can. It's really just a disruptive thing that I've got.' The intention was clear but the implementation was unsuccessful.

Alongside this inconsistency in rule enforcement is a harsher style of relationship. Praise is rarely used and Miss Baker is frequently critical of the same two target pupils, Darren and Lloyd, even when they are not mis-behaving. On one occasion during a PE lesson she drags Lloyd across the hall floor by his legs, shouting at him to be quiet and sit still. Two children giggle. Later she sends him out of the room. He stands by the doorway. 'Remove yourself from that doorway.' He eventually moves. She sends Darren out. Then, when he is leaving the room, she calls him back. He leaves anyway. In interview she says of Lloyd, 'He tends to put on affection. He comes up and cuddles you, but it's all put on, trying to creep to you, attention-seeking . . . otherwise it's conflict with Darren all the time.'

Miss Baker's relatively low task involvement level and higher deviance rate seem to be related to two principal related factors: the inconsistent application of classroom rules – applying them harshly one moment, ignoring them the next – and negative interpersonal relationships, with few examples of good work being recognised. The only occasion she was seen to smile was once at the end of a school day when all but one group of children had been dismissed. Her answers to the questions posed in the photographs were also more diffuse than Mrs Abel's. For the third picture, where the girl has called the teacher 'old cow', she admitted that this had happened to her, but said she might ignore it, or try to defuse it by saying she did look like an old cow. Mrs Abel, by comparison, felt it was natural to react angrily, but that teachers' anger must be expressed in a proper manner.

During a school year children may spend a thousand or more hours in the company of their class teacher. The cumulative effect of patterns of high involvement and low deviance, or low involvement and high deviance, can be considerable. Mrs Abel's average task involvement score was 84, and her range was from 79 to 94. This means that, typically, out of thirty children, about twenty-three would be observed to be highly involved in their work, about four would be medium involved and two not involved. Given that children must sometimes wait, and that no one concentrates for sixty minutes in every hour, this is a high degree of application.

By contrast Miss Baker's average task involvement score was 38, with a range of from 28 to 53. In practice this means, in a class of thirty, about seven pupils highly engaged in the task in hand, nine would be medium involved and fifteen would not be engaged, a quite different picture. Mrs Abel's average deviance score was 2, with a range of 0 to 4. This means that one pupil might be mildly misbehaving, say distracting a neighbour. Miss Baker's average deviance score was 20, with a range of from 10 to 26. This would involve say nineteen pupils not misbehaving, ten engaging in minor misbehaviour, and one behaving more badly, perhaps hitting another pupil.

So in one room in the school virtually everyone is working on the task in hand and behaving well; a few doors away, with pupils from a similar social background, about half are not involved in their work and a third are chattering or moving around the room when they should not be. Contemplating one such hour multiplied by 1,000 over a school year may help to explain some aspects of the differences in learning achievement by two classes in similar circumstances at the end of a school year.

Chapter 6

Supply teachers

Whereas experienced teachers in permanent posts and student teachers on teaching practice usually have several weeks during which to get to know their new classes, establish and fine-tune relationships and rules of behaviour, and decide which subjects and topics to teach at what time, many supply teachers have little opportunity to operate in stable conditions over a lengthy period of time with the same class.

They are often telephoned at short notice and asked to come in and take over a class, acting as substitute teachers. We decided that it would be interesting to study the approach to class management supply teachers adopted, especially those who had to arrange numerous first encounters with classes they had never met. It seemed likely that, since they had more opportunity than most teachers to establish themselves with several different classes, some might have developed skills which would be of interest to all teachers, even if others had simply learned coping strategies. An opportunity sample of twenty supply teachers was selected from one local authority in the South-west of England. A semi-structured interview schedule was used (Trotter and Wragg 1990). All but two of the interviews, which lasted at least an hour and usually much more than that, were tape-recorded and transcribed, and in the other two cases extensive notes were taken.

There have been very few studies of supply teachers (Loveys 1988), and those that are undertaken are often surveys of teacher absence and the use of supply cover. A one-day snapshot survey of the Inner London Education Authority looked at teacher absence and cover arrangements (ILEA 1989) and found that 40 per cent of that day's absences were covered by supply teachers. The short-term and long-term absence rates were 10.1 per cent and 3 per cent of the teaching force respectively. Supply teachers help maintain and lubricate the system. Without them, some schools, faced with severe absence or recruitment problems, would grind to a halt.

The twenty teachers in the sample were mainly women, only two being men, and had an average seven years of regular experience in schools before taking up supply work, though the actual range was from one teacher who had taught for twenty-three years first, to another who went straight into supply teaching without any other experience. The most common reasons offered for becoming a supply teacher were flexibility, financial advantage, interest and enjoyment, and as a springboard to a permanent post. They had spent about five and a half years on average as a supply teacher, and the range was from one person who had done it for nineteen years to another who was in her first year of it. The median number of different schools they had worked in was roughly six, though the distribution was skewed, with one in particular having experience of 'about fifty'. More typically, teachers had a more restricted number of schools likely to ring them up.

Emmer *et al.* (1981) and Evertson and Emmer (1982) are amongst several investigators who have highlighted the importance of preparation and planning in class management, yet supply teachers often report lack of time for this very matter. In order to elicit what thoughts and strategies supply teachers had developed, the main part of the interview schedule concentrated on their thoughts and actions before meeting a new class; what image, if any, they sought to project of themselves when they met a new class for the first time; what relationships they tried to establish; what and whose rules applied; what they did when disruptive behaviour occurred. In this last case, we again used the photographs of disruptive incidents described in chapter 5.

First meetings

It was quite clear, from almost all the interviews, that there were many occasions when supply teachers had little time to prepare. One respondent described how she was hired by the head as she took her own daughter to school:

He [the head] grabbed me and said, 'Someone's not feeling well, can you do it?' So I had no idea that I was going to teach that day and I went straight in. I didn't have anything with me. I just went straight into the classroom.

It is not surprising that, in the circumstances, some teachers develop deft strategies for coping with the lack of preparation time. One teacher told how she kept a bag for infants and a bag for juniors in her bedroom. As soon as she received a phone call and knew the age group she would be teaching, she seized the appropriate holdall and set off to the school. Another told of how she dreaded the 7.40 a.m. phone call, as she knew it would be a head ringing up, since that was the only kind of call she received at that morning hour.

Once supply teachers arrive at school they are aware of their marginal status. Some teachers used the expression 'lowest of the low' to describe it, and one described herself as 'one grade up from the dinner lady'. Another said:

You are at a disadvantage by the fact that you are a supply teacher. You're just a couple of notches above a student, aren't you? Children know that you are a supply teacher . . . they don't have the same respect for you as they do for people who are on the permanent staff.

Others complained at being called 'the supply' rather than being addressed by name, and of not receiving relevant information about the national curriculum, about class projects, or school rules and conventions.

This lack of knowledge could lead to problems, especially as the teachers did not know children as individuals:

> I once made a child who wasn't very bright – and I didn't realise it – look extremely silly and I've never forgotten that and afterwards I felt dreadful . . . He was messing about, I'd given them a tables test . . . it was a tables sheet and he was messing around and being silly and, of course, when it came to marking them he'd only got a few. And I sort of said to him, in front of all the class, 'If you hadn't been so silly, you might not have got such a low score.' And afterwards I found out that he really wasn't very bright. I'd only been put in there for a little while and obviously he was being silly, I suppose, to cover up for the fact that he couldn't do it. He really was at the rock bottom for brains – and quite a nice lad, actually – but I suppose I'd put him on the spot unfairly and I hadn't realised that and afterwards I felt terrible . . .

The supply teachers were asked how they prepared for these first meetings with a new class, given the shortness of notice and lack of familiarity with the people involved. One described how important the image of efficiency was to her:

> Basically, if I'm approaching a new class, I'm getting myself ready to get in there fairly early – I'm usually in a half-hour, forty minutes before I actually meet a class . . . because you want to put over the idea that you're well organised and a together person. I think the worst thing that a supply teacher can do is to be dithery in front of a new class – it's important that you are competent and confident with taking a register and you know how the dinner money is slotted in and things like this, even if you are thinking 'Well, they don't do their dinner money like so-and-so; this is totally wrong or something' . . . You've got to get a bit of street credibility fairly early on, I think.

Others echoed this need to be as well-prepared as possible in the circum-stances. This involved not only preliminary organisation, but also knowing what questions the teacher needed to ask when she arrived about school routines, like assembly or playground duty, so that her own preparation could dovetail with the school's normal practice:

> I will have planned out exactly what I'm going to do the night before – well, that's if you know the day before – if I've had that [notice] then I will have planned out what I'm going to do with them. So an hour before I

would be making sure that I'd got all the materials that I knew [I needed], up to lunchtime, I think. I would make sure that I'd got all the paper and the pencils and any books that I was going to need . . . I would have found out whether it was playground duty [and] if there were assemblies . . . Not all classrooms have a timetable up, but you need to know if you've got any mother-helpers coming in, if there's an assembly or if there's apparatus [or] television programmes. I would have found that out to begin with, and then fitted that in with what I'd planned to do.

One teacher's strategy was to rehearse her first lesson in her own mind about an hour before meeting the class, to go through the children's books to see what level and type of work would be appropriate, to set out paper, pencils or equipment, and then to stand in the room and think through what she was going to do. Four teachers admitted experiencing feelings of panic that rendered rehearsal unlikely, and felt that it was difficult, in the circumstances, to be constructive. Most, however, used early arrival to find out about the normal structure of a school day, the timetable, if there was one, what resources were available, and what the class's regular teacher had done recently.

Although some respondents claimed not to think too deeply about anything other than survival, one saying 'I do work, I don't think,' it was quite clear that a great deal of thought accompanied first encounters, even if teachers could not always articulate it. All were asked specifically what image they would like to project, and sixteen of the twenty had no difficulty at all describing what this was. They were able to describe in detail their vision of how they wanted children to perceive them and what they did to establish this favoured image in a consistent manner. 'Firm but friendly' was a commonly used expression. One who described this as needing to look 'efficient, organised, firm but reasonable . . . reasonable/friendly' went on:

I don't ever want to come over as being too hard, so I tend if I am being harsh or delivering 'rules', in inverted commas, or the way I feel it needs to be for us to get on, I try to say it in a very reasonable sort of voice because I think if you're delivering the sting in the tail and you're doing it with a really sort of harsh teacher-type voice, they often turn off before you've even started.

The need for strictness tempered with kindness was mentioned in particular by those used to working in difficult conditions. In really challenging situations, toughness would prevail over kindness, in order for the teacher to survive:

There's one particular class down at ——— where they're really tough – or they can be. They really 'monkey' about and I know they're like this, so I go right in, and as soon as some poor kid moves, that's it, because otherwise they would just make your life a misery. So I suppose the image I would project there would be as somebody tough.

In these circumstances, establishing dominance was seen to be paramount by others. One explained that there were clear rules she expected the pupils to adhere to and they should know that 'if they didn't, learning couldn't go on, and there was a nastier side to my nature'. The four supply teachers who said they did not consciously try to project any particular image felt it was unnecessary to be anything other than natural.

Establishing relationships and rules

Establishing positive relationships was seen by nineteen out of the twenty teachers as an important first step, or second step once dominance had been established, where this was thought to be a necessary first step. Time was mentioned as one major constraint working against the establishment of good relationships, as a supply teacher might only take a class for as little as a single afternoon.

Great emphasis was placed on the process of establishment. Most respondents used a deliberate settling-down period on first meeting the class, sometimes with the children sitting on the carpet, on other occasions with them sitting at their tables, during which a dialogue would take place, what one teacher described as a half-hour of 'pure conversation'. The physical proximity of having children grouped closely around the new adult in their lives was mentioned by several as a deliberate and precisely managed parent-like bonding ritual:

> perhaps it's about body language and things like that, really. I just feel I can relate more to them by being . . . to have a bit more physical nearness. I suppose it's the closeness, and it's also having a chat with them, isn't it? And the talking and really getting to know them and how they are as a group as well.

Some reinforced the parental nature of the bonding by talking about their own role as parent, one teacher saying, 'I usually talk about my own children, particularly with young children, so that they know I've got children and I'm used to children.' Perhaps supply teachers, given that many stated in interview that they had chosen this option because of the flexibility it offered them to fit in with their own children's lives, can adopt this parental style of bonding ritual more easily than others.

Conscious of the need to do more than merely establish a relationship, some teachers described strategies they had developed for assessing which children might cause them problems, because they have learning or behaviour difficulties. One described how she would talk to each of the pupils individually in her very first lesson so she could appraise them:

> They all have a silent reading book and they all know how to do that, so I get them very settled with their silent reading book and then I will just talk

to them and, depending on their age or the mood or whatever, I'll just talk to them about something that will interest them, so that we will just feel the relationship together, so that I am somebody there today to help them and I would like them to work with me. At the same time, I am doing quite a lot of assessments ... I am sifting out ... where the difficult children are, the disruptives. You can spot them within the first minute, they stand out. So I do my survey, first of all looking for those children, and then I look for the needy children who might be quiet but are slow learners. Once I've got those two groups charted the rest of the children just fall in, really.

There was a distinct division of opinion and practice on the matter of classroom rules of behaviour and procedure. Eleven out of twenty teachers made a conscious effort to apply rules from the outset, either their own or those they detected to be customary within the school. The others preferred to be reactive, to wait until circumstances required a rule to be stated or restated. This could, however, be at the very beginning of the first minute of contact. One of the common rules identified in the research literature (Wragg and Wood 1984) is 'No talking while I'm talking' in public situations. It was quite clear, in talking to one teacher, that this was, for her, an implicit classroom rule, and she revealed, in this account of a well rehearsed introduction, how she would establish it via a formal centre-stage, publicly enacted display of authority, emphasising the use of her eyes:

I do not go in and say 'These are the rules.' I might, but not to every class. It all depends on how I sense the situation. If I think it's a really bubbly sort of class, if I sense danger to the health of the lesson, to the on-going of the lesson, if I think I detect some elements that might hinder the development of the lesson, I will say, 'Good morning, everybody. Will you pay attention, please. I wish to speak to the class. Now, I don't think everybody is looking this way.' And I look. 'Would you please not fiddle with your ruler? That's right, just put it to one side. Thank you.' And I look. I don't know how I appear, but I wait until everybody's hands are free and they are looking. I do not proceed until that applies.

Procedural rules could cause some difficulty, especially if the supply teacher's practice was different from that of the class's regular teacher. Some simply imposed their own conventions from the beginning. One teacher always established her own rule about queuing at the teacher's desk. She set up a 'fast' side for spellings and a 'slow' side for problems needing a longer explanation. Another teacher, however, stressed the need to follow existing rules, commenting that 'it would be pointless trying to make out that it was *my* classroom'.

Handling disruption

Skilful teachers prevent disruption wherever possible, but all teachers have to manage deviant behaviour at some time during their teaching, so we decided to use, as a stimulus, colour photographs of classroom misbehaviour in order to elicit what the supply teachers would do in the circumstances. The responses to two of these photographs are described here.

Incident 1

The photograph shows children pushing each other as they run into the classroom. Each respondent was shown the picture and asked, 'It is time for the second half of the morning on your first day with this class. They come running back into the room, pushing each other squealing, laughing. What, if anything, do you do?' There was little hesitation from any of the teachers, as they were well used to this happening in real life. All agreed that some kind of action would have to be taken, and no-one suggested ignoring what happened. Most (thirteen out of twenty) would send the children out and make them re-enter in an orderly fashion, some stressing that they would become very authoritarian, using both voice and eyes:

> I would wait until they were all in the classroom, then I would use my assertive, cross voice and explain that in my class nobody comes into the classroom behaving like that; that we don't run into any classroom, that we walk into a classroom. And I would send them all outside and make them line up until there was absolute silence and then I would make them walk in, in an orderly manner, and sit down on the chairs properly.

The territorial aspect (*my* classroom) was echoed by another teacher, who would also use voice and eye contact to establish authority, saying:

> Your behaviour was disgraceful, disgraceful. Never again shall you enter my class like that – *my* class, by the way: I am your teacher today. Never again enter a class like that. Oh, and by the way, look at my face – I'm not smiling, I'm dead serious.

Those who would not send children outside talked about some activity that would settle the class, preferring to look ahead to the lesson in hand, commenting only briefly on the poor behaviour. One teacher of infants was used to the boisterous entry and was also well prepared for it:

> They've obviously come in really high and excited from playtime and I would have a quietening-down [activity], either a story or else a little game or something on the easel, either a number or a language thing. You can put up things like 'What can you tell me about the number 10?' and they have to think of sums about the number 10 or rhyming '-ing' words. But I think

I would do something all together and say that they hadn't come in very nicely and perhaps next time to see how nicely they came in, without jostling each other because somebody's going to get hurt.

Incident 2

In the second photograph a girl is seen standing in front of the class, a boy sitting near by is laughing. Teachers were told, 'In the afternoon you catch this girl scribbling on someone else's book. You tell her off in front of the rest of the class and, much to your surprise, she mutters, 'Old cow,' under her breath. You do not think the majority of the class heard it, but those sitting near by start to snigger. What, if anything, do you do?

All the respondents found this challenge to their authority much more difficult to handle. First reactions revealed this. 'Oh dear,' 'My God, how am I going to cope?' 'Panic!' 'That's difficult.' Most decided that their reaction would be determined by the kind of child involved, and fifteen teachers emphasised the importance of being seen to take action by the rest of the class. Some distinguished between the way they would respond as a class teacher, taking the child to one side, because they would know her, and how, as a supply teacher, they would react in a much more peremptory manner:

> in a supply situation where she might have just done it and that's it – she's said a comment and somebody's heard and they snigger – the whole thing could escalate. I think I would ask her to repeat what she had said and say, 'I thought that's what you said. Go out of my classroom, because I'm not having somebody talk to me in that tone of voice.' I'd send her outside the door and I'd ask her to come in when she felt she could apologise to me.

A number of teachers expressed the view that supply teachers were more likely to be the subject of a 'try-on' than regular teachers, and some gave examples of what they had done in real-life situations when subjected to verbal abuse:

> I said 'Do you use that . . . sort of language at home?' and he said, 'Yes'. I said, 'Who to?' He said, 'My mum.' I know what it was – he said to me, 'Stuff it.' I said, 'I beg your pardon?' He didn't repeat it, and I said, 'Don't you ever say that to me again.' I said, 'When did you say that to her?' He said, 'Well, she wouldn't let me go swimming the other night, so I said it to her.' I said, 'What did your mum say?' He said, 'Nothing,' and I said, 'Well, I'm saying something. You say that once more and you'll be in trouble, because I shall take you straight down to [the head teacher] and sort you out . . .

Some teachers sought to defuse the event by taking the girl outside, away from her audience, talking to her quietly later, but only the one inexperienced teacher in the sample, in her first year, said she would ignore it completely, though four others said they would play down its importance.

Supply teachers' strategies

That much of what supply teachers said about their preparation, rules, relationships and handling of misbehaviour was not unlike responses from teachers in other studies is understandable. They were, after all, experienced teachers in every case but one. What distinguished them, however, was their lack of knowledge of the particular school and classroom conventions and of individual children. In order to compensate for this, they had developed coping strategies, preparing for several eventualities, like the 'infants' bag and the 'juniors' bag, usually arriving early to find out about routines and set up their class, and even to rehearse their opening.

They tended to see their role as the maintenance of someone else's system, but could quickly become territorial and talk about '*my* classroom' or '*my* rules' to impress on the class that, though they might be transient, they were real teachers who were in charge. Most had developed routines that they could transplant, such as the 'fast' queue for spellings and the 'slow' queue for bigger problems. All were aware of the importance of their very first encounter, during which most tried consistently to project an image of being firm but fair. Many established a parent-like bonding ritual, mentioning their own children, asking pupils about brothers and sisters, sitting in close proximity on the carpet. Alongside this friendliness was a strong need to establish dominance should the occasion arise, by reacting quickly to misbehaviour, taking a more authoritarian stance than they might if they were the class's regular teacher. They were, in most cases, acutely aware of rules, routines and standards of behaviour, reflecting the observation of Brophy (1987) that teachers are like those circus performers who keep plates spinning at the top of sticks, managing, monitoring events continually and responding quickly when breakdowns threaten.

With their ability to be pro-active inhibited or curtailed by their lack of detailed knowledge of the children in their classes, supply teachers tended to make quick appraisals and treat some children as exemplars of certain stereotypes of behaviour or ability. Lacking the fully developed mental maps and file cards that would provide the knowledge available to the class's regular teacher, they often have to resort to typificatory knowledge (Brophy 1987), that is, intelligence about children at large, acquired in different circumstances, which then has to be used to meet particular events and incidents.

Expediency decrees that supply teachers should be able to respond quickly, behaving as experienced rather than novice teachers. This can involve a degree of stereotyping, of labelling certain types of child or behaviour in terms of parallel experience elsewhere, assuming that what is encountered is illustrative of a whole genus of comparable events elsewhere. Most supply teachers tempered this pressure to respond instantly on the basis of generalisations with a genuine desire to get to know children as individuals, but this was only possible when they had a longer period of time with a class, rather than the single day or half-day which some experienced. In the circumstances, it seems regrettable that those supply teachers who needed most support, in return for lubricating the school system, were often given least support and were, in most cases, unable to attend any training courses or even obtain copies of national curriculum documents.

Thus there are some aspects which make supply teaching atypical. On the other hand, there is much to be learned from those who cope well in sometimes unenviable circumstances, especially about preparation, presence, and the quick establishment of fair and effective rules and of positive relationships.

Chapter 7

Pupils' views of management

Relatively little research into teaching has solicited pupils' views. Yet they will spend several thousand hours sitting in primary school classes, and the German social psychologist Kurt Lewin (1943) claimed that children as young as 3 or 4 could be even more sensitive than adults to certain situations. One early survey of 672 studies of teacher effectiveness by Domas and Tiedeman (1950) reported that only seven of these had used some form of pupil rating. Only in higher education, particularly in the United States, has the student's evaluation been given any prominence (Marsh 1985).

The reluctance to use pupil perceptions is understandable. Most primary pupils have only experienced one school in one particular social setting, and they have a restricted view of teaching and of what adult life or the secondary phase of schooling may hold for them, so they will often favour the familiar. Were one to base a school or classroom system entirely on pupil opinion it would probably be ultra-conservative. On the other hand, even with limited experience from their interactions with and perceptions of others, from their reading, conversations, and viewing of television, children are capable of asking questions or making observations about classroom practice. Whilst few would advocate basing teaching entirely on pupil opinion, it is difficult to justify ignoring it completely, especially when such research as exists reports certain consistent findings.

It has commonly been found that pupils, when given a list of teacher behaviour or characteristics, will rate competence in key professional skills most highly. In one of the earliest studies Hollis (1935) gave over 8,000 pupils seven statements about teacher behaviour. Highest ranking was given to the teacher's ability to explain difficulties patiently, though the format of that particular study does not allow one to infer whether it was the explanation or the patience that was most valued. Nearly fifty years later Wragg and Wood (1984) analysed the responses of 200 pupils aged 11 to 16 on a checklist of thirty-two items using a five-point Likert scale on their concept of 'the best teacher in the world'. The most highly rated statement was 'This teacher would explain things clearly.'

Research into pupils' perceptions has been summarised by several writers.

Evans (1962) concluded that pupils seemed to prefer personal characteristics such as kindness, friendliness, patience, fairness and a sense of humour. They disliked sarcasm, favouritism, domineering and excessive punishment. Nash (1976) used a repertory-grid technique to elicit constructs from young secondary pupils and found almost exactly the same characteristics: good discipline, explaining skills, interest in pupils, fairness and friendliness. Summaries by Meighan (1977), Cohen and Manion (1981) and Wragg and Wood (1984) reported a similar picture. The empirical study by Wragg and Wood also found that teachers were expected to be firm but fair. Teachers who were bossy or punitive were not esteemed, but neither were those who were too permissive. 'This teacher would let you mark your own tests' and 'This teacher would do something else if that's what the class wanted' were both statements which received very low ratings on the 'best teacher' schedule.

Despite the paucity of research into the pupil perspective on classroom life, there is, nonetheless, a tenable view that teachers ought to know what pupils think about teaching, not so that they can abdicate their own responsibility for setting and maintaining an agenda, but so that pupils' concepts of teaching can be a legitimate part of classroom teaching and learning. Weinstein (1983) argued the case strongly: 'Being aware of students as active interpreters of classroom events forces teachers to examine more closely the effects of their own behaviour on the recipients of these interventions.' It was decided, therefore, that we would interview pupils as part of the Leverhulme Primary Project, so that there would be a pupil perspective from children in the very same classes of teachers we had observed and interviewed, rather than from a separate sample. In all, 460 primary pupils were interviewed, thirty as part of a pilot project and 430 in the main study.

Primary pupils' views – the pilot study

Interviews with young children about teachers and teaching can be difficult, as some find it hard to be specific, tending to offer vague generalisations like 'It's all right,' so we decided to use photographs and a semi-structured interview schedule. A pilot study was conducted in a school which recruited pupils mainly from a large council estate. Thirty pupils from the two oldest classes were interviewed individually. Five photographs, some of them the same as had been used in the interviews with experienced supply and student teachers reported in other chapters of this book, were shown to each child and the interviewer recorded answers to set questions, which were similar in wording to those asked of the teachers.

Photograph 1 shows two pupils pushing each other at the end of a classroom. The interviewer said, 'A teacher is sitting with her back to this group when she hears a noise. She turns round and sees two children who are not working. She has already told them off once that day for not getting on with their work. What do you think the teacher will do?'

The most common response was that the teacher would move the children, ten saying they would be sent out of the room, nine suggesting that the pupils would be separated from each other and made to sit elsewhere. Four pupils thought a telling-off would suffice, but only one child suggested further action: 'Probably, after school, she'd have a talk with them and ask what they were doing and who started it and that, and then she might send a letter back to their parents.'

Photograph 2 shows children rushing into a classroom. The story line was: 'After playtime this class go running into their classroom pushing each other, squealing and laughing. What do you think the teacher will do?'

Almost all respondents suggested the children would be sent outside and made to re-enter in an orderly manner, usually with a reprimand, one saying 'Do it again and again until they get it right.' Two pupils embroidered their explanation of 'telling off' by suggesting the teacher would give a reason for it, one girl saying 'The teacher would get angry and I think she'd tell them to sit down and give them a good talking to and explain why they shouldn't be doing it, because someone could get hurt, or work could get knocked off the table and get damaged, or anything like that.'

Photograph 3 shows a girl standing at the front of the class looking sullen and resentful. The interviewer said, 'The interviewer caught this girl scribbling on someone else's book. When the teacher tells the girl off in front of the class, the girl says something rude about the teacher. Not everyone in the class could hear what the girl had said, but the teacher and those sitting near by certainly did. What do you think the teacher will do?'

Such an insult to the teacher was seen as a major school offence by virtually every pupil, and eighteen thought she would be sent to the head. The others thought the teacher would deal with it herself and administer a punishment, like writing out a hundred lines 'I will not say rude words again' or even suspension from school, a power not actually vested in individual teachers.

Photograph 4 depicts the tail end of a queue of children waiting to enter the hall. The children were told, 'A class is going into the hall for a PE lesson and this is the back of the queue. The class teacher is at the front. When they arrive at the hall Bobby, the boy in blue, is crying. When the teacher asks him what is wrong he says that Jason, the boy in yellow, had thumped him in the back. The teacher had not seen what had happened this time, but she has seen Jason thumping and nipping other children before. All the class are watching the teacher – what do you think she will do?'

What was interesting about many of the responses to this picture was that several pupils assumed that Jason would lie about the event, denying he had done anything, and thus causing difficulties for the teacher. Their responses, therefore, included suggestions about how the teacher might need to keep him in after school until he confessed. If he did confess, then, it was believed by respondents, it might be easier for him, but the teacher would almost certainly shout at him. There was great insistence on the teacher sorting out the problem properly, pupils clearly identifying with the 'victim' in such circumstances and wanting protection, as this girl indicated: '(The teacher should find out the truth) because Jason keeps on going round hitting people and he should stop it and the teacher ought to find out if he's still doing it.'

This notion of terminating aggressive behaviour to protect the rest, bringing in parents if necessary, was echoed by others:

> They'd just have to try and think of a way of trying to get it out of them [Jason and any friends who cover up for him] because . . . if he keeps on doing it to other children and they won't admit it, he's just going to get worse and keep on doing it to other children . . . If he does keep doing it, they'll just have to get hold of his parents and tell them to come down because it's bad behaviour.

Few doubted Jason's guilt and some went so far as to suggest that both pupils would be kept in after school, on the grounds that such events are often two-sided, rather than isolated acts of aggression by unprovoked individuals.

Photograph 5 was of two pupils making paper aeroplanes instead of getting on with their work. The story line was: 'Just before home time the teacher is called out of the classroom to deal with a problem. When she comes back there is quite a lot of noise, two children are making paper aeroplanes and others are watching them. What do you think she will do?'

Half the respondents thought this was likely to be punished with a detention after school, and most ignored the role played by the observers. Eight children suspected that the paper aeroplane would be thrown in the waste bin, and one boy said that the teacher would reprimand them for wasting paper. This incident was probably the mildest of the five in the eyes of most pupils, and would have earned little more than a reprimand.

What was striking about these responses by thirty children to five picture situations, 150 replies in all, was that only one pupil said, 'Don't know,' to one picture, and the other 149 were usually clear and gave immediate replies to the stimulus of the picture, even though the interviewer had made it clear to the pupils that they could have as much time as they needed. The rudeness to the teacher in photograph 3 was clearly a major school offence in the eyes of most pupils and required higher authority. Few children suggested teachers would give reasons for their reactions, most assumed it would be instant and self-justifying. Leniency and humour were almost never mentioned, the common assumption being that teachers would react immediately and severely.

The main study

It was decided that the main study would not use all five pictures, as interviews would become extremely time-consuming. Instead we concentrated on the first three pictures, showing the two pupils pushing each other, the class rushing into the room, and the child insulting the teacher, as these had provoked an interesting mixture of responses and had been used with their teachers. We also decided to interview children across the whole primary age range, from 5 up to 12, and to add further questions about class management.

A sample of 430 pupils aged 5–12 in twenty classes in eight different schools was selected. The schools were in the North-west and the South-west of England and in London. They represented a mix between inner-city and rural schools, were all in schools where we were studying teachers, and were almost equally divided between boys and girls, with 52 per cent and 48 per cent respectively. The additional interview questions asked, after an explanation of the purposes and nature of the interview, were: 'Can you tell me what things you are allowed to do in the classroom?' 'Can you tell me what things you are not allowed to do?' 'Do you think children should be allowed to talk to each other during lessons?' (Why?/Why not?) 'Imagine the best teacher in the whole world, someone who is absolutely brilliant at teaching. What do you think this very good teacher would be like?' (Followed by 'Imagine the worst teacher in the whole world,' etc.) 'What sort of things do children do in class when they are naughty?' 'What happens when children do that?' (Whatever the child replied.) 'Are you ever naughty?' 'What do you do?' and 'What happens?' These were designed to allow children to give their own perceptions of effective teaching, of inappropriate behaviour, and their own accounts of what they themselves do.

One important strategic decision about the interviewer's wording when introducing the three photographs was to substitute 'What do you think happens next?' for the previous final sentence, 'What do you think the teacher will do?' This was in order to permit a wider range of possibilities than just action by the teacher. As in the pilot study all children interviewed were told that there were no 'right' or 'wrong' answers, that they were to say what they really felt, and that no teachers or fellow pupils would be told what they had replied.

An interesting feature of the pupil perspective is that, because pupils related to the children in the picture, whereas the teacher respondents reacted as a teacher, they would often give replies that were focused on what pupils do. For example, no teacher in our sample said, 'I would not notice (or would ignore) what happened, and, as a consequence, the pupils would continue to mess about because I had taken no action.' Yet this kind of outcome was seen in classrooms, and pupils do offer suggestions like 'The pupils will fight' or that they would carry on fooling around, as table 7.1, giving the responses of the 430 pupils to photograph 1, reveals.

Children use their own natural language when asked about classroom events. 'Telling off', the most common response, was often unspecific, as children assumed that everyone must know what a telling-off means. Youngest respondents, particularly 5 year olds, simply used the expression

Table 7.1 Percentage of responses in ten most frequently occurring categories to photograph 1 (two pupils pushing each other)

	Predicted outcome	Percentage of pupils
1	Teacher will tell them off	30.4
2	They will be sent to the head	25.3
3	They will be sent outside	7.9
4	They will be sent elsewhere	7.4
5	They carry on messing about	6.7
6	They get into trouble	6.7
7	The teacher will split them up	6.3
8	They will fight	4.4
9	They will get on with their work	4.2
10	They will be kept in after school	4.0

'get told off', whereas older pupils were often more specific: 'The teacher would tell that one off,' said one 12 year old, pointing to one of the pupils he judged to be more at fault. Some pupils were aware of a choice of possible outcomes: 'They get sent to wait outside and they go to the headmistress, and they get told off, and the headmistress gets their mum to come in and speak to the teacher.'

Experienced teachers tended to give as their most common response that the children would be moved, but only 6 or 7 per cent of pupil respondents mentioned this. 'She'll put them in a corner' and 'She'll stand them at the wall' were two suggestions from 6 year olds, but it was usually older pupils who offered variations of the reply of the 10 year old who said, 'She'll be very angry with them and she might move them apart from each other so they'll get on with their work.'

Amongst responses from pupils which were not present in teachers' replies are several suggestions that the teacher would be ineffective: 'They fight again,' 'They didn't get on with their work,' 'When the teacher turns her back again, they start messing about again,' 'They start having a fight and messing about again. They get told off and go to the office.' These kinds of replies mirror quite accurately what we sometimes saw during observations of lessons. On most occasions teachers did respond with reprimands and orders to cease, the 'telling off' reported by pupils, and on some occasions they failed to respond before the misbehaviour had escalated or even, rarely, failed to respond at all. Pupil responses confirm this mixed pattern. Four 5 year olds said the children would be smacked by the teacher, but we witnessed no corporal punishment in schools, and these young children probably based their surmise on home rather than school experience.

Photograph 2, of the children rushing into the room after break, also produced 'telling off' as the most likely response, but external authority was rarely cited on this occasion. Pushing and shoving were deemed to be part of everyday school life, and the teacher was most likely to shout and scold rather than involve higher authority, an option only mentioned by one per cent of respondents. Table 7.2 gives the breakdown of most common responses. Some of the minor categories, too small to figure in table 7.2, are of interest here. About 2 per cent of pupils suggested the teacher would give reasons why the behaviour was unacceptable, and 2 per cent also suggested that the bad behaviour would continue.

Table 7.2 Percentage of responses in ten most frequently occurring categories to photograph 2 (children rushing into classroom)

	Predicted outcome	Percentage of pupils
1	Teacher will tell them off	29.5
2	Teacher will shout at them	17.7
3	Teacher tells them to sit down	12.6
4	Teacher makes them come in again	11.9
5	Teacher tells them to be quiet	10.9
6	Children will fall over	9.8
7	Someone will get hurt	9.1
8	Children get on with their work	7.9
9	Children will sit down	2.8
10	Teacher will tell children to stop	2.3

There was a huge difference in the responses of teachers and pupils on the matter of re-entry. The most frequent response from teachers, at 77 per cent, was that pupils would be made to re-enter in an orderly fashion, but for pupils it was about 12 per cent. This may mirror actual practice, and we found numerous examples of close fit between practice we had observed and children's responses. There was one teacher in our sample who, both in her observed behaviour and in her interview response, was very keen on orderly entry, saying in her interview, 'Get them to do it again quietly. I feel you can do that preventively.' In her class nineteen out of the twenty-six pupils gave the re-entry outcome as their own reply, a much higher proportion than for the whole sample.

Children readily empathised with other children seen in the pictures, and the pupil responses showed quite an awareness of safety and the possibility of injury:

One of them falls over and everybody's going to run over him.

(Ten year old)

One of them gets hurt. There'd be a bundle. They wouldn't be able to get through the door. They'd have to back out and come back in one at a time.

(Seven year old)

Somebody might get hurt or somebody might fall over or they might bang their head on one of the tables if they do fall over.

(Nine year old)

In their replies to the third photograph, of the girl who has scribbled on children's books and called the teacher an 'old cow' (the children were told that the child would 'say something rude'), there was an interesting focus not just on the girl, but on the rest of the class, which was not so noticeable in the teachers' responses. Table 7.3 shows the distribution of replies over the ten most commonly occurring categories. The pupils were well aware of the notion of 'audience' in their replies, for they are, after all, sometimes the audience for such events themselves. There was quite a deal of talk, therefore, about other pupils being reprimanded, not just the girl. For example, a boy is visible in the picture smiling at what is happening, and many respondents commented that he would be told off for laughing. Also about 10 per cent of children said that a pupil would tell the teacher what the girl had said. This was regarded as a serious offence, with 17 per cent of pupils saying the girl would be sent to the head, yet this is lower than the 25 per cent who thought the two boys pushing each other in picture 1 would be sent to the head. The interviewer did not raise this specifically, so as not to put ideas into the children's heads, but it may be that higher authority was thought to be necessary for two aggressive boys, less so for one rude girl pupil. A further study would be needed to elicit this.

Table 7.3 Percentage of responses in ten most frequently occurring categories for photograph 3 (girl calls teacher 'old cow')

	Predicted outcome	Percentage of pupils
1	Teacher will tell off girl and/or other pupil(s)	37.7
2	Girl will be sent to the head	17.2
3	Teacher asks pupil(s) why they are laughing	9.5
4	Pupils tell teacher what girl said	9.5
5	Girl will get into trouble	6.7
6	Girl will be sent into corner	5.3
7	Girl will be sent out of room	4.0
8	Teacher will shout/show anger	4.0
9	Teacher will speak to girl/others	3.7
10	Teacher will give reasons why behaviour wrong	3.5

The pupils' responses are not exactly comparable to the teachers' replies, as the former were asked what would happen next and the latter what they themselves would do. However, it is clear that pupils expect to be told off for misbehaviour, to be sent to the head for more serious misconduct, and to be moved, sent outside or shouted at if they act anti-socially with others. They are also aware that teachers' best intentions to curb misbehaviour are not always fulfilled and that deviance can and will escalate if unchecked. There were numerous other close matches between what we observed in a particular teacher's classroom and what the pupils responded. Five classes whose teachers tended to shout when they misbehaved showed a higher incidence of 'teacher shouts' responses and four classes showed a higher than average tendency to use the 'teacher tells to sit down' category, which was consistent with the teacher's normal behaviour.

In addition to the photograph response, pupils were asked a series of questions about behaviour in the classroom and about what teachers do, and a sub-sample of 105 of these detailed responses, consisting of one class each of 5–6, 6–7, 7–8, 9–11 and 11–12 year olds, are reported here. The intention of the first question, asking what pupils are allowed to do, was to generate positive rather than negative responses. The five most common responses were (1) work, (2) talk to each other, (3) play when we've finished our work, (4) choose something we want to do and (5) walk freely in the classroom (with a reason). This mixture of work and choice came out clearly in several responses, some respecting the freedom, others not:

> We've got to do our work, then sometimes, in the afternoon, if we do all our work we're allowed to play with the Lego and we're allowed to write letters over there (pointing) to people when it's their birthday or something.
>
> (Seven year old)
>
> We're allowed to get on with our work, sort of on our own. We don't have to do everything, we don't have to do the same things all the time.
>
> (Eleven year old)
>
> You're allowed to talk quietly, but you're not allowed to shout, which is what everyone usually does instead of getting on with their work.
>
> (Eight year old)
>
> We're allowed to choose. We're allowed to play in the house, we can play in the big sandpit or the little sandpit, which is out there, or we can play outside or do some writing or drawing.
>
> (Six year old)

Play was principally mentioned by the 5–6 and 6–7 year olds. It was perceived as play by pupils, but teachers saw it as school work with choice.

When it came to asking children what they were not allowed to do the list of responses was much longer. In first five places were (1) shout, (2) be silly/ mess about, (3) fight, (4) throw things, (5) run. Even younger pupils had a well shaped sense of what the teacher's rules were:

> We're not allowed to muck about, we're not allowed to fight and we're not allowed to yell at the top of our voices, and a few other things which I can't remember. We've got quite a lot of rules – loads.
>
> (Eight year old)
>
> We're not allowed to scream, we're not allowed to shout, we're not allowed to throw things around the classrooms, not allowed to be naughty, we're not allowed to do mean things to people, like scratch and punch and kick, and that's it really.
>
> (Seven year old)

You're not really allowed to copy, you've got to do your own work. When you [are] working with someone, you're to discuss it with them and not shout at them. If you haven't finished and you've had a long time to do a certain piece of work then you've got to stay in at break and finish it, and if it's like near the end of the day, then you've got to take it home and finish it for homework.

(Ten year old)

The concern with shouting reflects the category of misbehaviour we observed most frequently, namely noisy chatter. Pupils were clearly divided by age on the matter of whether talking in the classroom should be permitted at all. Table 7.4 shows how they responded, and the older pupils took a more sophisticated view of classroom talk than the younger pupils, who usually assumed it must be wrong. Of the thirty-six 9–12 year olds who replied 'Yes', 16 qualified it by adding that it was legitimate only if related to work or if done quietly. The reasons for replies were mainly, for those who replied 'Yes', because it helped you with your work, stopped you getting bored, helped concentration and allowed you to check your answers. Those who saw it negatively said it interfered with work, you got told off, you wouldn't hear the teacher and it interrupted others. Some of the more aware pupils in the 'it depends' category gave a balanced view of the pros and cons:

If it's about work, then yes, and they're not making too much noise, but if they're mucking about or talking about what they did at the weekend, then no, because they're not getting on with their work properly and they'll probably get told off and get extra work.

(Ten year old)

Table 7.4 Replies to question, 'Should children be allowed to talk to each other in lessons?'

Response	5–6	6–7	Age group 7–8	9–11	11–12	Total
Yes	4	2	8	19	17	50
No	13	15	12	2	0	42
Sometimes	1	1	1	2	2	7
It depends	0	2	0	3	1	6
Total	18	20	21	26	20	105

The question about the best and worst teacher in the world produced responses not unlike those reported in other studies described earlier in this chapter. The best teacher in the world would, according to this sample, do interesting activities and also let you choose, be 'nice', kind and 'good at teaching', which was variously interpreted as a combination of subject knowledge ('brainy', 'understands a lot') and professional skill ('explains', 'good at teaching you about computers' (seven pupils, all in the same class)). The best teacher in the world would be quite strict, 'not let you get away with things', but not too bossy, and would have a sense of humour. This general picture of pupils' perceptions obtained from these interviews is almost exactly what other studies have found, confirming that the pupil perception literature is astonishingly consistent across time and age groups.

Younger pupils tended to name a teacher quite naturally, often their current teacher, assuming she must be the best. Some twenty seven out of thirty eight 5–7 year olds named a teacher, and eleven of these were their current teacher, whereas only five of the sixty seven older pupils named a teacher, of which three were their own. When it came to the 'worst teacher in the world' stereotype only thirteen pupils named a teacher, again mainly younger ones, and only one of these was the child's current teacher. The responses here were often the obverse of the good teacher stereotype, and the most disliked characteristics were shouting and yelling at children, not allowing you to talk, telling people off all the time, often unfairly, not knowing how to teach, being 'nasty' and over-bossy, not letting you do things you like, being rude to children, setting work that is too hard and using excessive punishments. The greater sophistication and more abstract discernment of the older pupil and the more concrete, specific world view of the younger pupil are well illustrated by these two responses expressing a similar view:

> They'd get cross at the slightest thing and they'd go round not really noticing, they'd go round teaching people and they'd get cross if you got things wrong, instead of seeing how you got it wrong and making sure you understand. They wouldn't talk to you about it, so they'd just snap at you.
>
> (Eleven year old)
>
> The lady who's in there (pointing to a teacher in another room) she kept on shouting at us and we couldn't get on with our work. But I done it good, so I didn't get told off.
>
> (Six year old)

The questions about what naughty children do in class and how the teacher responds reflected and reinforced answers we had received to earlier questions. There were clear views on what constitutes naughty behaviour, and, as previously, these reflected violence to another person and noise. Kicking, pushing, fighting, shouting, screaming, throwing or flicking things, messing about and damage to property were all mentioned frequently, closely followed by illicit talking, swearing, not working, fidgeting and running. The most reported responses from the teacher were a telling-off, being sent to the head or sent outside, told to get on with your work, punishing with extra work, shouting, getting cross and warning about future conduct. In classes where teachers actually dealt with misbehaviour in a positive manner this was greatly appreciated by children, who often spoke spontaneously in approving terms, like this 7 year old:

What naughty pupils do '. . . punishing other people. Like Miss Brown [class teacher] says, if they swear at people they're getting bitchy. That's what Miss Brown says.'

What happens 'We have a circle time [when the pupils and teacher sit around in a circle] and ask people what they do to people. Then Miss Brown tries to sort it out and mostly she gets it all sorted out and she's really good at it. She's good at sorting it out.'

About half (fifty two out of 105) the children admitted to being naughty in class, with older pupils showing few inhibitions about admitting it and younger pupils responding more warily. Only three out of the eighteen 5–6 year olds in the sample replied 'Yes,' whereas seventeen of the oldest twenty children replied in the affirmative. The contrast is revealed by these two responses from a younger and older pupil:

Are you ever naughty?
No. I get on with my work and I don't talk.

(Five year old)

Are you ever naughty?
Sometimes.
What do you do?
Throw rubbers and paper.
What happens?
I don't know, I've never been caught.

(Twelve year old)

Most pupils were well aware of the consequences of misbehaviour and could describe them in great detail, appreciating such matters as confidentiality or the significance of status, even when the teacher or the school had intricate rituals, often involving the school hierarchy in an elaborate chain of events:

I got a yellow card. It's just a warning. You get one when you get told off. The first card you get is normal, and then if you do it again you go into a corner or another class, and then you go to the headmistress and then you get a letter home to the parents.

(Eight year old)

Well, Miss Gibbon normally takes them [naughty pupils] outside and talks to them so no one else can hear, and they have to sit outside and then the headteacher comes along and gives them some hard work.

(Ten year old)

Even very young children had a clear understanding of the borderline between what the teacher would regard as acceptable and what would be regarded as deviant. Fighting was the third most frequently mentioned 'naughty' behaviour, but there was a clear distinction between the real thing and rough-and-tumble role-played versions:

I just plays on my own with my cousin and some of my friends. We plays a little fight, it's not a real fight, it's a play fight. You just pretend to punch like that (demonstrates mock blow), and that's pretending. You won't get told off. . . . You stand near the wall when you're naughty. I don't stand near the wall. I don't be naughty outside.

(Six year old)

This part of our enquiry showed that children have a perspective on misbehaviour that is often different from that of the teacher, though they can repeat the school's official policies on discipline with clarity and apparent consent. Spending up to thirty five hours a week in school ensures that they experience their teachers' management rituals and routines numerous times. There is little ambiguity in the minds of even the youngest pupils about what is expected, and what will ensue if they transgress. Yet their vantage point is different from that of teachers. They see shouting and telling off as a normal part of classroom life, to be expected even, whereas teachers tend to be more embarrassed at mentioning these, from their point of view, cruder responses.

Not surprisingly aggression features high on their list of concerns, as they are well aware that a fellow belligerent pupil can easily knock them over in a rush, hit them, or cause them some other mischief, and they appreciate teachers who, without themselves being over-domineering, are clearly in charge when it comes to dealing with over-aggressive behaviour. It confirms the popular child stereotype of successful teaching reported in other enquiries – in charge, firm but fair, knowing their craft, able to explain clearly, pleasant to be with, good-humoured and good-natured – and loath to shout.

Chapter 8

Explaining and explanations

Explaining is not only a professional skill which is highly esteemed by children. It is an aspect of communication which lies at the centre of human discourse in many fields: parents explain things to their children; radio and television presenters explain what lies behind news stories to listeners and viewers; pilots explain the cause of delay to air travellers. In the case of doctors and patients there can be, as in teaching, reciprocal explanations: the patient first explains symptoms to the doctor, and the doctor then explains causes and treatments to the patient. Explaining is not, however, a uni-dimensional activity, and the words 'explain' and 'explanation' are used in many different ways. For the purposes of this research we took as an operational definition the statement: 'explaining is giving understanding to another'. This interpretation allows the notion to embrace strategies other than imparting information directly, as it can include, for example, asking questions which encourage pupils to reach their own conclusions, engaging in practical work or giving a demonstration.

Explanations can help some to understand a concept like 'density' or 'prejudice', and the notion may be new to the learner, or already partly familiar. They can also illuminate cause and effect, for example that rain is produced by the cooling of air. There are many other possibilities, such as the explanation of procedures, including both those within the subject domain, like how to convert a fraction to a decimal, and those to do with the management of the lesson, such as ways of ensuring that no one has an accident in a gymnastics lesson. There can be explanations of purposes and objectives, when a teacher explains why children are going to embark on a study of their own village, or what they will have learned at the conclusion of some activity; of relationships between people, events or the different parts of something, like why bees and flies are insects but spiders are not, or what religious festivals like Christmas and Easter have in common; of the processes involved in the working of a piece of machinery or the behaviour of people or animals. Explanations often answer real or imaginary questions based on common interrogatives like Who? What? How? Why? Where? When?

Numerous investigations have sought to assemble a typology of explanations, and Brown and Armstrong (1984) have summarised work by Swift (1961), Bellack *et al.* (1966), Ennis (1969), Smith and Meux (1970) and Brown (1978). They produced a chart (Table 8.1) which compares three views of the process of explaining. Research into explanations in the classroom has been summarised by Crowhurst (1988). Such research is sparse compared with enquiry into other teaching strategies. Smith and Meux analysed transcripts of eighty five lessons given by seventeen teachers in five high schools. They split the lessons into a series of 'episodes' and found that describing, designating and explaining were the three operations that occurred most frequently. Tisher (1970) used the classification scheme developed by Smith and Meux to analyse the relationship between teachers' strategies in nine science classes and children's understanding in science. Explaining ranked as fourth most frequently used strategy after designating, describing and stating.

Brown and Armstrong (1984) used their own system for analysing discourse to elicit which features distinguished the lessons of twelve student teachers explaining biological topics to children. They used independent ratings of videotapes of the lessons and pupil learning as measured by post-tests to identify the more 'effective' explanations. These were shown on analysis to be characterised by more 'keys', that is, central principles or generalisations which help to unlock understanding. The more successful explanations also had more framing statements which showed the beginnings and endings of sub-topics, more focusing statements emphasising the key points, and used the rule–example–rule structure – e.g. an insect has, among other characteristics, six legs (rule), a fly is an insect (example), so insects have six legs (rule) – which had also been identified by Gage *et al.* (1972) as effective. However, the rule–example–rule pattern seemed to work best in interpretive explanations, when technical terms were being explored. In reason-giving and descriptive explanations, when processes were being explored, the example–rule–example model seemed to be effective.

The matter of cognitive level is also relevant to research into explaining, and this topic will be dealt with again in the report of the research on questioning in chapter 9. The level of thinking involved in classroom teaching and learning has been discussed by Bloom (1956), whose taxonomy of educational objectives in the cognitive domain has frequently been used or modified. Bloom formulated a hierarchical view of learning at six levels, starting with knowledge and then going on to comprehension, application, analysis, synthesis and finally evaluation. The assumption was that one needed the lower levels in order to achieve the higher levels: you need to have knowledge in order to comprehend, and you must comprehend in order to be able to analyse, synthesise or evaluate. Taba (1966) devised a similar set of thought levels in her work at San Francisco State College helping teachers move children up to higher levels of thought, though there is no

Table 8.1 Three typologies of explaining

After Hyman (1974)	After Smith and Meux (1970)	After Brown (1978)
Type I Generalisation – specific instance		
		Reason-giving, answering the question 'Why?'
Empirical The effects of pressure on the volume of gas	*Empirical-subsumptive* Seasonal changes on mammals	Why does the volume of a gas decrease as pressure increases? Why do certain mammals hibernate in winter?
Probabilistic Relation between lung cancer and smoking	*Judgmental* Causes of higher crime rate in urban areas	Why do heavy smokers have a greater risk of contracting cancer? Why is there more crime in inner-city areas?
Non-empirical A verb agrees with its subject	*Normative* The proper use of knives and forks	Why do we say, 'He runs,' but 'They run'? Why do we hold a fork in the left hand?
Type II Functional		
		Interpretive, answering the question 'What?'
Purpose The motives behind Lord Jim's actions	*Teleological* Birds of prey as efficient hunters	What led Lord Jim to become the strange character he was? What uses do talons and curved beaks serve in birds of prey?
Function Unions and their members	*Consequence* Inflation and our money	What can unions do in an industrial dispute? What are the effects of a high inflation rate on the currency?
Type III Serial		
		Descriptive, answering the question 'How?'
Sequential Making a sponge cake	*Sequential* Constructing a perpendicular to a given line	How do you make a light sponge? How can a perpendicular be constructed using compass and ruler?
Genetic Differences between cats and dogs	*Mechanical* The operation of a car engine	As animals, how do cats differ from dogs? How does the internal combustion engine work?
Chronological Events leading to the war in Vietnam	*Procedural* Conducting a formal meeting	How did colonial history lead to the Vietnamese war? How does the chairman lead a meeting?

conclusive research evidence that operating at higher levels is inevitably associated with 'better learning', a topic which will be discussed again in chapter 9.

The present study of teachers' explanations

It was decided to study teachers explaining new subject matter to primary pupils in two major domains of the school curriculum, science and English, as this would enable us to investigate the field in two distinctive and contrasting subject areas. Preliminary informal observations in the class-rooms of five teachers in three different schools were made, and lessons whose subject matter ranged from mathematics to country dancing were studied. Examples of explaining episodes were collected. There were also extensive interviews with the teachers concerned. The pilot study involved asking teachers to explain a variety of topics, such as 'the water cycle', 'erosion', the difference between 'their' and 'there', mathematical concepts such as 'parallel' and 'perpendicular', to small groups of children of different ability.

The pilot study confirmed that explaining took place regularly in lessons, that teachers appeared to use a variety of strategies, that explaining to individual pupils caused some management problems, like children waiting with hand in the air, or standing in a queue if the teacher was explaining at her desk, and that it would be worthwhile studying explanations to children of different levels of ability. The pilot also revealed that several explanatory episodes were related to misbehaviour and class management, like 'why we need to wipe our feet when we come in on a wet day'; that it was not too difficult to test more able children and those of average ability, but that testing low-ability children, particularly in younger age groups, caused great difficulty, as written forms of assessment were often not appropriate and oral forms were extremely time-consuming. Indeed, teachers in the pilot com-mented on the difficulty of explaining basic concepts to lower-ability pupils generally, about the time taken and the disappointment when little seemed to be understood.

Following the pilot it was decided to concentrate on two topics, one in English, one in science; to study in particular high and medium-ability pupils, as lower-ability pupils would really need a separate study; to give a post-test of learning; to limit the time available for the 'explanation' to ten minutes, as this had been shown to be the sort of time teachers devoted to public discussion of a new topic; and to give teachers a completely free hand in the strategies they used. It was also decided to confine the study to 8 and 9 year old pupils, on the grounds that they were old enough to be able to write and were in the middle years of primary education, and to have four children in each group, as these could be monitored effectively and four was a size of group to which teachers had often been seen explaining something.

Thus the research was part experimental and part naturalistic. It was experimental, in the sense that the researchers controlled the amount of time available for the exploration (up to ten minutes maximum), the amount of time the children had to complete the post-test (up to fifteen minutes maximum), the two topics in English and science, the ability levels of the children and the number of children in each group (four). Furthermore there was a control group of children who took the post-test but had not been given the teacher's explanation first, as we wanted to see what differences having an explanation appeared to make. The research was also, in part, naturalistic, in that the children were from the teacher's regular class, the explaining took place in a location near the normal class with which children were familiar, say the library, or another classroom, and teachers had a completely free hand in deciding how they explained the topics.

A total of thirty-two teachers from sixteen schools in both urban and rural areas took part in the research. The sample was virtually random, as only two schools approached did not wish to take part. Every teacher gave four explanations, two to groups of four children each consisting of two boys and two girls (1) of above average ability (IQ range 110 to 120) and (2) four children of average ability (IQ range 95 to 105). The control group consisted of four children of average ability, so that their test scores could be compared with the experimental average-ability group. It would not always have been possible to have a control group of above average ability, owing to small numbers in some classes. Two topics were selected: firstly a factual scientific topic, 'Insects', and teachers were told that children should, at the end of the explanation, be able to identify insects and know the parts of an insect; secondly, there was an explanation of an imaginary island (figure 8.1) called the Island of Zarg, which was to be followed by children writing a story entitled 'My Adventure on the Island of Zarg'. The design was thus a very balanced one and the order of teaching was randomised, so that the topic and the ability range were not always taught in the same order by different teachers, otherwise artefacts might have been produced that were relevant to the order in which groups were taught. A summary of the design is given below.

No. of schools: sixteen.

No. of teachers: thirty two (sixteen of 8 year olds, sixteen of 9 year olds).

No. of topics: two, 'Insects' and 'Island of Zarg'.

No. of pupils:

    Experimental groups: 128 above-average, 128 average ability.

    Control groups: 128 average ability.

    Total: 384 pupils.

Total number of explanations: four for each teacher (two on 'insects', two on 'Zarg'), 128 in all.

Order of teaching groups and topics randomised.

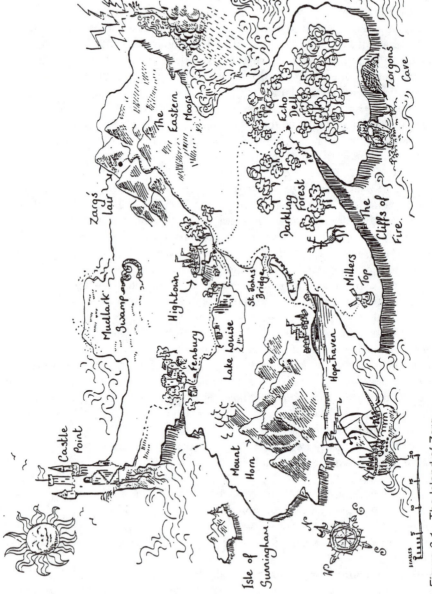

Figure 8.1 The Island of Zarg

The research instruments

A great deal of data was generated in the study and several forms of analysis for both process and product data were used (Crowhurst 1988). In the case of the process data, that is, the actual analysis of the classroom explanation, all the explanations were observed live by one of the research team, and an observation schedule, Teacher Explanation Observation Schedule (TEXOS), was developed, which was first piloted in schools and then used in the main study. The TEXOS schedule was a category and sign system derived from observations made at the pilot stage and from ideas in other observation instruments such as those used by Galton (1978) and Brown and Armstrong (1984). All explanations were recorded on sound cassette for further analysis and corroboration.

The first section summarised background information about the teacher and the class, the second part was a coding system for tallying the nature of questions, pupil responses, teacher responses, linguistic moves, such as using analogies, examples, or giving or eliciting summaries and pauses, social moves such as humour, praise or chiding, and visual aids. Five two-minute lesson segments were coded, with the observer recording whether or not each form of behaviour took place in a two-minute segment. There was also an 'opportunity to learn' section, in separate form for 'Insects' and 'Zarg', in which the observer noted whether such matters as number of legs, number of wings, spiders not being insects, and features of the Island of Zarg were mentioned during the explanation by pupil or teacher.

The third section made use of the critical events technique described in chapter 3. One event was recorded which seemed to the observer to be related to an important aspect of that particular explanation, followed by an interview with the teacher about it, during which the teacher was also asked about the teaching approach used and, after the final observation, whether any conscious distinction had been made between the explanation to the above-average and average groups of children. There were also seven bipolar opposite rating scales of teacher characteristics which included warm/aloof, dull/stimulating and items which rated eye contact and fluency. Inter-observer (between two people) and intra-observer (each observer with self, before and after research) agreement coefficients were calculated from observations of videotapes. These were high and correlations of 0.779 to 0.934 were obtained for intra-observer agreement and of 0.674 to 0.723 for inter-observer agreement. The higher levels of agreement were, in each case, on the Insects topic, which seemed easier to code than the more discursive Island of Zarg explanations.

The product data were of two kinds. First of all there was a test of insect recognition, which involved pictures of several real insects and other creatures, like arachnids and crustaceans. There were also questions about insects and an invitation to describe them freehand. Secondly, for the Island of Zarg, children had to write a free composition entitled, 'My Adventure on the Island of Zarg'. The insects questions were scored according to a scheme devised during the pilot study, giving a maximum score of thirty points. The correlation between two independent markers was a very high 0.941.

The creative writing piece scoring system was influenced by the work of Wilkinson *et al.* (1980) and Bennett (1984). It consisted of a series of five-point scales covering imaginativeness, mention of island features, coherence, sentence complexity and story length. Correlations between independent markers were 0.778 (island features mentioned), 0.784 (sentence complexity), 0.789 (coherence), 0.791 (imaginativeness), 0.841 (overall impression) and 0.920 (length).

Research findings

Lesson observation

Analysis of the strategies used by teachers revealed a fascinating range of tactics, with short questions, short responses and teacher repetition of pupils' replies lying at the heart of many explanations. Table 8.2 shows the most frequently occurring features of all explanations recorded using TEXOS. In each case, the range is from a minimum of 0 if the behaviour had not occurred at all, to an absolute maximum of 5 if it had occurred in every single one of the five lesson segments observed in each explanation. The pattern confirms that questioning is a frequently used strategy which leads to shorter or longer pupil answers. Table 8.3 shows, by contrast, the ten least frequently recorded categories.

The common pattern of teacher question, short answer, teacher repeats, teacher probes was observed in both science and English explanations. For example:

Insects

Teacher   What sort of things does an insect have on its head?
Pupil   Big round eyes.
Teacher   Big round eyes, yes – and why do you think an insect needs big round eyes?

Island of Zarg

Teacher   What is a Zarg?
Pupil   He's a big, black, furry monster.
Teacher   A big, black, furry monster. And what sort of monster is he? Is he friendly? Or fierce, perhaps?

Table 8.2   Ten most frequently occurring categories for all explanations
(n = 128)

TEXOS category	Frequency (max. = 5)
1 Short pupil responses	4.4
2 Teacher repeats pupil answer	3.8
3 Teacher open question	3.7
4 Spontaneous pupil response	3.7
5 Teacher probes	3.4
6 Teacher closed question	2.9
7 Long pupil response	2.9
8 Teacher pauses	2.6
9 Teacher rephrases	2.6
10 Teacher summarises	2.5

Table 8.3   Ten least frequently occurring categories for all explanations
(n = 128)

TEXOS category	Frequency (max. = 5)
1 Teacher rejects pupil response	0.2
2 Use of analogy	0.4
3 No pupil response	0.5
4 Teacher elicits summary from pupils	0.7
5 Teacher chides	0.8
6 Teacher explains links	0.9
7 Teacher elicits example from pupils	1.1
8 Teacher corrects pupil	1.4
9 Teacher gives example	1.4
10 Teacher gives verbal cue	1.4

The results of the analysis of the processes of explaining show that teachers tended to control the interaction quite carefully, making many of the significant moves themselves, like summing up, questioning, repeating answers, probing. At the same time, there was considerable interaction, and rarely was there no response from pupils, even though their answers were likely to be short. Relatively little use was made of analogies and examples. Analogies occurred mainly in the insect explanations, when referring to the exo-skeleton as being like a suit of armour, or when talking about the eye:

> The surface of the eye looks like lots of marbles packed together in a plastic bag.

> It looks like lots of TV screens put together side by side.

The patterns of interaction were further analysed to see what predominant moves occurred. The most highly significant product–moment correlations between the more frequently occurring categories of the TEXOS data are given in Table 8.4. All are significant at beyond the 0.001 level of probability, that is, they would have occurred by chance less than once in a thousand times. There were high correlations between some of the less frequently occurring categories, but these have been omitted as there can often be spurious correlations between infrequently occurring pieces of behaviour. This analysis confirms the predominant question-and-answer pattern of interaction, with a variety of questions, some occurring in sequences, followed by short rather than long responses from the pupil (though spontaneous contributions from pupils were more likely to be long, rather than short). The following exchange was typical of this common pattern:

Teacher   Is a woodlouse an insect?
Pupil 1   Yes.
Teacher   Does it look like an insect?
Pupil 1   Sort of.
Teacher   What about its three body parts? Can you find the head, thorax and abdomen?
Pupil 1   I can't find the thorax and abdomen.
Pupil 2   It looks like it's got lots of little body parts.
Teacher   Ah! How many legs has it got?
Pupil 2   More than six.
Teacher   More than six, and lots of body parts. Is it an insect?
Pupil 1   It can't be.

Table 8.4   Highest correlations between most frequently occurring process variables (all significant beyond the 0.001 level).

TEXOS features correlated	Correlation
1 Long pupil responses and spontaneous pupil responses	+0.65
2 Teacher repeats pupil responses and short responses	+0.62
3 Teacher probes and sequenced questions	+0.60
4 Teacher probes and open questions	+0.56
5 Sequenced questions and teacher repeats pupil responses	+0.56
6 Open questions and short pupil responses	+0.53
7 Teacher corrects and short pupil responses	+0.50
8 Sequenced questions and short pupil responses	+0.50
9 Open questions and teacher repeats responses	+0.49
10 Closed questions and teacher repeats responses	+0.44
11 Sequenced questions and closed questions	+0.43
12 Closed questions and short pupil responses	+0.43

Comparisons between science and English lessons

It was hypothesised that science and English lessons would be different in explanatory styles adopted by the teacher, but this might not have been the case. Analysis showed that there were notable differences, however. Tables 8.2, 8.3 and 8.4 above show the mean category scores for both topics combined, but when we compared the type of explaining categories used by teachers for the two topics separately, some quite spectacular differences emerged. In order to investigate what differences there were between explanations in the two topic areas of Insects and the Island of Zarg, as well as between explanations to older (9 year old) and younger (8 year old) pupils, and to above-average and average pupils, we used analysis of variance. The F ratios for these comparisons are shown in the tables below. The higher the F ratio, the more significant the difference between the groups.

One of the most spectacular differences was in the category 'Teacher engages pupils' imagination'. Although it was not unknown in the Insects topic, for example, when a teacher occasionally asked children to imagine what it must be like to be an insect, the science topic was usually dealt with in a much more factual manner. Almost all the examples of engagement of the imagination, therefore, occurred in the English lessons on the 'Island of Zarg' map. The F ratio was a massive 531.4, the most significant of any obtained, well beyond the 0.001 level of significance.

Most highly significant differences of this kind, however, occurred in the opposite direction. Table 8.5 shows the greatest differences where there was a much higher incidence in the category of behaviour concerned in the Insects lesson. 'Use of visual aids' figures prominently, because teachers rarely used additional visual aids in the 'Zarg' lesson, as the map of the island was provided, though a few did occasionally amplify the map with additional visual aids. All the categories in table 8.5 occurred more frequently in the Insects lessons at a degree of statistical significance beyond the 0.001 level.

The two differences where the incidence was higher in the English lessons on the Island of Zarg are worthy of comment. Table 8.6 shows the hugely significant difference in the category 'teacher engages pupil imagination', but also the higher occurrence of verbal cues, where the teacher 'nudged' the

Table 8.5 Most significant differences between Insects and Zarg explanations (in each case higher frequency of occurrence being in the Insect lessons, all differences significant beyond the 0.001 level)

	TEXOS category	F ratio
1	Teacher gives example	239.9
2	Teacher elicits example	158.6
3	Teacher gives summary	85.1
4	Teacher elicits summary	64.0
5	Eye contact	34.8
6	Closed questions	16.9
7	Teacher praises	15.3
8	Organisation	13.4
9	Clarity	12.5
10	Teacher explains links	7.3

Table 8.6 Most significant differences between Insects and Zarg lesson (both significant beyond the 0.001 level)

TEXOS category	F ratio
1 Teacher engages imagination	531.4
2 Verbal cue	7.5

pupils along with a helpful word. Though the F ratio is much lower, it too is significant at beyond the 0.001 level.

These quantitative data confirm other observations made above. The format of many explanations of insects was essentially that of programmed learning, with a short 'frame' of information, a closed question, a short answer, a reinforcement (usually praise) or repetition, and sometimes a summary from the teacher. There was also much more eye contact, organisation and conceptual clarity on the rating scales. The English lessons, by contrast, were more discursive, with a challenge to the imagination being central, and longer answers also featuring.

Some of these and other more qualitative aspects of explaining the two topics can be illustrated from transcripts of lessons. The programmed learning format is implemented in the following rapid-fire exchange. The children were looking at a centipede:

> *Teacher*   What makes this different from insects? What did we say an insect has?
> *Pupil 1*   Six legs.
> *Teacher*   Right, how many legs has that one got?
> *Pupil 2*   Forty-two, I've counted.
> *Teacher*   So, is it an insect?
> *Pupil 3*   Well, I think it looks like one.
> *Teacher*   Have a look. Is its body arranged like that? (Shows pupils diagram of an insect body.)
> *Pupil 2*   Not at all.
> *Teacher*   So is it an insect?
> *Pupil 4*   No. But spiders have eight legs, so they're insects.
> *Teacher*   Are they?
> *Pupil 4*   I think so.
> *Teacher*   Well, are we going to say spiders are insects and spiders have six legs?
> *Pupil 4*   No, silly me. I always thought they were, though.

Despite the apparently neat programmed learning format, there is still some conceptual confusion. Pupil 1 has confirmed the prerequisite that insects should have six legs, but in the eyes of pupils 3 and 4 it is still a matter of intuitive 'feel' rather than criteria or 'must have' characteristics. Having what looks to be a tightly controlled 'information–question–pupil answer–

teacher response' pattern does not of itself ensure clear structure or universal understanding.

Another teacher used a similar clipped rapid-fire dialogue approach, but in a different manner, this time to probe and challenge, starting with a 'not' analogy (a camel not being an insect):

> *Teacher*   A camel is not an insect. Why?
> *Pupil 1*   It hasn't got antennae.
> *Teacher*   A snail has got antennae.
> *Pupil 2*   Insects have wings.
> *Teacher*   So do nightingales.
> *Pupil 1*   Insects collect pollen.
> *Teacher*   So do humming birds.

This challenging, slightly adversarial style raises interesting possibilities about teachers' reflections on teaching. Such is the speed of the exchange that there can be little time for reflection. Intelligent action by teachers may be based on deep and surface structures, the deep ones, laid down by reflection and experience over a period of time, determining the surface structures which are also influenced by rapidly processed context clues.

The features of high-scoring lessons will be discussed below, but here is an example of a teacher whose pupils performed particularly well on post-tests who used the same programmed short frame approach in her summary when she was revising the main points children would need to remember:

> *Teacher*   So, then, let's go back to my little friend here (pointing to a model of an insect she has made and used earlier). Who's going to tell me the names of the parts?
> *Pupil 1*   Head.
> *Teacher*   Head, yes.
> *Pupil 2*   Thorax and abdomen.
> *Teacher*   Well done. What are these?
> *Pupil 3*   Feelers.
> *Teacher*   And what are they for?
> *Pupil 3*   'Tasting' the air.
> *Teacher*   Yes, tasting the air, that's a good description.

In the case of the lessons on the Island of Zarg there were numerous examples of attempts to invoke the imagination. Some responses were elicited through open but focused questions, such as:

If there was something terribly dangerous on this island, where do you think would be a good place to hide?

Let's say that ship down there is a pirate ship. Imagine you are on that ship, arriving in Hopehaven. What's going to happen to you when you land?

Tell me where the best place on this island would be for me to have my holiday?

What does the name 'Darkling Forest' conjure up in your minds?

Verbal cues were more frequent in the Zarg explanations because teachers tended to give clues about what pupils might do just before they began writing. It should be pointed out, incidentally, that the two differing patterns described above were predominant tendencies, not exclusive patterns. Imagination was sometimes evoked in Insect explanations:

What must it be like to be an insect?'

Do you know that butterflies can taste with their feet? (Laughter.) Yes, when they land on things they can taste them using their feet. Wouldn't it be funny if we could taste with our feet?

Age and ability of pupils

The issue of matching tasks to pupils has been investigated by a number of researchers (Bennett *et al.* 1984). The task is, however, but one part of the matching process, for the other important element must be teaching strategies. One might expect that, just as there were significant differences between the strategies used for the factual Insects topic and the discursive Island of Zarg creative writing assignment, so too there might be differences in patterns of teaching average and above-average pupils and 8 and 9 year olds.

Analysis of variance was again used to elicit whether significant differences did occur between the TEXOS categories obtained for the various groups. In the case of age of pupils the most striking finding is that not one single element of the observation schedule reached even the 5 per cent level of significance. Given that there are more than twenty categories in the schedule, at least one difference at the 5 per cent, one in twenty, level would have been expected to occur by chance, but no such differences emerged. Furthermore the teachers of 8 year olds were not the same people as the teachers of 9 year olds, another reason why some significant differences might have occurred, yet none did. Perhaps the slight difference in the ages of pupils, only one year, may account for this similarity of approach. Had the study involved a wider age difference, say, 7 year olds and 11 year olds, the differences might have been more marked. The lack of contrast found in the quantitative reports was analysed. No differences of any note emerged here either. The inescapable conclusion, on the matter of the age of pupils, in this study, therefore, is that a small difference in age, like one year, appears not to be associated with different strategic approaches.

Whereas the non-significance of pupil age as a factor was not too surprising, the findings on pupil ability level were perhaps more noteworthy. Analysis of variance on the process data from the explanation given to average ability and those given to above-average ability showed astonishingly little difference, even though, in this case, it was the *same* teachers who were involved in both cases. Table 8.7 shows that only four elements of classroom process showed any significant difference at all. In each case all the differences were in the direction of more of the behaviour concerned occurring in the classes of the average ability group, and only one was highly significant at the 0.001 level, the other three being significant at the 0.05 level.

Table 8.7 Four process measures found to be most significant in the comparison between explanations to average and above-average pupils, in each case more occurring in the lesson with average ability pupils

TEXOS category	F ratio
1 Teacher corrects	7.7***
2 Teacher rephrases	6.4*
3 Teacher explains links	4.5*
4 Teacher gives summary	4.5*

Analysis of both interviews with teachers and lesson observation field notes confirmed that the differences in process were slight, confined mainly to the consequences of incorrect or partially correct responses in the Insects lesson, when teachers corrected, rephrased, explained links and gave summaries. Most teachers, however, confirmed in interview, when asked specifically, after the explanation had been given to both groups, 'Were you conscious of any differences in the way you explained to high and average-ability children?' that they had not consciously sought to vary their approach.

Only two teachers outlined different strategies for the two ability groups for the Insects topic, and only six for the Island of Zarg. Only one teacher said he used different strategies on *both* topics. One style changer was the teacher whose pupils obtained the highest scores of any in the sample on the test following the Insects explanation. He was a biology graduate teaching in a small village school in a not especially privileged area, where the ability of the children in the two groups was no different from that of children observed in other schools. He explained how he had deliberately made the explanation to the average ability group 'more concrete'. Whereas, with the more able pupils, he had discussed the characteristics of insects and then looked at specific examples, with the average ability pupils he began with a 'not analogy', an approach favoured by other teachers, which involves inviting pupils to compare an insect with a non-insect, like an elephant, a cow or, in this case, a bird.

> *Teacher* Is a bird an insect?
> *Pupil 1* No, that's silly.
> *Teacher* Why?

Pupil 1   Well, it's too small. A bird's bigger.
Teacher   So all insects are small, then, and all birds are big?
Pupil 2   No, you can have little birds . . . and big insects.
Pupil 3   It's got the wrong number of legs.
Teacher   Why, how many does an insect have?
Pupil 3   Six.
Pupil 1   No it doesn't. It's eight. A spider's got eight legs.
Pupil 3   A spider's not an insect.
Teacher   Well, let's clear that one up first.

The children went on to consider each part of the insect and then looked at actual insects. The matter of strategies used by teachers in higher and lower-scoring explanations is discussed below, but the most important issue here is that so few teachers did consciously opt for a change of approach. Even those that did sometimes found that circumstances brought about the change, rather than pre-planning. For example, one teacher who had obtained several responses from the above average group about the castle on the Island of Zarg found little response when he asked the same questions to the average ability group.

Teacher   Who do you think lived in that castle?
Pupils   (No response.)
Teacher   No ideas at all?
Pupils   (No response.)
Teacher   James, what about you?
Pupil 1   (No response.)
Teacher   Anybody? Well, I think perhaps it could be some important dignitary, either a king or a queen.

He then continued with an extended monologue, but in interview said that this was as a result of the poor response of the pupils, not through pre-planning. This finding that so few teachers opted for different styles of approach with pupils of different abilities could be explained by two factors. One is that the explanations were undertaken back to back, with the second group coming in about an hour after the first group, though the order of topic and ability group was randomised, so that some teachers explained first to higher ability pupils, others first to average pupils, and similarly with the order of the two topics. Given the slight artificiality of covering the same topic on the same day with two different groups, perhaps this imposed constraints which might not apply in a more naturalistic setting. Secondly it might be argued that the difference between the two groups was relatively small – mean IQ 100 in the average group, mean IQ 115 in the above-average group – and that, had two groups of mean IQ 85 and 115, or 80 and 120, been compared, the differences might have been spectacular. Nonetheless, it is worthy of note and will be discussed again in chapter 12.

Styles of explaining

One further analysis was undertaken on the classroom observation process data. In order to reduce a large set of data (640 lesson segments) to something more parsimonious and easier to interpret, as well as to corroborate or refute other forms of analysis, a principal components factor analysis and non-hierarchical cluster analysis were performed. A principal components factor analysis puts together those measures which correlate most highly and produces a smaller set of factors. Three factors were obtained which had latent roots above 1.0, with latent roots of 5.3, 4.5 and 2.1 respectively. These accounted for 20.3, 17.3 and 8.3 per cent of the variance.

Factor 1 (20.3 per cent of variance):   a programmed learning factor This factor loaded most heavily on all categories of questions, open, closed and sequenced, and on short pupil responses, teacher corrects, repeats, rephrases, praises, and on teacher summary. It was confirmation of the question–answer–reinforcement pattern described earlier, reminiscent of programmed learning principles.

Factor 2 (17.3 per cent of the variance):   a topic dissemination factor The second factor had both positive and negative loadings. The factor loaded *positively* on visual aids, teacher and pupil giving examples, summaries from teacher and pupils, and explaining links, and *negatively* on open questions, long pupil responses, teacher probes and rephrases, and engaging pupils' imagination. It reflects the essential differences between the more highly structured Insects explanation and the more discursive Island of Zarg lesson.

Factor 3 (8.3 per cent of the variance):   a pupil response factor The third factor also showed both negative and positive loading, and pupil responses figured in both. The factor loaded *positively* on no pupil response, pauses, sequenced teacher questions and probes, and *negatively* on long and spontaneous pupil responses. It confirms that a higher frequency of teacher behaviour, like sequencing questions and probing, was associated with a lower frequency of long and spontaneous responses from pupils. It does not mean that there is a *causal* link, however, As was shown above, teachers sometimes resort to reserve strategies as a result of poor pupil response, so it cannot be said that sequencing questions and probing *cause* a zero pupil response or low occurrence of longer, spontaneous pupil contributions, merely that the two go together. It could equally be argued that low pupil response might be a cause of the teacher using sequences of questions and probes, not the result of it.

The non-hierarchical cluster analysis took the whole explanation as the unit of analysis, so all 128 explanations were used to assemble a taxonomy of teaching styles. Whereas factor analysis puts together the various *measures* to form a smaller number of factors, cluster analysis puts together individual profiles of explanations to form a smaller set of groups or clusters. The procedure begins with 128 clusters and ends with one, when all have been combined. The four, five and six cluster solutions were inspected, and the four cluster solutions displayed the clearest, least diffuse model. The clusters, from now on called 'styles', were as follows:

Style 1 (containing thirty-nine explanations)   This style involved a higher incidence of pupil responses, especially long and spontaneous ones, more open questions, much more engaging of the imagination, more teacher rephrasing and much less use of visual aids. The emphasis is on pupil contributions to discussion. Not surprisingly the thirty-nine explanations in this style contained thirty-five from the Island of Zarg creative writing lessons and only four from the Insects lesson.

Style 2 (containing sixty explanations)   The style here was as described earlier in the description of the Insects topic, for all sixty were about insects, with greatest emphasis on teachers giving and eliciting examples and summaries. It was the more tightly structured factual topic approach, with far lower engaging of the imagination.

Style 3 (containing twelve explanations)   All of these were Island of Zarg lessons and most of the differences between this style and the rest are because of much lower occurrence of short pupil responses, summaries, praise, teacher repeats, asks closed question and makes personal references.

Style 4 (containing seventeen explanations)   These were also exclusively Island of Zarg lessons, and the distinguishing characteristics were both in a positive and in a negative direction, with much higher occurrence of engagement of the imagination and verbal cues, but much lower use of visual aids, sequenced questions, giving and eliciting examples and praise.

In general these multivariate analyses, like factor and cluster analysis, gave a similar picture to that described above, and certainly confirmed the significance of the relationship between type of topic and strategies adopted.

Pupil achievement and learning

At the conclusion of each explanation, tests of insect identification, knowledge of insect characteristics and ability to explain insects to others were given, as described above, and after each Island of Zarg lesson pupils were asked to write a story entitled 'My Adventure on the Island of Zarg'. The post-tests were scored by two independent markers whose scoring correlated highly, as was described earlier in this chapter.

There were three aspects of these outcome measures that were of particular interest. The first was the effectiveness of having had a teacher explanation at all. That would be resolved by inspecting the scores of the sixty-four children in the sixteen average ability 9-year old groups to whom the teachers had explained, and the sixty-four in the sixteen control groups of similar ability from the same classes, who had received no explanations. The scorers did not know which pupils were in which groups. In order to test the significance of any difference in scores a null hypothesis was adopted, that is, it was assumed that teaching would make no difference and the scores of the experimental and control group would be the same. A two-tailed t test of all outcome measures was then undertaken.

The second element of interest was whether having an 'opportunity to learn' made any difference. For example, if a teacher does not mention or elicit the fact that insects have six legs, then there has been no 'opportunity to learn' it, in that lesson at any rate. Pre-tests were not used, as the research design was quite complex and time-consuming, and adding extensive pre-testing might have alienated children and teachers, so conclusions are based on post-test assumptions only and must have some reservations attached to them.

The third area of interest was what distinguished high-scoring and low-scoring lessons. This is as near as one usually gets to measures of 'effectiveness' in research on teaching, but, given that the tests are short-term measures of learning, or may reflect prior knowledge and experience, again a caveat must be applied. The epithet 'effective' would have to be used purely within the limitations and constraints of this particular piece of research.

Did 'teaching' make a difference?

Table 8.8 shows the results of the t tests on the scores obtained by the experimental and control groups of average ability children. Although in general the experimental groups outperformed the control groups, this was

Table 8.8 Mean scores of experimental and control groups of average ability pupils on tests about insects and creative writing (sub-scores and total scores)

Test	Experimental	Control	t value
Insects	22.9	15.8	4.69***
Creative writing			
Length	2.8	2.0	2.5*
Sentence structure	2.6	1.9	0.56 (n.s.)
Coherence	2.9	2.2	2.6*
Features	2.9	2.4	1.4 (n.s.)
Imaginativeness	3.3	2.2	2.8*
Overall impression	2.9	2.1	1.8 (n.s.)
Total score	17.8	12.7	2.4*

*** Significant at <0.001 level, * Significant at <0.05 level, n.s. not significant.

not always the case. Some teachers had merely 'toured' the Island of Zarg in their explanations. This produced 'listing' responses which did not score high on the 'imaginativeness' dimension:

I started at Mount Horn and then I went to the castle and fell in the swamp and met Zarg outside his lair and he sent me to visit Zorgon in his cave. After that I went to Miller's Top, Fenbury, Hopehaven and sailed home.

On the other hand there were pupils in the control group clearly capable of writing imaginative stories with nothing more than the map of the island, as this extract from a high-scoring story shows:

Deeper and deeper we plunged into the cave. CRUMP! We hit the bottom. In the distance we heard a strange rumble as if someone was snoring very loud. . .

In general, however, the experimental groups did better than the control groups on each of the sub-measures of creative writing, though not all the differences reached statistical significance.

The scores in Table 8.8 show that having received an explanation was associated with higher achievement on every single measure in the whole set of post-tests and that in the tests of knowledge about insects the superiority of the experimental over the control groups was significant at beyond the 0.001 level. There was no statistical significance in the differences on sub-scores of creative writing, like sentence structure, mention of the island's features and overall impression, but in sentence length, coherence, imaginativeness and total score the differences in favour of the taught groups were significant at the 0.05 level. Having had an explanation did, therefore, seem to make a significant impact on pupils' learning and achievement in several important respects.

Opportunity to learn

The analysis above shows that having some sort of explanation appears, in general, to be better than not, but we wanted to see whether specific mention of certain aspects of insects' characteristics did appear to be related to their ability to recognise them accurately. The creative writing exercise was not scrutinised in the same way, as it would have been difficult to relate specific and discrete pieces of process data to such outcome measures as 'imaginativeness'. It was easier to inspect the analyses of the Insects explanations to elicit whether, for example, the teacher had mentioned that spiders were not insects, and whether this was related to pupils answering that question correctly.

A correlation analysis was undertaken, therefore, relating frequency of factually correct mentions of feelers, thorax, abdomen, number of legs, number of wings, and spiders not being insects, to number of pupils in the groups correctly identifying each of these in the post-test. Analysis of observation data showed that over 90 per cent of teachers made at least one mention of feelers, thorax, abdomen and number of legs during one of their explanations, whereas the figures for number of wings and spiders were 78.4 per cent and 64 per cent respectively. Table 8.9 shows the correlations obtained for all sixty-four lessons to 256 8 and 9 year old pupils receiving Insect explanations.

Table 8.9 Correlations between frequency of mention of insect features and number of pupils correctly answering relevant item on post-test

Feature mentioned	Correlation with test item
Feelers	0.29**
Thorax	0.46***
Abdomen	0.46***
Number of legs	0.05 (n.s.)
Number of wings	0.04 (n.s.)
Spiders not insects	0.38***

*** Significant at <0.001 level, ** Significant at <0.01 level, n.s. = not significant.

These results must be interpreted with caution. For example, if teachers feel that most children already know that insects have six legs, they may mention this feature less frequently than, say, 'thorax' or 'abdomen', which are likely to be new to 8 and 9 year olds. Also since correlations are of frequency of mention, not intensity or context, these quantitative measures do not distinguish on qualitative grounds, and are thus relatively crude, needing to be set alongside other kinds of information, like that in the section on high and low-scoring lessons below. Within these limitations it is of some interest to note that the correlations between frequency of mention of thorax, abdomen and spiders not being insects were significant beyond the 0.001 level.

High- and low-scoring lessons

A qualitative analysis was performed on the lessons of the teachers whose pupils obtained the highest and lowest post-test scores on both topics. The following cases show the flavour of some of these high-scoring lessons:

Mrs Archer (high-scoring Insect explanation)   The explanation began with Mrs Archer producing two large display cases full of insects.

> *Teacher*   Do you know what these are?
> *Pupil 1*   Bees and wasps.
> *Teacher*   Yes, that's right and what are these?
> *Pupil 2*   Bluebottles
> *Teacher*   Yes, bluebottles, greenbottles. They're all flies .... What about this beautiful creature?
> *Pupil 3*   He's a dragonfly.

At this stage one of the pupils wanted to talk about frogs, which also live by ponds. The teacher listened and then skilfully redirected and refocused.

One of the most notable features of her explanation was her use of voice intonation and emphasis, and pauses. At the end of the first phase of the explanation, she recapped with some vigour:

> All of these creatures (pointing to the display cases) are all so different, *but* (emphasis) (pause) they do have *one* (emphasis) thing in common (pause). They *all* (emphasis) belong to the family called (pause) insects (pause) – insects.

The main body of the explanation was devoted to covering each of the features of the insect body. When talking about the insect's feelers she used an analogy:

> The feelers are rather like radio aerials, they pick up all sorts of messages in the air around the insect.

Much of the explanation involved question-and-answer and reference to the insect display cases, but she also had a model of an insect she had made herself, and this featured frequently in the exchanges.

A high degree of learning in Mrs Archer's explanations appeared to be related to clear structure and explanation of key points through question-and-answer, skilful use of different types of visual aid, both simplified home-made insect shapes and cases of actual insects, refocusing discussion when it strayed off the point, eliciting a summary from pupils in which the main characteristics of insects were again illuminated, and effective modulation of voice, with emphasis and pausing for effect.

Mr Barlow (low-scoring Insects explanation) By contrast with Mrs Archer, the explanations in Mr Barlow's lessons lacked clarity from the beginning. What is more, they were also factually incorrect and confusing from the very outset.

> *Teacher* I'm going to give you the little word 'insect'. Immediately in your mind there's a picture of something, I expect. There is in mine. What sort of picture have you got, Cassandra?
> *Pupil 1* A spider.
> *Teacher* OK, you think of a spider. You keep the spider there. Peter, what about you?
> *Pupil 2* (No response.)
> *Teacher* When I say 'insect' what do you immediately think of – an insect?
> *Pupil 3* A ladybird.
> *Teacher* Yes, that's right.
> *Pupil 4* A worm.
> *Teacher* Yes – anything else?

Pupil 3   A snail.
Teacher   How do insects move around, Peter?
Pupil 2   Legs.
Teacher   How many legs has an insect got?
Pupil 2   Six.
Teacher   Yes, six; but do insects get around any other way?
Pupil 2   Some insects fly.
Teacher   Yes, some insects use wings. Can you think of an insect that flies?
Pupil 2   An eagle.
Teacher   An eagle? Is that an insect? No, it's a bird. A bird is definitely not an insect.

The factual inaccuracies and lack of conceptual clarity, with shape, movement and example confused and blurred, were compounded at the end of the lesson when Mr Barlow summed up for the pupils what had supposedly been learned.

Teacher   So we've thought about a whole set of different insects today: snails, centipedes, ladybirds, caterpillars and wood lice, and we've also found a lot of ways in which these insects move about – crawling, walking, sliding, swimming, flying and hopping.

The low degree of learning during Mr Barlow's explanation appears to be related to a lack of distinct key points which would have given conceptual clarity, and factual inaccuracy, a topic which will be discussed further in chapter 10. He establishes that insects have six legs, but never returns to the spider mentioned by Cassandra, nor explains why such creatures as worms, centipedes or snails are allowed into the genus when they do not have six legs. It was not surprising, therefore, that the concept 'insect' in the children's minds wrongly included gastropods, arachnids and other unlikely members. The pupils' test responses showed that their concept of an insect was anything smallish that crawls, swims, flies or hops around and is not a bird.

Mrs Charles (high-scoring Island of Zarg explanation)   In the interview following this lesson Mrs Charles modestly said, 'I reckon they could have managed quite well without me.' Yet this explanation was located in Style 4 in the cluster analysis, emphasising the stimulation of pupils' imagination and verbal cues. She concentrated in her exposition on encouraging children to use their imagination about the features of the island and on extending or exploring their vocabulary, as this exchange shows:

Teacher   Can you see anything that attracts you about the island? Anywhere you'd like to visit, David?
Pupil 1   Castle Point.
Teacher   Why would you like to go there?
Pupil 1   It's exciting.

Teacher   Yes, it's exciting. Have you found anywhere you'd like to go, Emma?

Pupil 2   I think . . .

Teacher   No, it's Emma's turn. I'd like to hear what Emma has to say.

Pupil 3   Eastern Moors. There's a creature . . . it's . . . it's . . .

Teacher   There's something up there that Emma's found. What has she found coming out of the sea?

Pupil 4   A monster.

Teacher   Yes, it could be. What's coming out of his hand?

Pupil 2   Lightning.

Teacher   What else has he got coming out of him?

Pupil 2   Rain.

Teacher   Rain and thunder, so it's almost as if he's in control of the . . .?

Pupil 2   Weather.

Teacher   The weather, yes, I think so . . . What would be a good word to describe Darkling Forest?

Pupil 2   Spooky and creepy.

Teacher   Better than 'spooky and creepy'?

Pupil 1   Strange and weird.

Teacher   Yes, strange and weird. How about a word beginning with two e's? Do you know it?

Pupil 1   Eerie.

Teacher   Yes. What does 'eerie' mean?

Pupil 1   Scary.

What the transcript does not show is the high degree of pleasure, signalled through voice, intonation and facial expression, at the pupils' responses. The exchanges were fairly rapid, the responses brief; however, the management was benignly but tightly controlled. The level of excitement was high, like the pace. This enthusiasm, pace, regular involvement of pupils, albeit with short replies and discriminating response to their answers, which were not automatically accepted, may all be related to the quality of the children's written work, which was scored very highly by the markers. If these explanations were snapshots of what had happened over a longer period of time, it would appear that the effect of these strategies may well be cumulative. Children do not become skilful writers overnight, or after one such lesson. In interview Mrs Charles stressed the importance of the initial stimulus: 'They need a starting point. Once they have that, their story can take them anywhere.'

Miss Dogger (low-scoring Island of Zarg explanation)   It soon became clear in Miss Dogger's lesson that the story the pupils were to write was one she would provide, not one that they would invent. The transcript shows that her explanation was a mixture of 'Guess my story' and 'Here's what you're going to do'. This was evident from her opening:

> *Teacher* In a minute I'm going to ask you to write a story. Do you think your story is going to be about modern days or olden days?
>
> *Pupil 1* About olden days 'cos there's a castle on the island.
>
> *Teacher* Oh, well, you see lots of castles around today. No, there was one thing I thought gave it away. Can't you see it?
>
> *Pupil 2* The windmill.
>
> *Teacher* No.
>
> *Pupil 3* The ship.
>
> *Teacher* Yes, that's right – the ship.

She gave more information about the ship, and then the first and only spontaneous response came from a pupil:

> *Pupil 2* Hey, there's a monster there.
>
> *Teacher* Yes, I don't think he's a monster though, I think he's supposed to be some sort of rain god. Look – there's rain coming from his hands.

No further spontaneous responses occurred, and the children listened patiently as she elaborated more detail of what was essentially her own story that they were to attempt to reproduce:

> *Teacher* You're on that ship, and it's called *Gull*. You're sailing over to the island, when there's a storm and you're washed overboard. You get washed up here at Mudlark Swamp. Now, the inhabitants of Hightown are unfriendly, but up in the hills you'll see a cave – Zarg's lair. Now, Zarg is a fearsome creature, a bit frightening, but he's friendly.

The approach was a contrast to that of Mrs Charles, who often sought precise vocabulary but was open-minded about story lines. The children's low scores in Miss Dogger's group seem to be related to restrictions on their imagination imposed by this more prescriptive approach and the lack of enthusiasm and drive which was a feature of the lesson of Mrs Charles.

Summary of features of high-scoring explanations

The main points that emerged when two separate analysts went through the explanation tapes and transcripts are a little different for the two topics. The highest-scoring Insects explanations were, in general, clearly structured, with the 'keys' or central ideas made distinct and linked to one another in a logical sequence and shape, often with a teacher or pupil review at the end of the section or the whole explanation, and the teacher's subject knowledge was factually correct. Language choices were sensible, neither too banal nor at too high a level of abstraction, an appropriate register being employed. Voice was clear and well modulated, with effective movement, facial expression and animation, and there was fluency and pace. Good visual aids to learning were employed and the occasional illuminating example or analogy was given or, more likely, elicited. There was an overall simplicity of structure which gave clarity. Indeed, one high-scoring teacher, who began with a simple line drawn on the blackboard, said in interview, 'You just need the very basics in an explanation like this, other pictures would have confused the children.' Another, who started by establishing why insects were a distinct group, stated in interview, 'I thought it would be a good way to go from the general to the particular. I wanted the children to be sure that "insects" is the name of a group of animals early on.'

In the creative writing lessons on the Island of Zarg, some of the above applied, but personal characteristics like enthusiasm and voice being used to create or evoke an atmosphere of mystery or curiosity figure prominently. Questions and statements that provoked thought and stimulated the imagination were notable ('A thick fog comes down,' said one teacher), but both prescriptive and exploratory approaches could be successful. The effectiveness of this single lesson was probably a reflection of the cumulative effect of strategies which led to skilful writing being employed over a period of time.

Other features of high-scoring lessons were the occasional use of humour which was relevant to the topic, as opposed to gratuitous humour. The use of the 'advance organiser' (Ausubel *et al.*, 1978) sometimes occurred, when the teacher employed what broadcasters call a 'tease' at the beginning of their explanation, to give shape or to arouse curiosity:

> *Teacher*   If I told you in, say, a bucket of earth there were hundreds of them. They're in the air, they're even in ponds and rivers. There are millions of them in a tree. They live all over the world, except at the North and South Poles. There are over a million different types of them. There are 200,000 different types in this country alone. Some of them can fly, some can swim, some make holes in the ground, and some make holes in wood. What do you think I would be talking about?

As is often the case, however, despite some communalities, high-scoring explanations were also different from each other, with their own unique qualities. The general conclusions above are not universal prescriptions, but rather interesting illuminations from one intensive study.

Chapter 9

Teachers' questions

In daily adult life, if we were to ask one another questions to which we clearly knew the answer, this kind of behaviour would be regarded with suspicion. It would be extremely odd, for example, if one person were to say to another, 'What's the weather like today?' when both could clearly see it was pouring with rain. Equally, if one adult were to ask another a series of probing questions, it would be regarded as socially rude and insensitive, invading the other's privacy, the sort of behaviour only permitted when the person interrogated is suspected of having committed some criminal act.

Yet in classrooms questioning is one of the most regularly employed teaching strategies. Questions are asked to individual pupils, to the whole class, to small groups. In some parts of lessons there may be five or even ten questions in a single minute, and most teachers will ask hundreds of questions within a few days. Even as early as 1912, Romiett Stevens found that two-thirds of questions being asked required children to recall the sort of information that could be verified from textbooks. Other early studies reported similar findings. Haines (1925) analysed the demands made on twelve 13 year old pupils by teachers' questions and concluded that 70 per cent required factual recall, whereas only 17 per cent made demands on pupils' thinking that went beyond pure recall.

When Gall (1970) reviewed research on questioning, there seemed to be a 3:1:1 split between different types of questioning, with 60 per cent asking for the recall of facts, 20 per cent demanding a higher mode of thinking, and 20 per cent dealing with the management of classes or individuals. The ORACLE study of primary schools (Galton *et al.* 1980) found that 12 per cent of time in class was devoted to questioning, and the ratio was rather different, more like 2:1:1, but this time most questions came into the category of management, with, 47 per cent. The figures for factual recall and questions about ideas were 29 per cent and 23 per cent respectively.

The reasons why teachers ask questions are varied. Turney (1973) produced a list of twelve, covering such purposes as to arouse curiosity, focus attention, develop an active approach, stimulate pupils, structure the task, diagnose difficulties, communicate expectation, help children reflect, develop thinking skills, help group reflection, provoke discussion and show interest in pupils' ideas and feelings. Brown and Edmondson (1984) asked forty secondary teachers to state their reasons for asking questions. The five most common responses, in order of frequency, were: to encourage thought and understanding; to check what pupils knew and could do; to gain pupils' attention to the task in hand; to review, revise or reinforce what had been learned; to help with class management.

As was described in the previous chapter on explaining, with which this chapter has a great deal in common conceptually, some researchers have concentrated on levels of thought and related their study of questioning to these. Sadker and Sadker (1982) built much of their training programme in questioning skills on Bloom's taxonomy (Bloom 1956). Trainees were encouraged to ask questions in each of the categories of the taxonomy in the cognitive domain. A question at the first level, 'knowledge', might be 'Who wrote Hamlet?' At the second level, 'comprehension', the teacher might ask, 'What is the main idea that this chart presents?' This continued up the levels until level six, 'evaluation', was reached, where an appropriate question might be 'Which picture do you like best and why?'

The problem with this approach is that it often presupposes that higher order questions are in some way qualitatively 'better' than lower order questions, yet the research evidence on this is divided. Even those who have summarised research into questioning have disagreed about whether there is a causal link between the asking of higher order questions and pupil learning. Two reviews of similar studies came to opposite conclusions, partly because they used different methods for aggregating findings. Whereas Winne (1979), who analysed experimental studies of questioning where teachers deliberately asked certain types of question, concluded that there was no causal link, Redfield and Rousseau (1981), who did a meta-analysis of most of the same studies, decided that there was a positive association between higher order cognitive questioning and pupil learning.

The findings from research may not always be consistent, but some features of it are. There does seem to be evidence that questioning is an important strategy which teachers usually employ; that it can occur with some frequency; that teachers' questions are of several kinds – some to do with the management of the lesson, others dealing with the substance of it; that questions serve different purposes and demand different levels of response, though what is arguably 'higher' and what is 'lower' order is a matter of some disagreement.

There is little work on pupils' questions, though Barnes and Todd (1977) studied children working in small groups and found that they generated more exploratory questions, hypotheses and explanations when a teacher was not present than when one was. Other aspects of pupil perspective have also been studied, and Tobin's (1987) review of 'wait time', that is, the effect of a teacher pausing for longer to allow pupils to respond, shows that pausing can elicit longer answers, encourage more pupils to take part in answering questions and produce more questions from pupils. Much of this work goes back to the seminal studies of Rowe (1978), who found that teachers frequently allowed less than a second before breaking the silence by asking another question, giving more information or redirecting, restating or rephrasing the original question.

The finding by Adams and Biddle (1970), who analysed several hours of videotaped lessons, that most of the action was directed at children sitting in a V-shaped ledge in front of the teacher's favoured position in front of the class, also has relevance to work on questioning, in that it suggests that children on the periphery, or those sitting outside that V-shaped wedge, could be out of the action. Given the degree of self-selection of seating in many classes, there might be a tendency therefore for those pupils most keen to answer questions to select those 'busy' central seats, and for quieter pupils to choose seats in areas of the classroom where they are less likely to be called on during whole-class teaching, thereby reinforcing the predominant behaviour patterns of both the eloquent and the silent.

The present studies of questioning

During the Leverhulme Primary Project we undertook four studies of questioning. In the first we asked a group of twenty-eight primary teachers in twelve primary schools to keep a log of some of the questions they asked during their teaching. Fourteen schools were randomly selected, of which all but two agreed to co-operate. Each school was asked to find either two or three teachers to volunteer to take part. Six schools provided three teachers, four found two volunteers and two produced one teacher. All the studies of questioning in this chapter are of teachers who agreed to take part and, as with all cases in this kind of research, they may not be typical of teachers at large. Nonetheless, the view of observers was that the teachers in the sample did not appear to be different in any perceivable way from other teachers, except that they chose to volunteer to participate.

The second study described below is of over 1,000 questions asked by a group of seven teachers who were observed during the study of class management described in chapters 4 and 5. They agreed that the observer could return to do a further study of their classroom, in which all questions asked during several half-hour periods would be logged. Again this is an opportunity sample of teachers willing to be observed taken from a larger sample of teachers in another study. The third enquiry into questioning involved the observation of the classes of twenty teachers in ten schools which had been chosen randomly and which, in all cases, agreed to participate. In each school, two volunteer teachers were observed, their lessons recorded and transcribed, and the questioning episodes in them were analysed. In all three studies the use of questioning by a total of fifty-five primary teachers was studied. The fourth study was the analysis of the questions asked during explanations described in the previous chapter.

All analyses were undertaken by two members of the research team. Three tests of agreement on categorisation where questions were coded as 'managerial', 'higher order' or 'lower order' showed a mean agreement of 95 per cent. Three sets of 100 questions were selected randomly and agreement was 95, 94 and 96 per cent respectively. All questions about which either coder had any doubt were rated until agreement was reached.

Study 1   The teachers' log of questions asked

The twenty-eight teachers who agreed to take part in this study were asked to keep a log of questions they asked under several headings. Each was given a structured diary in which to record, as soon as possible after the event, what kinds of questions they asked and what the responses were. In the first section, teachers were asked to record three questions asked to the whole class, a small group, or an individual child on one particular day. They wrote down the actual wording of the question, the context in which it occurred, the main purpose of the question, and the response and outcomes. The second section asked them to record a sequence of questions, consisting of at least two and not more than five questions asked one after another. Again, they had to record the essential features of wording, context, purpose and outcome. Thirdly, they answered attitude and frequency questions on five-point scales, and these are reported in tables 9.1 and 9.2. Finally, they were asked what tips they would give to student teachers about questioning. Some teachers recorded several lessons and took the diary entries down from the cassette, some recorded just one lesson, about half did not record at all but wrote their report from memory.

The overall total of 187 questions recorded by the twenty-eight teachers were of different kinds, and those asked in sequence followed various patterns. Questions were coded as 'managerial' if they were to do with the organisation and management of the lesson, 'lower order' if recall of information was predominantly what was required, and 'higher order' if more than remembering facts was needed. Teachers recorded a far lower level of managerial questions than is normally witnessed in classrooms, as well as far more higher order questions. This is because they found it more interesting to record and comment on the questions which provoked thought or activity, as is to be expected if one asks a teacher to select and analyse in some depth particular questions asked during a day. The 187 questions logged and analysed consisted of ten managerial, seventy-eight higher order and ninety-nine lower order questions. This study certainly does not, therefore, portray a random sample of questions, but rather a set of questions teachers themselves selected for further analysis.

There was, as one would expect, considerable variety according to the age of the children. Half of the teachers taught infant age children from 5 to 7, and the other half taught juniors from 7 to 11. Teachers of reception class and early years pupils often said in interview that they believed in keeping their questions simple, and one, talking about her own philosophy of questioning, said, 'Always use simple, understandable words. Try not to embarrass the child by asking too difficult a question.' Her own questions were indeed simply phrased, her chosen sequence of five questions being entirely about colours: (1) 'What are the names of these colours [of the rainbow]?' (2) 'Which colour do you like best?' (3) 'How many people like red [the child's answer] best?' (4) 'Can you think of anything else that is red?' (5) 'Can you see anything red in our classroom?' It was a funnelling style of sequence, based entirely on simple colour questions, not so much raising levels of thought as focusing them.

Some infant teachers asked simple questions, but used their sequence to extend and lift thought, as advocated by Taba *et al.* (1971). Another teacher of 5–6 year olds again began with colours, but for a purpose. She showed a picture of baby birds in a nest and began with two lower order questions: 'What colour is this egg?' and 'How many more eggs are there in the nest?' Her main theme is about bird life and her next three questions became more demanding than just recall as children were asked to use their powers of reasoning and imagination: 'Does the mother bird look after her chicks?' 'Why didn't this egg hatch – what do you think?' 'How does the mother bird feed her chicks?'

The strategy of extending and lifting was seen with older pupils as well, and often pupils' responses helped determine the nature and level of each succeeding question. One class of 7 year olds was studying 'forces', including magnetism and gravity. The children were looking at a paperclip attached by a thread to a block of wood on a table. By holding a magnet above it, the teacher appeared to make it float. Her questions grew in complexity and were highly responsive to children's replies:

What force is making the magnet stay in the air? (Replies: 'The magnet,' 'It was trying to get the magnet,' 'No, the magnet was trying to get it,' 'The paperclip was metal and the magnet was pulling it.')

Were there any other forces acting on the paper clip? (No coherent replies.)

When you moved the magnet a bit further away, what happened to the paperclip? ('It fell down,' 'Oh, gravity,' 'Gravity made it fall down.')

Was gravity pulling it all the time? (Reply: Yes.')

So why didn't the paperclip fall straight away? (Replies: 'It wanted to get to the magnet,' 'The magnet was stronger,' 'It was strong when it was near.')

Was there anything else stopping the paper clip doing what it wanted?

(Replies: 'The string wouldn't let it,' 'It did stretch a bit,' 'The block,' 'The weight of the block.')

The path of extending and lifting was not smooth here, as the teacher tried to lift the level too rapidly by asking about forces the children had not identified. However, by giving a specific concrete example, of moving the magnet away, she allowed the class to focus on gravity and the downward pull.

Some funnelling sequences were skilfully sculptured so that decisions could be made on the basis of shaped reasoning. A teacher of 10–11 year olds recorded a set of five questions in a music lesson which helped children learn to discriminate sounds. She began with two chords played on the piano, asking the class if the chords were the same as each other or different. The chords were a C major and a C minor. In response to the first question, four children thought they were the same, four were not sure and the rest all believed, correctly, that they were different. Her second question, 'How do you think the chords are different?' was too diffuse and only one child could give any impression of a sound being 'lower'. She next played the chords as an arpeggio (as two sets of four separate notes) and asked, 'Tell me which note you think is lower. Is it the first note, the second, the third or the fourth?' and then checked out each with 'Is it the first?' which four children believed to be correct, and 'Is it the fourth?' also believed to be correct by four pupils. Finally, she checked out the middle notes, by which time the great majority of the class correctly identified the second note as being the one that was lower. This was an interesting example of a funnelling strategy that went from the diffuse to the precise in a small number of steps.

Sometimes it was not until a later question that class discussion became animated and discussion flourished. Another teacher of infants aged 4–6 described her sequence with groups of children who were making a house from blocks. Her first question was a disguised command: 'Can you go and choose the boxes that you think you will need to make your house?' Early responses called most blocks 'cubes' and only distinguished 'big ones' from 'little ones'. Initially the children in the group wanted to stick the paper boxes together as whole blocks, but her fifth question, 'Do you need scissors?' focused their attention on the actual shapes and what the test really entailed. She reported:

> This resulted in much more interaction and discussion . . . thoughts on size, angles of cutting and how easy/difficult it was to get surfaces to fit and stick together. The last question was in fact the one that really got the task under way and questions/answers flowing from the children with a sense of them working together, rather than individually, which I felt the activity was leading to before this point.

All twenty-eight teachers in the sample completed the structured questionnaire parts of the teachers' log. Each item was based on strategies observed by members of the team carrying out classroom observations, or from statements given by teachers in interview. The first set, shown in table 9.1, dealt with attitudes to questioning, and responses were on a five-point Likert scale ranging from 1 = strongly agree to 5 = strongly disagree, with the mid-point 3 = neutral. Thus the lower the score in table 9.1 the higher the agreement. Scores are shown in descending order of agreement, so statement 1, about putting the question back to the same pupil, attracted most agreement.

The responses in table 9.1 show a clear preference for allowing pupils to answer questions if they have failed at their first attempt and a degree of support for calling on non-volunteers to answer but ambivalence over the issue of involving other pupils in correcting many answers. There is an equally clear rejection of the notion that written questions are superior to oral ones and that teachers' questions should be confined to those to which they themselves know the answer.

Table 9.2 shows a different set of strategy statements designed to elicit frequency of behaviour. Again, a five-point scale was used, with 1 = always,

Table 9.1 Responses of all twenty-eight teachers to attitude statements in descending order of agreement (on five-point Likert scale from 1 = strongly agree to 5 = strongly disagree).

	Statement	Mean score
1	If a pupil does not understand a question it is better to rephrase it for him rather than put the same question to another pupil	1.71
2	During whole-class teaching the teacher should nominate pupils to answer, not just rely on volunteers	2.43
3	If a pupil gives an incorrect answer it is best to ask someone else in the class to correct it	3.04
4	Teachers should not ask a question unless they know the answer	4.04
5	The important questions have to be set and answered in written form rather than discussed orally	4.68
	Overall mean score	3.18

Table 9.2 Frequency of questioning behaviour in descending order of occurrence (on a five-point scale from 1 = always to 5 = never).

	Statement	Mean score
1	I praise correct answers	1.54
2	I address questions to the whole class	2.61
3	I get children to ask each other questions	2.89
4	I call on a pupil by name to answer a question	3.14
5	I ask questions systematically around the class, calling on each pupil in turn	4.39
	Overall mean score	2.91

2 = frequently, 3 = about half the time, 4 = occasionally, 5 = never. The order in table 9.2 is in descending order of frequency, so praising correct answers was thought to be the most frequent occurrence.

Statements in attitude questionnaires often produce paragon ideal assertions of good intent, rather than accurate portrayals of actual behaviour. A number of replies given by teachers in this study do not match what we actually observed in lessons in other parts of the Leverhulme project. For example, seventeen out of twenty-eight teachers gave the response 'always' to the item 'I praise correct answers,' yet none of the teachers we observed invariably praised answers that were right. Twelve teachers replied 'Always' or 'Frequently' to the statement 'I get children to ask each other questions,' yet this was something we rarely observed. There seems to be a strong tendency to reply in the affirmative to these two child-centred statements, in contrast with what we actually observed in live observation of classrooms. On the other hand, the endorsement of asking questions to the whole class was something which did conform to what we observed in lessons, where it was the second most frequent occurrence, after asking questions to individuals, which was in first place (see below).

On the matter of advice to student teachers on questioning, teachers responded in a disparate manner with relatively few communalities. Teachers of younger pupils stressed simplicity: 'Always use simple, understandable words – keep the question short. Try not to embarrass the child by asking too difficult a question,' 'If you only want one answer, then [your] question must be short and precise.' The most common advice, in descending order of frequency of mention, was:

1 Use a variety of both open and closed questions.
2 Get the language right and choose words carefully.
3 Listen carefully to children's answers.
4 Be prepared to rephrase questions and redirect them.
5 Keep questions brief and simple.
6 Start from what pupils know.
7 Admit when you don't know yourself, but then find out answers.
8 Hands up and one at a time to answer.
9 Give everyone a chance to answer at some time.
10 Watch for diversions or 'silly' answers and discourage them.

The main emphasis was on variety, and avoiding asking only one style of question, and on empathising with the pupil, that is, choosing the most suitable language register, listening carefully to answers, as these give valuable information, and being flexible and responsive enough to rephrase or redirect a question which was not quite in its best form, or did not evoke a response in its initial form.

Study 2   Observations of over 1,000 questions asked in teachers' lessons

Whereas the study just described was of teachers' self-reports on questioning the other two studies of questioning reported in this chapter involved live observation and recording of teachers' lessons. The first of these was an analysis of 1,021 questions asked by seven teachers. It was based on an actuality log of questions asked during several half-hour periods of observation. A trained observer who was a member of the research team observed the teachers in the sample for several half-hour sessions, and wrote down in a sequential log all the questions asked by the teacher during the period of study, as well as information about the responses, whether the question was managerial, lower or higher order, as described earlier in this chapter, and whether it was addressed to an individual, a group or the whole class. Two raters coded all the questions separately, agreeing on 95 per cent of occasions, with the remaining 5 per cent discussed until agreement was reached.

Table 9.3 shows the overall categorisation of the whole sample of questions. The high incidence of managerial questions and the low occurrence of higher order questions is not unlike the study of transactions in secondary classes reported by Kerry (1984), which found 54 per cent, 42 per cent and 4 per cent respectively using a similar categorisation of 'managing', 'informing' and 'stimulating'.

Table 9.3 Percentage of questions (n=1,021) in each of three categories.

Type of question	Percentage of questions
Managerial questions (to do with running of lessons)	57
Lower order (information/data recall)	35
Higher order (more than data recall)	8
Total	100

Table 9.4 shows the distribution of questions to different targets. Two-thirds of all questions were directed to individuals. Table 9.5 combines the two in a single 3×3 contingency table and shows the distribution of each type of question to each of the three targets.

Table 9.4 Percentage of questions to different targets

Target of question	Percentage of questions
Individual	66
Whole class	22
Small group	12
Total	100

Table 9.5 Percentage of questions over categories and targets

Type of question	Individuals	Whole class	Small group	Total
Managerial	37	12	8	57
Lower order	24	8	3	35
Higher order	5	2	1	8
Total	66	22	12	100

There are numerous interesting inferences to be drawn from just these tables alone. Teachers asked relatively few higher order questions and addressed few questions to small groups. Questions related to the management of the lesson predominated, and most of these were addressed to individuals. The managerial questions were of different kinds, as the examples from the question logs given below reveal. Details of pupil and teacher responses are given in tables 9.6 and 9.7.

1 *Managerial – organisation – target whole class – acceptable pupil response – neutral teacher reply* 'Has anyone got any book club money?'
2 *Managerial – pupil behaviour – target individual – non-acceptable pupil response – neutral teacher reply* 'Martin, how is it you manage to join in every conversation I'm having?'
3 *Managerial – disguised command/reprimand – target class, no pupil response, no teacher reply* 'Could you all please stop fussing?'
4 *Managerial – sequence – target class, acceptable pupil responses, positive teacher reply* 'OK, who got ten out of ten? 'Who got nine?' 'Who got eight?' 'Anybody less than five?'
5 *Managerial – threat – target group, acceptable pupil response, neutral teacher reply* 'Who else wants to stay with me?' (threatening to keep pupils in after school if they misbehave).
6 *Managerial – sarcasm – target individual, no pupil response, no teacher reply* 'Did I say go and do a quick scribble?' (to a pupil whose work is unsatisfactory).
7 *Managerial – miscellaneous* 'Are you a girl today or a boy?' (said with humour to a girl pupil who was supposed to have left the room with the rest of the girls, and now found herself the only girl left in the room). 'Are you a school dinner?' (sorting out who has a packed lunch and who goes to the dining room for a cooked meal). 'Have you hidden your tongues?' (asked with humour to a group of children who had not replied to a question).

The second largest category, involving the recall of information or data, was also of diverse kinds. Frequently such questions were closely related to the immediate subject matter and produced simple, often one-word, replies. Some involved number ('What number is it?'), others the naming of people

('Who can remember what Jesus's mummy and daddy were called?') or of properties such as colour ('What colour is the chimney?'), the articulating of words ('What does that say?'), and the repeat or recall of information just given ('What do you think an adverb does?' 'What did he find when he found the star?' 'Who was this big fat lady?').

There were several examples of sequences of questions that moved from lower order to the less frequently occurring higher order category. A group of children were observed measuring the distance travelled by various-sized toy cars rolled down a ramp. The sequence began with a simple observation question, but went on to a higher, more complex reasoning and hypothesis-stating level:

1 'Which one went the furthest this time?'
2 'Which one might go the furthest next time?'
3 'John, why do you think the green one might go furthest?'

Higher order questions occurred in various forms, the most frequent of which was introduced by the 'Why?' interrogative. ('Why do you think it would make her happy?' 'Why did he go to Wales?') Sometimes the interrogative 'Why?' was simply used on its own to extend a brief pupil answer to a previous question. A 'Why?' question was not always a precursor to higher order thinking, however, Management questions like 'Why are you sitting there?' were disguised comments/reprimands and rarely an invitation to give reasons. Some higher order questions involved pupils' imagination, as in the case of a group of pupils learning about the Second World War, who were asked, 'What do you think you'd have to take into an air raid shelter?', which required a great deal of thought about human needs, survival, what was available in the 1940s and the nature of war. In general, however, there were very few questions that required an imaginative leap.

There were a few examples of higher order questions within the management category, and this occasionally posed a coding problem, as personal and social education can be regarded as a legitimate 'subject' within primary education. There were very few disagreements between researchers about categories for coding, but two of the questions about which coders disagreed were of this kind, as both involved the teacher asking pupils to empathise with her: 'Can anyone tell me why I get cross when I see people kneeling on their chairs?' and 'How do you think that makes me feel?' Eventually both were coded as management, as they produced very short answers and appeared to be principally admonition rather than an invitation to reflect.

This shows the importance of context in the analysis of questions. Questions cannot be understood in isolation, and because question logs and recordings were available and, as one of the analysts had observed the lessons live, the context was available to the investigators. A question like 'What is the question?' can only be understood when one knows that the class is studying number bonds and looking at the six-times table. The children have been asked 'What is three times six?' or 'What is five times six?' but now the teacher reverses the process, gives an answer like 'Thirty-six', and asks the children what the question must have been to produce this response.

The humorous question 'I'm not such an ogre, am I?' occurred when the teacher discovered, at the end of the lesson, that one child had not understood something but had not asked the teacher to explain. The question was preceded by the teacher encouraging the child to ask in future, and the good-natured suggestion that children had nothing to fear if they did not under-stand seemed to the observer to have been well received by the child concerned.

Children's and teachers' responses to questions also varied considerably. Table 9.6 shows the breakdown of pupil responses into three categories: (1) no verbal response, (2) correct or acceptable response, (3) incorrect or unacceptable response. The double categories correct/acceptable and their obverse are necessary because an answer can be deemed to be factually 'correct' ('What colour is this?' 'White.' 'That's right.') or 'acceptable', like when the teacher said to her class, 'What do we say to Mrs Smith?' (Mrs Smith was a classroom assistant who had just helped a group of children make some buns for one boy's birthday) and the pupils replied, 'Thank you,' which the teacher felt was an acceptable response.

Table 9.6   Types of pupil response

Type of pupil response	Percentage of occurrences
No verbal response	36.5
Correct/acceptable response	56.5
Incorrect/unacceptable response	6.9
Inaudible response	0.1
Total	100.0

The category 'non-verbal response' does not indicate no response at all by the pupils, though this might be the case, it merely shows that no one spoke in reply. When one teacher, on showing the class a picture, said, 'Can you see?' no one replied verbally, but body posture showed that she needed to turn the book round to face some of the pupils, which she did.

Once pupils had responded (or not done so, as the case might be), the very next act by the teacher was what we called the 'teacher reply framework'. This can be a very important part of the whole questioning process, as it sets the climate and offers important signals to pupils about the accuracy of their replies, or how they have been received by the teacher. The teacher's responses to pupils' answers were coded under 'neutral framework' (which includes no responses, giving further information, changing to another activity, but not giving an evaluative reply to the pupil's response); 'positive framework' (e.g. praise, assent); 'negative framework' (e.g. criticism, dismay); 'immediately asks another question' (including repeated and rephrased questions), and 'inaudible'. Table 9.7 shows the distribution obtained. About half the teacher replies were within a positive framework and relatively few unacceptable pupil responses and negative teacher replies were recorded, but then, as stated earlier in this chapter, most questions asked were simple and straightforward, and only a few involved complex levels of reasoning.

Table 9.7   Teacher reply frameworks following pupil responses

Type of teacher reply framework	Percentage of occurrences
Neutral framework	20.2
Positive framework	49.4
Negative framework	12.8
Immediately asks another question	17.4
Inaudible	0.2
Total	100.0

Study 3   Questions in factual and discursive lessons

The second live observation study, of twenty teachers, involved recording a sample of two of their lessons, one on a largely factual topic, the other on a more discursive one such as creative arts or writing a story. Each teacher observed was asked to give the observer a time when such lessons could be observed. Analysis of lesson transcripts confirms many of the points made about questioning in this chapter and in chapter 8 on explaining. Several dimensions of questioning were identifiable, not dissimilar to some of the points made in the analysis of explanations, as one would expect, since the two are related. These included:

Narrow/broad

Most questions asked were narrow or closed, though in the more discursive topics broader or more open-ended questions were more common. Most of the narrow questions produced very short answers. A discussion on fruits with 5–6 year olds, for example, where the teacher asked children the names of fruits produced the following twenty successive answers, only one of which is longer than three words: 'No,' 'Lemon,' 'A melon,' 'A big fruit,' 'Yellow,' 'Lemon,' 'Bruised,' 'Gone off,' 'There's white stuff in the middle,' 'A lemon,' 'Duck,' 'No, duck,' 'A duck,' 'Yeah,' 'Orange,' 'Apple,' 'Apple,' 'Tomato,' 'Cut them up,' 'Eat them.' Often page after page of transcript showed a similar pattern of short, clipped responses. Word counts of several segments of lessons revealed that on some occasions 90 per cent or more were uttered by the teacher, though more commonly it was about three-quarters.

Yet even in these factual episodes some teachers' questions and reactions to responses could elicit longer responses. This teacher used a broader question followed by enthusiastic reinforcement of good longer responses and an acceptance and enhancement of pupils' ideas, which together produced considered replies from 8 year olds talking about air pressure:

Teacher Where's the pressure?

Pupil Inside the cup, and then there's pressure in the balloon. It's kind of like a piece of steel and a magnet going together, and there's a bit of something in the middle that they can't get through and that means that they keep on sticking together.

Teacher What a wonderful explanation, what a wonderful idea . . . What about the air around here, what about the air pressure around here, because you mentioned the air pressure in the balloon and the cup – do you think there's any air pressure round here?

Pupil Well, if it's air pressure and it's pushing down, it's . . . helping it to not let any air out, because it's trying to get in and all the air is trying to get out of the side of the cup. The air pressure is trying to push it in.

Teacher Isn't that a good idea!

Observation/recall/thought

There is a close relationship between observation and recall in education. When children are asked to observe, they are also, by implication, asked to recall facts and constructs within which to place their observation. While it is possible to ask children to recall facts without using their senses to make an observation, the two acts are often combined. Indeed, lessons often begin with recall and observation and then progress to thought and reflection:

Teacher Let's just recap a little bit what we've been doing. We started off . . . making what?

Pupil Gliders.

Teacher Gliders first of all, right? . . . Can anyone remember what we learned about that?

Pupil 2 If it had a pointed nose it was aerodynamic.

Teacher Right . . . what does aerodynamic mean, then?

Pupil 3 The wind can pass through.

Teacher Is that right?

Pupil 4 Cut over it.

Teacher (holding up paper dart) Cut over it, yes. Do you mean the dart itself will cut through the air, right? We'll move on from there . . . Now, there's something else I want you to do. When air gets hot it moves up.

Pupil 5 Like steam.

Teacher   Right. Well, we won't talk about water just for now . . . Do you remember a moment when something went 'click' in your mind and you thought, 'Ah, that's it'?

Pupil 6   I didn't think that these spirals would spin round in hot air. I thought they'd just kind of bounce up and down.

Teacher   Was that a surprise? Why did they spin round?

Pupil 6   It was kind of catching on it so it took up . . . kind of goes up and makes it spin round.

After the lesson the teacher said in interview how he had deliberately checked out what pupils remembered, then encouraged them to engage in analytical and imaginative thought, though he felt disappointed at some of the responses, and finally had gone on to creative practical activity:

'I was quite pleased at how much they'd remembered, and they came out with words like 'streamlining' and then understood about parachutes and gravity and weight . . . The disappointing bit was, having primed them all and brought them carefully on to the idea that hot air rises, when I came on to say, 'OK, what could we devise?', the children had no idea at all, so . . . I had to start to spoon-feed them a bit . . . [but] the practical work that followed up was quite inventive.

Confused/clear

Sometimes questions were very clear, phrased in language which the children understood and which seemed appropriate for the context. On other occasions questions were embedded in an envelope of extra information, or even in other questions, with the result that confusion would almost invariably follow, or the teacher would need to rephrase what had been asked. This confused sequence emerged from an unclear question about two eggs asked of a group of 6 year olds. Unsure of the purpose or focus of the question, the pupils eventually became distracted:

Teacher   That was the first egg. What is the same about this one?

Pupil 1   It's smaller.

Teacher   No, what's the same?

Pupil 1   Bigger.

Pupil 2   Shell.

Teacher   They've got the same shell. What do you mean by the same shell?

Pupil 2   Same colour.

Pupil 3   It's outside.

Teacher   And it's outside?

Pupil 3   Out of the egg.

Teacher   'Cos it's a shell it's outside, that's right.

Pupil 4   A peacock might come out.
Teacher   Shh! Alex, Alex . . . Let's see what happens when we open it
. . . Let's try not to shout, and that means Alex and Royston.

The key point the teacher was trying to elicit, that one egg was cooked and
the other egg was raw, only emerged later, when the two eggs were cracked.

By contrast the same teacher skilfully constructed a painting activity by
encouraging children to mix paints and then asking them questions about
each colour choice. The concepts of how to make a colour lighter or darker,
how to name the new colour and how to mix paint were all developed by
clearly focused questioning and practical activity:

Teacher   Let's see how many lovely colours you can make. What
happens to your colour [blue] when you add yellow to it?
Pupil 1   It goes dark green.
Teacher   How many colours have you got here? They're all green, but
they're different, aren't they?
Pupil 2   I've got two greens now.
Teacher   So you have. What did you add to it? Blue or white? . . . What
happens when you add white to it?
Pupil 2   Light.
Teacher   It's a light green, that's right. (To another pupil) That's a
super green, how did you make that one?
Pupil 3   Yellow and dark green.
Teacher   That's like a spring green, isn't it, very bright . . . Lovely . . .
Dip your brush in there, make it clean and then take some more powder.
Wipe it on the side, then pick up more powder.

These three studies of questioning strategies have produced a set of interesting
conclusions which will be discussed again in chapter 12. Certainly primary
teachers might like to reflect on the large number of managerial and lower
order questions we noted and the relatively low incidence of higher questioning that required analytical, evaluative or imaginative answers. Equally
the skilful way in which the more skilful communicators can raise the level of
thinking, reflection and practical activity, the place of clearly structured
sequences of questions and the large number of very short answers sometimes recorded, provide patterns for consideration which will be discussed
further in chapter 12.

Chapter 10

Teachers' subject knowledge

The two national surveys

In chapter 8 it was shown how, when teaching a topic like 'Insects', which requires teachers to have a secure foundation of knowledge themselves, children's own conceptions could be unclear when the teacher was not himself sure what characteristics distinguished insects from such creatures as arachnids and gastropods. During the Leverhulme Primary Project we undertook two national surveys of 901 and 433 primary teachers respectively. In the companion book to this one, *Learning to Teach* (Bennett and Carré 1993), there is a full description of the research undertaken by Neville Bennett and his team into student teachers' subject knowledge. This chapter describes the research conducted as part of the class management enquiries into how primary teachers cope with teaching a fresh topic for the first time, when their own subject knowledge is insecurely founded.

In the first stage of a two-part national survey of primary teachers in England, following the 1988 Education Act, which introduced a structured national curriculum for the first time, a stratified random sample of 901 teachers in 152 schools replied to a lengthy questionnaire which sought information about how competent teachers felt to teach the ten subjects in the primary curriculum with their existing subject knowledge (Wragg *et al.* 1989). The response rate was 72 per cent (152 out of 212 schools approached). Teachers were asked about the nine subjects in the national curriculum – art, design and technology, English, geography, history, mathematics, music, physical education and science, as well as religious education, which had been a compulsory subject since the 1944 Education Act. Two years later, follow-up questionnaires were sent to many of the same schools, though not to all, as some had indicated that they did not wish to take part in a second survey. Sample loss was inevitable, as some teachers had moved schools, and fresh schools had to be drawn randomly from the *Primary Education Directory*. Of the 131 schools which participated in the second survey in 1991, there were fifty-six which had also taken part in the first. The second survey produced replies from 433 teachers, of whom 223 had taken part in both surveys. A separate analysis of teachers who had participated in both surveys revealed that there were no significant differences in the patterns of response compared with the total sample, and this applied in terms of both statistical significance and direction of change (Bennett *et al.* 1992).

The questionnaire not only asked teachers to respond to the subject overall, but also invited self-ratings of competence on specific topics within maths, science and English. In each case, respondents were asked to use a four-point rating scale:

1   Yes, I feel I am competent with my existing knowledge and skills.
2   Yes, I feel competent, with some help from colleagues.
3   Maybe, I'd feel competent with in-service help from colleagues.
4   No, I feel I would not be competent without substantial in-service support.

This kind of response allowed analysis either as categoric data, for example, how many readers needed substantial in-service support, or as continuous data, permitting mean scores to be compared.

The results of the two surveys on the question about each of the ten subjects primary teachers are required to teach are show in table 10.1. Only Category 1 responses are shown, that is, those believing they are competent to teach the subject with their existing knowledge. Relatively little movement was noted in half the subjects, the rank order of English and maths (first and second), physical education (sixth) and music and technology (ninth and tenth) remaining the same. Science moved up from eighth position to third in the two-year period, explained to some extent by the fact that many teachers had spent two years teaching the new science curriculum, but technology remained rooted firmly at the bottom of the list at 14 per cent. The percentage of teachers feeling competent dropped in all the other eight subjects, and this was especially noticeable in history (54 per cent down to 38 per cent) and geography (48 per

Table 10.1   Percentage of teachers feeling competent with existing knowledge and skills in each of ten subjects in 1989 national survey and 1991 follow-up

Subject	1989 survey (n=901)		1991 follow-up (n=433)	
	Cat. 1	Rank	Cat. 1	Rank
English	81	1	77	1
Mathematics	68	2	62	2
History	54	3	38	5
Geography	48	4	36	7
Art	48	5	40	4
Physical education	47	6	37	6
Religious education	45	7	33	8
Science	34	8	41	3
Music	27	9	23	9
Technology	14	10	14	10

cent down to 36 per cent), where the final subject syllabuses, both of which were wide-ranging and full of subject knowledge demands, were published just before teachers filled in the follow-up questionnaire.

It was not surprising that teachers demonstrated such low confidence in their own knowledge in subjects such as science, music and technology. Analysis of the main subject specialisms of teachers in the first sample had revealed that only 8 per cent had majored in science, only 7 per cent in music, and a tiny 0.3 per cent in technology. Over half had an arts/humanities background. Study of responses to specific topics in science and technology showed a wide range, from about 75 per cent feeling able to teach the 'water cycle' or 'looking after living things' with their existing knowledge down to 10 or 20 per cent for topics such as 'adding to a database' or 'using graphics to develop new ideas' or 'using microelectronic kits'. Under half felt competent to teach electrical circuits or the use of power sources.

Comparisons between groups of respondents showed that male teachers expressed greater feelings of competence than female teachers in science and technology, and women felt more competent than men at art, English, music and religious education. All these differences, in t tests, were significant at the 0.01 or 0.001 level. When we scrutinised the responses of teachers of different ages, ratings declined with age in subjects like science and technology. Teachers with over thirty years of experience rated themselves much lower than those with under five years. In technology, only 6 per cent felt competent, compared with 13 per cent of the youngest teachers, and in science it was 27 per cent compared with 37 per cent. Teachers in medium-sized schools (101–300 pupils) rated themselves as more competent in science and technology than those in large or small schools, both differences being significant at the 0.05 level. Junior school teachers also rated themselves more competent than infant school teachers in science, technology, geography and history, all significant on t tests at the 0.001 level, except science, which was significant at the 0.05 level.

In view of the special problems in science and technology, we decided to study a sample of teachers who were teaching certain topics in these fields for the very first time. There were two separate studies. The first involved teachers who had little or no experience of teaching a topic like electricity. Twelve schools in one region, randomly chosen from lists of schools in each of four categories, were approached. The four categories were large urban, small urban, large rural and small rural. Ten teachers of 7–11 year olds who had never, or only rarely, taught physical science topics such as magnetism and electricity agreed to be observed and interviewed about their experiences teaching the topic 'electricity'. In addition we studied two teachers teaching technology to 6–8 year olds for the first time. In the second piece of research there was a four-strand study of teachers using the BBC videos on primary science, which involved such topics as 'levers', 'stiff shapes' and 'floating and sinking', most of which were new to the participants.

Study 1   Teaching science and technology

Most of the twelve teachers in the sample were apprehensive about teaching physical science and technology topics they had not taught before. As few primary schools had all the necessary equipment we decided to provide sets of circuit boards and components. Only two of the teachers felt they would have been able to make a start on the teaching of electricity with their school's existing equipment. Four basic kits were provided, consisting of circuit boards, batteries, bulbs, switches and wires. Written notes for sets of activities, which covered four of the attainment statements of the national curriculum, were also offered. Teachers had a free choice about how they taught, some choosing to teach the topic as a self-contained set of activities, others incorporating it into a project on 'energy'. The two teachers who were observed teaching technology had a completely free hand in their choice of topic or activity.

Interviews were held before the teaching began and after the observation of lessons. Teachers were asked how they decided on their approach, how effectively they felt they had handled the lessons, what difficulties they had encountered, how the pupils had responded, how they handled children's questions and what support they had found or felt they would have needed. Classroom observation, in this case, was not structured, except that trained observers made extensive field notes and looked for, and recorded, 'illustrative events', that is, incidents or aspects of practice that seemed worthy of further scrutiny and questioning in interview. The observation was non-participant, except in the case of one of the teachers of technology, who was a member of the research team.

There was considerable apprehension before the teaching began. Comments included: 'Horror! I haven't taught it before,' and 'It's a challenge. Everything in education is a challenge. Children . . . they've got to meet it, so why not the staff?' Most teachers turned to other people for help, rather than to books. Few found the children's books available in their library to be adequate for the pupils, let alone themselves, but in any case their greatest need was for a *person*, usually the school's science co-ordinator, but it could also be any fellow adult who was knowledgeable, so a spouse, a pupil's parent, a school governor who was a science graduate, and a teacher from a nearby secondary school who came in to answer questions once a month, were all cited as sources of information.

Some teachers confessed their ignorance to the class immediately. One began, 'Look, I've got to be honest with you. I know nothing about electricity. I can just about change a fuse.' Classes of up to thirty six were observed and teachers established groups of from two pupils up to six to work on the units. It soon became clear that most teachers had to spend a great deal of time on preparation, except for one who said, 'It's dreadful' (laugh). 'It's dreadful for two reasons. One, I haven't spent a lot of time preparing for it.

It's one of the many things that are going on . . . um, what else? . . . I just feel so lacking in confidence about the whole thing . . . I don't know what I would do without David' (a former school governor who had offered to help).

The two most perplexing problems faced by these teachers were first of all not knowing the relevant scientific principles, and secondly inability to cope with pupils' questions: 'Loads of questions. "Why is this happening?" "Why isn't this working?" Mostly to do with the practical and lots of questions about the actual theory of it.' One teacher simply referred children back to the written notes when any query came up and asked them to see if they could find the answer themselves. Others were perplexed and bemused by the mysteries of electricity: 'I can't understand why, when one battery [of three] is put in backwards, the lamp still lights up.'

Despite their anxieties some teachers were quite prepared to take on adventurous-looking projects which took them and their class way beyond their own subject competence. The routes through the specified attainment statements were varied, but some classes went on to make a burglar alarm or doll's house lights, and one teacher even strayed, unwittingly, into topics normally covered by much older pupils, like series and parallel circuits, electricity generation and distribution to domestic and industrial premises.

The actual attainment statements which teachers had to cover included eight mentions of specific cognitive skills, such as knowing, understanding, describing and recording. There were also the practical skills of constructing a simple electrical circuit, varying the flow of the current, and observing what was happening. Most teachers gave emphasis to the actual practical activities, but little systematic checking of understanding was observed. On the other hand teachers' own observations influenced their judgement about how effective the lessons had been, some commenting specifically on children's enthusiasm, or the value to lower-attaining pupils: 'James did *very* well the first time. He's not a high achiever usually, but I presume that was previous knowledge that he'd had. He set up a circuit very, very quickly and got the switch in, and a light-emitting diode.' Less able children performing well on a practical activity where the teacher herself was not secure was a great surprise to some teachers. One commented on the case of a boy with special educational needs who showed such manipulative skill he was appointed 'leader' by the rest of his group, an event that had not occurred previously. Another low-achieving pupil asked if she could take away bulbs and batteries so she could work on them at home.

Aware of the many demands on them once the lesson started, most teachers prepared in far greater detail than for other activities in their day. One teacher described how she stayed up until past midnight practising with the electricity kits until she felt confident enough to supervise their use by others. Even then she simply omitted reference to topics or concepts she did not herself understand: '. . . amps, volts, wattage, atomic structure . . . Perhaps I should have. I would have gone to the *Oxford English Dictionary* if I'd had to teach it.'

Experiments in technology were similar. One teacher was observed working with children who were designing an egg holder. When one pupil decided to use the centre of a kitchen roll to hold his egg and then had to pack enormous amounts of plasticine around its base to hold it firm, eventually having to give up and even tape the egg on the top to prevent it falling off, she never discussed design principles or such notions as 'centre of gravity'. Yet in other subject areas she was competent and proficient.

Another technology lesson involved the making of kites, where children first designed and then made kites out of wood veneer and tissue paper. Seven year old children were not, in this school, allowed to use sharp scissors, so there was considerable frustration amongst them as they found the delicate paper tearing when they cut it with blunt round scissors. The teacher had little idea whether to intervene and cut out the shapes for each child, or to give them extra paper so they could try again. Nor were explanations forthcoming about why some kites flew well and others did not.

Despite the difficulties most teachers claimed afterwards they had enjoyed the experience:

We're all so excited. We've loved doing this.

In the main (it has gone) quite well. But, left to their own devices, we got some very complicated circuits. Everyone enjoyed it.'

I'm quite excited about it now, because you can see their results . . . what they can discuss with you. So now I say to colleagues, 'Well, now look at me. I'm a prime example of someone who panicked. I'll look forward to doing it again.'

The picture in this story is a clear one. Most teachers were enthusiastic, if still apprehensive, about their experiences teaching a new topic for the first time, but their own lack of knowledge raised problems. Outside the classroom these were resolved through lengthy preparation and recourse to people such as the science co-ordinator, governors, parents even, who possessed the knowledge they lacked. Inside the classroom most were perplexed by not knowing the relevant scientific principles and by pupils' questions, many of which were unanticipated or unpredictable. The most common coping strategies were evasion, that is, avoiding altogether subject matter not properly known, and turning children back on their own devices, asking them to improvise a solution themselves, or offering to find out for a future lesson. Particularly bewildering, if gratifying, to some teachers was the unexpected competence of certain of their pupils, thought to be slower learners, when faced with a practical activity in which the teacher herself was not well schooled. These findings raise several issues which will be addressed again in chapter 12.

Study 2   Teaching and learning with science videos

During interview teachers sometimes said that they would like high-quality video material to help them teach topics that were new to them, so we decided to investigate how teachers used videos, what they themselves learned from them and what they then did with the pupils. The BBC had produced a set of primary science videos for teachers on topics like 'levers', 'floating and sinking' and 'stiff shapes'. It was decided to conduct a four-strand investigation of the first two of these topics. A questionnaire survey of users constituted the first strand. Case studies of four schools, a large and a small urban, a large and a small rural, which had ordered the videos was the second strand. The third strand was of four different schools, selected, as in the second strand, but this time from schools which had not ordered the videos. In this case the four schools were given the videos. It was decided to adopt this particular strategy as teachers in schools that send away for videos might be especially competent or keen. The fourth strand involved a study of student teachers to elicit what they themselves learned from watching the videos.

The questionnaire survey was of seventy three schools throughout the country which were, according to the BBC, the first set of schools to order the videos. It became clear that many schools reported they were under such pressure they had not yet had time to use the videos at all, in some cases not even to look at them. These constraints of time and over-demand are real at a time of rapid curricular change in primary schools. Heads and science co-ordinators had usually placed the order for the videos, and the main target for them was said to be 8–9 year olds or upper juniors. Fewer than a third of respondents had had time to use them properly. Most teachers had watched them at home or as a group after school. Many felt that preliminary viewing had helped clarify scientific principles in their own mind. What they most wanted, they reported, was three things: an enhancement of their own scientific knowledge, practical ideas for classroom work and high-quality out-of-studio visual material, showing, for example, why lifeboats do not sink, or examples of levers in everyday life.

The case studies of four randomly chosen user schools involved interviews with teachers and observation of lessons. Semi-structured interviews were held and these were tape-recorded. Observation, as in the earlier study in this chapter, was freehand, with collection of 'illustrative events'. Most difficulties caused for teachers, as in the earlier study, arose from pupils' questions, especially those involving a request for information about underlying scientific principles, usually 'why?' questions. Why, for example, was it easier to raise two people close to the centre of a ladder than two sitting at the extremes; why a whole apple floated, but when the same apple was cut into pieces they sank; why most grains of sand fell to the bottom of a water tank, but some stayed floating on the surface. Teachers readily confessed their ignorance of 'density', 'surface tension' or 'Archimedes' principle', which were central to an understanding of these phenomena. Several said they had not themselves realised, for example, that scissors were levers, so they welcomed a video which gave a wider set of illustrations than they would have selected themselves: 'We needed the videos for the principles. Bill [top juniors] knows a lot about science, and even he found them helpful. We need the scientific principles. The videos pinpoint the principles.'

Some teachers felt having greater security on principles, as well as powerful visual ideas about science in the world surrounding their pupils, had given them confidence they might not otherwise have had. One group visited a lifeboat station after seeing a scene in which a lifeboat is shown being submerged and then righting itself. Another group had visited a canal and been on a boat. Like other groups they had taken the topic 'floating and sinking' as part of a larger project on 'water', which had involved studying the water cycle, the use of waterways, water in our daily lives as well as floating, sinking and other scientific aspects. Other teachers incorporated 'levers' into their project on 'toys'.

Once more, teachers spoke appreciatively of people who helped them. One science co-ordinator produced a booklet of ideas to go with the videos. Another had been through the videos noting down the tape counter references for each scene and offering suggestions for use within the school's pattern of project and topic work. Teachers insecure with their own subject knowledge welcomed this sort of practical help, which left them more able to concentrate on classroom process, especially as most expressed problems about using videos, ranging from the difficulty of having to move learning equipment to their own classroom, when the television area was not free, to coping with children's questions about the video scenes. One teacher in a large rural school, winding forward to a particular scene, suddenly found Wimbledon tennis being transmitted on the regular channel as the video recorder was locked on fast forward. It ruined the concentration of the 8–9 year olds in the class: 'You see, it's all right for the first bit' (showing the first scene). 'When you set it up, that's fine and it's ready to go, but if you want to use the effective bits afterwards – particularly if they're short snippets – well, you saw what happened.' When teachers are teaching unfamiliar material, logistical or equipment problems merely compound their difficulties.

In the third strand, when four schools were selected which had not bought the videos, similar observations were made, but there were also additional ones. These schools were not especially enthusiastic about science, unlike the strand two schools, where some key person had been keen and knowledgeable enough to track down and order science videos. One of the schools, in the London area, contained several teachers who had been on primary science 'booster' courses in the previous two or three years, so those teachers felt more confident than the teachers in the other urban school and the two rural schools who had had no such courses. Indeed, most teachers confessed, in interview, to being especially worried about physical science topics and about scientific processes in general, like testing hypotheses, or conducting a 'fair' experiment. The relationship between 'density' and 'flotation' was one that was mentioned as a source of mystery by many of those interviewed and observed.

Some teachers said they needed help with absolutely basic ideas. 'I have no idea at all how a buzzer works,' one teacher confessed, 'yet my children are supposed to use one.' One teacher found a problem when the class tried to imitate a scene from the video in which a balloon floated. The class found the balloon also floated when it was empty and the teacher was lost for an explanation, admitting that she even had no idea which principles to investigate, let alone explain.

In one of the rural schools that had several new members of staff there was the advantage of fresh teachers who were keen and willing to experiment. A number of them felt the videos had made them realise there was much more to topics like 'flotation' and 'levers' than they had realised on their own. Video materials can help solve problems by giving teachers and children a firm foundation of scientific fact, high-quality visual images, illustrating principles in action, and practical ideas for classroom practice, but they can also create problems by exposing teachers in areas where they are insecure and by provoking questions from pupils that teachers cannot answer. The more self-confident teachers cope with this and use words like 'challenge' in interview, whereas ones less confident see it as yet another potential pitfall in an already hazardous occupation.

If teachers are themselves still learners in some subjects, then it is important to know what they might learn from the same video materials seen by their pupils. In the fourth and final strand of this study we decided to study a group of twenty-one primary trainees. All were near the end of a one-year postgraduate teacher training course, and only one of them was a science specialist. They were given tests of scientific knowledge and teaching ideas immediately before and after watching the videos. Some fascinating differences emerged, not all predictable.

Levers

Respondents were asked, before and after, to identify levers commonly found in the home. All were able to give at least one example beforehand. The trainees were able to cite on average 2.85 more examples after watching the videos, usually though not always examples shown in one film, like nut-crackers, doors and scissors. When asked to define the purpose of a lever the results were more mixed. Six were able to give a correct definition before and after about half the group produced a more correct response after viewing. Four, however, still gave the same or a different incorrect response after viewing the film.

The most difficult question for respondents was about a gate which was closed, and students were asked the position one would pull the gate open to which would need the least force. This topic was not covered directly in the video, and most people gave the same answer before and after, about half being correct and the others being incorrect. Only two people changed their thinking from incorrect to correct. Finally, there were two questions about the fulcrum. Students were asked to identify where, in a bottle opener, the fulcrum was located. Most identified it incorrectly before and after, four were correct before and after. Of the remaining four students, one moved from incorrect to correct, but the other three gave a wrong answer after the film, having given the correct answer beforehand. When asked to explain the relationship between force applied and distance from fulcrum when using a lever, half were able to give a better definition after the viewing, the others did not improve.

Flotation

All students were able to name correctly objects which floated and sank before and after viewing. More objects were named afterwards, but also previous answers were refined: for example, 'bottles' became 'empty bottles', 'cups' became 'empty cups placed the right way up', and 'plastic bags' became 'plastic bags filled with air'. When asked to explain why a polystyrene brick floats, but a brick sinks, most students compared the densities of the two objects, but did not refer to the density of water. Only four students referred to the importance of air in flotation.

In the next section, students were asked to comment on the correctness or incorrectness of four statements. The results of the twenty students who were not science graduates were as follows:

1   'Light objects float, heavy objects sink' (false). Sixteen correct before and after, remaining four correct after.
2   'Large objects sink, small objects float' (false). All twenty correct before and after.
3   'The shape of an object can make it float or sink' (true). Seventeen correct before and after, two incorrect before and after, one incorrect before but correct after.
4   'Metal objects always sink' (false). Eighteen correct before and after, one correct before, incorrect after, one incorrect before, correct after.

A high degree of prior knowledge clearly affected these responses, as was the case in a question which showed four different balls floating in a tank of water, some sitting higher than others. When asked which balls were the most and least dense, all responded correctly, but in response to the question asking which ball had a density nearest to that of water, eight incorrectly chose a ball which was half in and half out of the water. This did not change after viewing the video on floating and sinking. Finally, when asked to explain why an empty bottle floats, but a full one sinks, eight improved their original definition after seeing the video, usually by mentioning the importance of air, eight gave equally good before and after responses, three gave poorer replies after the video and one did not give a second explanation.

When asked about teaching ideas, most felt they had gained a much wider understanding of levers and would be able to give pupils more examples of levers in everyday life, mentioning in particular bottle openers, traffic barriers, the beam engine, the mobile TV camera on a boom, scissors, a door opening and the human arm. About half mentioned an appreciation of the points made in the videos about children explaining to each other. Many were still not clear about the fulcrum. Observations on flotation involved a better awareness of high and low floaters, the acquisition of ideas for using parachutes, raising a sunken plastic bag by blowing air underneath it, doing tests with air in cans and testing children's hypotheses. There was still some admitted confusion about density, buoyancy and Archimedes' principle.

These studies reveal aspects of a matter analysed in greater detail in the companion book of research findings from the Leverhulme Primary Project (Bennett and Carré 1993), that teachers' subject knowledge can be an important constituent of effective or ineffective teaching. It is clear, both from our national surveys and from our case studies, that large numbers of primary teachers admit their own subject knowledge in science and technology is insecurely founded. This research has shown that most teachers manage this deficit by extensive preparation outside the classroom, by recourse to people rather than books, and occasionally by evasion and pressing pupils to fall back on their own resources inside the classroom. It has also revealed that teachers can themselves learn from good-quality video material, in terms of both understanding the scientific principles (though film can also occasionally generate confusion) and acquiring practical teaching ideas, but that these may be limited. Sometimes this will be as a result of the failure to apply a scientific principle learned in one context to a novel or unpredicted situation, like a pupil's question, but on other occasions it can be simple constraints to do with logistics and equipment. If teachers working for the first time in unfamiliar territory are to become more effective, then several messages can be drawn by those responsible for policy and practice, a matter which will again be addressed in the final chapter of this book.

Chapter 11

Student teachers' professional skills

As is the case in virtually all professional and vocational training, student teachers must complete periods of field experience in which they work in conditions close to those surrounding full-time practitioners. These may vary from opportunities to teach individuals or small groups on an occasional half-day or whole-day basis, up to block practices lasting a term or longer, usually on a reduced timetable. Novices on teaching practice have often been studied by researchers. Wragg (1972) documented 578 lessons given by 102 student teachers during a ten-week practice and found that many students had fairly fixed patterns of interaction which hardly altered during the practice. Fink (1976) used diaries, questionnaires and lesson observations in her study of twenty-five student teachers, showing that they became more custodial towards their pupils as the practice progressed. Preece (1979) found that students' anxiety fell during teaching practice when he studied 100 students on a postgraduate secondary course.

Partington and Hinchliffe (1979) conducted fifty six case studies of students thought to be especially good or poor at managing classes and reported that the establishment of good personal relationships, effective preparation, skilful organisation of group and individual work, clear questioning and explaining, and effective presentation of self were all associated with 'success' as perceived by tutors and supervising teachers. Wragg and Dooley (1984) observed 204 lessons given by thirty four secondary postgraduate students and found that most of the deviant behaviour which occurred was of a minor nature, most commonly noisy chatter punctuated by requests or commands to desist. Few students had serious discipline problems, though many lessons sank into minor chaos with prolonged mild deviance, which occurred most frequently during transitions from one activity to another. Wragg and Wood (1984) observed 210 lessons given by twenty eight undergraduate or postgraduate secondary students during their first encounters on teaching practice, and compared these with 103 lessons given by thirteen experienced teachers. The students were less likely to be rated 'confident', 'businesslike' or 'stimulating' and made less use of their eyes to sweep the room or engage individuals in eye contact. They were less certain about classroom rules and expectations and less deliberate about learning pupils' names, though they identified themselves more closely with pupils than did the experienced teachers.

There have been several reviews of research on teacher education and student teachers, including some covering a wide field (Wragg 1982, Tickle 1987, Diamond 1991) and some dealing with specific aspects such as the supervision or mentoring of students (Little 1990). Much of the writing on teacher education is analytical, and a great deal is political or polemical, but relatively little is based on live observation of lessons given by students, though some has addressed closely related matters like attitudes or attitude change. We decided to base much of our Leverhulme Primary Project work on student teachers, in the strand of the project reported in this book, on studying their behaviour and experience in the classroom during teaching practice. Substantial research into cohorts of student teachers in the strand of the project directed by Neville Bennett is described in the companion volume to this one (Bennett and Carré 1993). This chapter describes three studies. The first is of undergraduate student teachers' first encounters on their final block teaching practice. The same procedures were used as for the study of experienced teachers' first encounters described in chapter 3. The second study is of students' teaching strategies during teaching practice and in particular their handling of disruption. The procedures used in this study are the same as those used in the observations of experienced teachers described in chapters 4 and 5. The third study is of student teachers' attitude change before and after their final block practice. The same set of photographs used in other research described in this book were used to elicit responses, and both freehand comment and answers to structured attitude statements were analysed.

Study 1   Students' first encounters

It was not as straightforward to observe the first encounters of student teachers as it was to study the first lessons of experienced teachers. At the beginning of the school year the new class teacher usually devotes her whole time to her new class from the very first moments of the first day. Student teachers tend to ease gradually into their role, perhaps observing for a few days, but also supervising a small group, working with individuals or taking the lead for part of a lesson shared with the class's regular teacher. It is much less likely that there will be a single clean 'moment of entry'; rather, first encounters will be diffuse, more phased than sudden.

A sample of undergraduate primary students on final teaching practice was selected largely at random, except that an effort was made to choose students in a mixture of small and large urban and small and large rural schools. A total of sixteen students were observed by trained observers, using procedures described in chapter 3. The observers spent the first three days in the students' classrooms, once the initial period of observation was over, but it was not always possible to ensure that the very first encounter of this blurred beginning was witnessed, for the reasons given above. Four students were not seen during their very first lesson, one because she had taught a lesson during her observation phase, one had taught several lessons during what was meant to be observation, a third had taught all the class but in separate groups, and the fourth was team teaching with the class's regular teacher from the beginning.

Preliminary interviews were held with each student during the last week of the term preceding teaching practice, the equivalent of the pre-observation interview with experienced teachers. All had had previous experience of eight weeks of block practice in two primary schools and several single days of school experience. All taught in the 7–11 age range, though two were in small village schools and so encountered occasionally a number of younger pupils.

Two said they had been given no preliminary advice by teachers, but others mentioned the sort of tips reported earlier in this book, most citing the 'firm but friendly' preliminary image favoured by experienced teachers in chapter 3. Students' description of hints and tips received included: 'Be firm but friendly; ignore unnecessary comments,' 'Be friendly, but be strict; better to be strict in the first few weeks.' 'Be firm from the very start, let the children know what you expect of them and what the rules are. Establish the rules with the help of the children,' and 'Be firm, don't smile too much. Best to establish that *you* are the boss and fully in control and they are thus to treat you as they would their regular teacher. Don't be an ogre, though.' Other commonly offered advice concerned getting to know names quickly, getting to know children as individuals, and starting with easy work that children can do.

Asked about their classroom environment, most expressed satisfaction at the space available for teaching but had reservations about shortage of storage space. Only one was very unhappy about this, as she had to teach thirty five children aged 9–10 in a cramped space. She had observed the class and was apprehensive about possible class management problems because so many children had to work in a corridor. Four of the students worked in open plan schools. Most had access to reasonable facilities, but fewer than half had classrooms or work bays with specialist areas for maths, science or reading. Five had no access to a sink for work with water or for washing up. In general the students were uncomplaining about lack of facilities, using terms like 'reasonable', 'adequate' or 'awkward'.

Interviewers asked students whether they would like to change the room in any way once they took over their teaching programme. Most said not, or expressed uncertainty, especially where teaching areas were shared with others. Two said they would like to create a carpet space for class discussion and one wanted to put up more posters, but the predominant reaction was non-territorial, a recognition that it was simply not their own territory, a complete contrast to those experienced teachers reflecting before the school year on 'my class', 'my classroom' or 'my rules'. This 'guest' status was further enhanced by the various other adults who, students already knew, would share the classroom, including the class's regular teacher, the head occasionally, classroom assistants and parent helpers. Only six were told they would be on their own.

None of the students, however, seemed apprehensive about support and assistance. All spoke of the positive attitude towards them when they had visited, and words like 'friendly', 'supportive', 'helpful', 'welcoming', 'co-operative atmosphere' and 'family atmosphere' were used by respondents in all the interviews. The main possible constraint mentioned was lack of specialist space, particularly for practical activities, storage and display, rather than people. Two students were apprehensive about team teaching, especially one who would be working with sixty children and two teachers in an area she had found very noisy and confusing when she had visited the school. One student was worried about the head, who, she said, used very long words and seemed to have a strange manner. All felt they had learned valuable information from their preliminary visits, especially about pupils with difficulties, the wide spread of reading ages in the class, the work schemes and the general ethos of the school. Most students had come away with a positive view of the class they were to take, though one said she had not been able to form any picture of them, and two were aware of social problems that might cause concern.

Students were also asked how they thought their management style might differ from that of the class teacher. Half said they were not able to judge. Some of the others mentioned that they might need to be more strict, do more practical work or teach in a more structured environment. One said she might find it a problem working with two other teachers in a team, as they had different styles from each other, and she was not yet sure how best to fit in. Students tended to be more concerned about fitting in with the work schemes than with the management styles, however, and all were aware of the need to be well prepared for what was a wide variety of approaches to the curriculum, some based on 'subjects', others on often widely differing themes from school to school. Topics like 'Roman history' and 'The countryside' were sometimes given to students by the school, but in most cases students would be expected to improvise their own schemes to fit in with the school's general approach to the national curriculum.

Fewer than half were able to describe in preliminary interviews what their first lesson might be and the following were the only responses which gave any indication of content or style: 'I may tell a story,' 'A brainstorm session on the topic "Invaders" and an outline of how I see the topic will run,' 'Let the children know exactly what I expect of them,' 'Introduce the topic "water", words which describe water.' Their replies to questions about how they would feel an hour before their first lesson varied from the domestic

'Getting my own children to school,' 'What to have for breakfast. I will be very nervous, worrying,' 'Whether I have packed everything in my bag – sandwiches, pens, money, lesson notes, bus pass, and whether my contact lenses are going to stay in,' to dress rehearsals: 'I will be thinking about lesson materials – have I prepared enough?' 'I'll be looking forward to it. I'll want to be enthusiastic, fun, likable, exciting, but also stand for no nonsense'.

The 'dress rehearsal' was particularly noticeable in the responses to the question about what they would be doing five minutes before their first lesson:

> How I am going to introduce myself. Talking to myself about what I'm going to say. Making sure I know how to organise the children. Re-read lesson plans and have them near by.

> Trying to remember the first couple of things I want them to do, so I don't have to look at my notes too much. Trying to relax and feel confident.

> Panic. Here goes. What to say at the beginning, how to make the lesson enjoyable.

Some of these comments reveal the kind of image the students hoped to project, but we had asked specifically about this. The same words recurred in the responses: 'Firm' (eight people) was the most frequently cited description, followed by 'confident' (five), 'friendly' and 'interesting' (four each). Some of this vocabulary recurred when questions were asked about relationships and rules. Most were eager to let children see that if they were firm, even severe, at the beginning they were also human:

> I want to get to know their names or characteristics as quickly as possible, by giving away information or impressions about myself and helping the children to see me as a person.

> I want to first establish my position as a teacher. When I have earned the children's respect then I can concentrate on building more of a friendship role.

There was a highly significant difference between students and experienced teachers on the matter of classroom rules. In chapter 3 there were nine categories of classroom rule, each with several examples of sub-categories, stated by teachers in interview, and, in the main, implemented in the classroom. The students in this sample were far less clear in their minds about their own classroom rules. Some mentioned generic headings, rather than specific rules, such as 'respect for others' or 'ensure harmony in the classroom'. Three mentioned 'no talking when someone else is talking' and two talked about respect for property. The great majority, however, used variations of the notion that existing rules would be enforced or rules would be established when needed:

At first I'll just observe to see what rules are already in force. I'll only establish my own if necessary.

The rules will come up naturally as the lesson proceeds.

Yes (I'll introduce rules) if I think I need them. I don't know what. I'll discuss it with the class, and I'll word them positively.

Altogether each of the sixteen students was observed for between six and eight sessions lasting up to 100 minutes, a total of 116 sessions altogether. Once the students began their teaching practice some of their intentions were overtaken by the pressure of events. One student who had expressed a relaxed view about the need for classroom rules found herself having to improvise them quickly in the very first lesson, when pupils rushed into the room noisily. There was not always a clean hand-over from the class teacher to the student, so it is not possible to make too many comparisons with the patterns observed in the classes of experienced teachers described in chapter 3. However, of the seventy three occasions when a clear beginning to a lesson could be observed, the student was already present on fifty seven occasions, the pupils entered the class first on twelve occasions, and in four cases the student and the pupils came into the room simultaneously. This is not too surprising, as, unlike the experienced teachers in the chapter 3 sample, the students did not have other responsibilities, such as playground duty, in these first few days.

In all cases the observer commented that the teacher seemed prepared for the start of the lesson. The one student, however, who spoke at greatest length in interview about the need for discipline and orderliness and how she would discuss rules in the very first lesson, actually did none of these, even though her class entered quite noisily. The first classroom entry of the children was quite varied, and, to some extent, in the very first encounter tended to reflect the pattern with the class's regular teacher rather than that of the newly arrived student. Only three classes were recorded as 'noisy' on entry to the first lesson. By the seventh and eighth sessions this had grown to five. One class which had been orderly on the first day had begun to rush in noisily from the playground. Another class had a group of boys who began to run into the room on the fourth session and were reprimanded by the teacher for noise and unruliness. This happened again in two of the following four entries. Three classes were described as noisy or disorganised after the lesson should have started, the others tended to settle down much as they had done for experienced teachers.

In almost all the lessons there was a task demand fairly soon after the pupils had settled down, and here was another big difference between students and experienced teachers. First of all there was no special emphasis in the school assembly on the new school year or on high expectations, none of those moral demands and exhortations that had characterised the first school day in September. Secondly the students felt able to move straight into lesson content. Few made any reference to rules or routines, for these had, by then, been established by the class's regular teacher. Most students secured a high degree of application to the task. Observers noted that in all except eleven sessions almost all the pupils applied themselves to the task in hand soon after the lesson had begun. One student only was recorded as needing more than ten minutes for the class to commence work. Only three students had sessions where a significant number did not become engaged in their work at the beginning of the lesson. One had three sessions when between six and ten pupils did not commence work, another had two sessions where six to ten and one session where eleven to fifteen pupils did not begin their task, and a third had one session with six to ten not occupied and two with eleven to fifteen not engaged in the task in hand.

Attention-getting behaviour by the students was a less confident, more shaky version of what had been observed for experienced teachers. 'Right' and 'Shhh' were common devices for opening, voice and position playing a prominent role. Some students lacked the conviction of the class's regular teacher, so they needed more than one attempt to get silence. One student even tried standing on a chair. Another confessed her learner status freely: 'I'm going to take the register now. It's my first time, so I'll need some help.' Others soon found resistance to their carefully planned lessons: 'Right, we're going to be doing aerobics' (groans from group of reluctant girls) 'so you might as well be enthusiastic' (more groans). 'You'll enjoy it. Right. Make two lines, please.'

It was not long before some students had to deal with misbehaviour. A student who said she would only establish rules if necessary began a session following a day when several pupils had misbehaved with a huge display of anger: 'Right!' (Slams file down on desk.) 'Yesterday was disgusting. Your behaviour was appalling. It will not happen today or else we'll not do anything interesting.' Another student who had expressed, in interview, a desire to make what she said worth listening to, so children would learn to accept her as their new teacher, found difficulty in commanding a hearing and was soon filling out the imperious stereotype she was eager to avoid, as she sought to establish social control:

> Right, then. You're not going to do anything till you're quiet. If anyone's going to be silly they can go straight back to the classroom. Put your money away, Peter. (Angrily) Now! Jonathan! We're waiting for your group.

Whereas most students had no difficulty controlling the class, and those that did generally asserted themselves, albeit with difficulty, one student was too nervous to take action when challenges to her authority occurred. She had said in interview that she would be nervous and would feel panic, and in an early session one boy began to yawn ostentatiously, eventually lying across his desk pretending to snore. She ignored it and carried on addressing the rest of the class. By the second day the observer noted that children appeared to wander off to an adjacent area where their normal class teacher was working, the classroom was generally noisy, no procedure for attracting attention by pupils or teacher had been established and there was no feeling that the student had actually taken over the class. Though she wandered round the room looking at pupils' work in a perfunctory manner, this did not reduce the misbehaviour.

In such circumstances pupils will sometimes, in the absence of clearly defined rules, seek a definition by testing the limits of misbehaviour, so that case law can be established. This is exactly what happened in this student's lesson. One pupil set off the alarm of his watch; there was no reaction. Another repeatedly sharpened her pencil, saying she did not feel like working; the student told her to sit down. One girl played with a doll and talked to four others, another pushed her table backwards and forwards, one pupil played with a hand-held computer game, two girls talked incessantly for ten minutes about matters other than the task, two boys donned sunglasses, another boy banged on the table to gain attention, a pupil persistently annoyed another, two boys put their feet on the table and began whistling. Many of these were ignored, others were met by an order to cease, but not in a convincing or assertive manner. The limits were not being defined, so pupils kept seeking some consistent reaction to what was and was not permitted.

One particular difficulty for student teachers was the individual pupil who was particularly badly behaved. The class teacher had warned one student that 'Three-quarters of these children are from broken homes' and that one pupil in particular was very badly behaved and had been expelled from two other schools. She was largely unable to cope with a succession of anti-social acts from him which made a considerable impact on the other pupils. He was seen to kick a ball in a girl's face, stamp his hand with a rubber stamp at the teacher's desk, dance on a chair, grab a pupil by the neck and shake him, take a girl's pencil, throw things across the room and numerous other attention-seeking or disruptive acts. The student tried using a rough and angry voice, but to little effect, so she kept a distance from him. On one occasion when he refused to write, saying he could not do the task, she replied, 'I'm sure you could if you tried. That's your trouble, you just don't try.' She did not, however, sit with him to see what his problem was, nor was she given any advice on how to cope.

As the case in the classes of experienced teachers reported in this book, most inappropriate behaviour was noisy or illicit chatter. This arose for different reasons. In one student's class the children's task was to plant cress in trays. She had explained what was to be done, and the class had been attentive, but she had not prepared the trays. As soon as the transition from whole-class to group activity occurred the pupils, uncertain how to get a tray, began to talk to each other. The teacher eventually gave out the trays, but by then there was a noisier working atmosphere; she ignored it and concentrated on one group at a time. In a later physical education lesson the organisation was even more complex, but she had learned from her previous experience, had all the equipment available, explained clearly what the class would do, set up demonstrations to reinforce what the task involved and used her eyes to sweep over the whole room and control the activity. There were no incidents of disruption.

Analysis of those lessons which had high levels of activity and orderliness showed that the more effective students had prepared the activities adequately, explained clearly what was involved, answered pupils' questions, monitored the work of individuals or groups, but kept an overview of the whole class and were especially vigilant during transitions, curbing misbehaviour before it escalated. They also were more likely to devise lessons and tasks which engaged pupils' attention. Obversely the lessons with more disruption and inattention were usually well prepared in terms of content, but less so in organisation. Misbehaviour recurred most frequently at the beginning and end of lessons and during transitions from one activity to another. Younger pupils especially became restless at the end of the longer sessions, and one student had problems because she overestimated the ability of the class and devised work which only the more able would do, resulting in large queues of pupils at her desk with a succession of queries, and resultant obscuring of the rest of the class from her view. Another student put some sheets on the blackboard that were so small children had to get out of their seats to see them. The more robust students learned immediately from their organisational or procedural misjudgments, but the more nervous or less perceptive took little or no remedial action.

The primary differences between the students and the experienced teachers were principally lack of clarity about classroom rules and the limits of inappropriate behaviour, a less confident and convincing manner when dealing with disruption, a lower level of whole-class vigilance when working with individuals or whole-class groups, fewer coping strategies when organisation or relationships went wrong, and less attention to the rules of behaviour in the very first encounter. Student teachers gave almost all their planning time to subject matter, less to organisation and little to 'tone' or desired classroom atmosphere. They were especially keen to work with individuals and small groups and gave a great deal of attention to these. This close identity with the individual child before professional socialisation has taken place was also noted in the study by Wragg and Wood (1984) of secondary trainees.

Study 2   Students on teaching practice

Once student teachers have completed the first few days of their teaching practice they have to sustain and enhance their class management over several weeks, usually under the supervision of the class's regular teacher. In chapters 4 and 5 there was a description of the management strategies of a sample of experienced teachers in London, the North-west and the South-west. We also observed student teachers, using the same research procedures, and twelve out of the sixty teachers in the sample were second-year students on their first longer six-week block of teaching practice. They had already experienced one day a week in school followed by a three-week block practice in their first year. It would have been interesting to follow through the group of students observed during their first encounter, but researchers must nowadays be sensitive to the pressures on schools and not outstay their welcome. Intensive observation of lessons can be intrusive on a school when many novelties and rapid changes in curriculum consume the time and energy of teachers.

It was decided, therefore, to follow a different group of students, using exactly the same procedures as were employed for experienced teachers, except that, on the observation schedule, the category 'another teacher' was expanded to incorporate the intervention of the class teacher whilst her student was taking the class. We had intended that some of the class teachers would themselves agree to be observed as part of our study of experienced teachers, and only two of them declined, so in the case of ten students in the sample we had observation data in exactly the same classroom environment collected from their class teachers after they had left. In each case the same class management observation schedule was used during four visits. There are thus four sets of five structured two-minute observation blocks for each participant, four sets of deviance and on-task measures, four sets of freehand observation notes, critical events, as well as interview data for both student and experienced teachers. Altogether forty sessions were observed for both students and teachers, making 200 observation blocks in each case.

In quantitative terms, therefore, table 11.1 shows comparisons between the two groups for exactly the same number of lessons observed using identical procedures, as the two students whose class teachers did not wish to be observed have been excluded. The figures in table 11.1 show the principal activities in which students or teachers were engaged. These could either be teachers acting solo, for example addressing the class, teacher–pupil

Table 11.1   Percentage of each activity during structured observation of 200 lesson segments in the classes of experienced and 200 in the classes of student teachers

Principal type of activity	Experienced teachers	Student teachers
Teacher solo	6	13
Teacher–pupil interaction	15	33
Pupils working, teacher monitors	69	51
Pupils working, teacher does not monitor	4	2
Transition with movement of class	1	1
Transition without movement of class	5	0

interaction, pupils working with the teacher, either monitoring what they were doing or not, and transitions from one activity to another, with or without movement. In each case the predominant type of activity was recorded. The most striking differences between the two groups lie in the greater amount of teacher–pupil interaction seen in students' lessons and the consequent lower incidence of pupils working with teacher monitoring. Student teachers feel more of a need to present themselves, to rehearse their presentation skills on teaching practice, hence also the higher incidence of 'teacher solo' in which students often explained content or procedures to the whole class.

There were some notable differences in the occurrence of misbehaviour. Table 11.2 shows the frequency of deviant behaviour in lessons. It needs to be borne in mind, of course, that observers noted any mildly deviant act, including illicit chatter, and that having one or two such acts does not mean classroom mayhem.

Table 11.2 Percentage of lesson segments (out of 200 for each group) in which different numbers of pupils were observed misbehaving

Number of pupils misbehaving	Experienced teachers	Student teachers
0	55	40
1	19	12
2 to 4	10	18
5 or more	16	30

It was much more likely that students would have a small cluster of pupils not attending to the task, often the children at one table. There were also differences in the nature of misbehaviour, as table 11.3, showing four of the commonly observed types of deviant behaviour, reveals. As one might expect, students have more occurrence of noisy chatter than the class's normal teacher, but the category of children moving when they were not supposed to is the same (twenty two). There was also a difference in responses to deviance. Student teachers responded in 98 per cent of cases, whereas experienced teachers did so in 90 per cent, preferring sometimes to ignore it. The responses to deviant behaviour shown in table 11.4 are also based on percentages, to help comparison, as there were more responses from student teachers because there was more misbehaviour overall. In table 11.4 A1 to A3 figures show the target of the responses, B1 and B2 the timing of the intervention, C1 to C12 actual strategies, and D1 and D2 the length of the response. There are several similarities between student and experienced teachers, but the most striking differences are to be found in the students' greater tendency to address their response to groups of pupils, issue an order to cease the misbehaviour and use facial expressions, whereas the

Table 11.3 Percentage of lesson segments (out of 200 for each group) when four categories of pupil misbehaviour occurred

Type of behaviour	Experienced teachers	Student teachers
Noisy or illicit pupil talk	22	45
Inappropriate movement	22	22
Inappropriate use of materials	8	11
Defiance fo teacher	5	8

Table 11.4 Comparison of experienced and student teachers' responses to misbehaviour (figures show percentage of all responses to misbehaviour by each group)

Teachers' responses to misbehaviour		Experienced teachers	Student teachers
A1	To whole class	35	41
A2	To group	19	35
A3	To individuals	46	24
B1	Before escalation of misbehaviour	95	97
B2	After escalation of misbehaviour	5	3
C1	Order to cease	65	90
C2	Pupil named	64	64
C3	Reprimand	43	41
C4	Involve pupils in work	43	14
C5	Proximity (going over to pupil)	18	21
C6	Touch	10	12
C7	Praise	9	3
C8	Gesture	9	9
C9	Facial expression	8	21
C10	Pause	6	8
C11	Pupil moved	5	0
C12	Threat	5	3
D1	Teacher response brief	71	87
D2	Teacher response sustained	29	13

experienced teachers were far more likely to address individuals, seek to re-involve pupils in their work, and use praise and to make sustained responses.

The outcomes of these interventions are shown in Table 11.5. Rows A1 to A3 give the pupils' reactions, B1 to B4 reveal whether the misbehaviour increased, decreased, remained the same or ended, and C1 to C3 show whether the teacher appeared calm, agitated or angry. There are few large differences, experienced teachers being slightly more likely to secure pupil acceptance of the action (e.g. 'Yes, miss') and to see the misbehaviour ending, though, paradoxically, they were also slightly more likely to see it sustained. These differences, however, are too small to be of any interest.

Two measures of on-task behaviour and deviance were computed, as

Table 11.5 Outcomes of experienced and student teachers' interventions (shown as percentages of all responses by each group)

Outcome of teacher intervention	Experienced teachers	Student teachers
A1 Pupil(s) silent	80	90
A2 Pupil(s) accept(s) teacher's action	16	6
A3 Pupil(s) altercate(s) or protest(s)	4	4
B1 Misbehaviour ends	76	71
B2 Misbehaviour lessens	15	24
B3 Misbehaviour is sustained	9	5
B4 Misbehaviour increases	0	0
C1 Teacher calm	92	90
C2 Teacher agitated	5	9
C3 Teacher angry	3	1

described in chapter 4, by studying each pupil in the class separately, producing scores ranging from 0 to 100. In the case of the on-task index, a score of 0 would indicate that no one was on task at any time and a score of 100 would mean all pupils were on task all of the time. A deviance index score of 0 would mean no child ever misbehaved, whilst a score of 100 would indicate that every child misbehaved badly on every occasion. Table 11.6 shows for each class the comparable on-task and deviance scores for both students and teachers. All the comparisons are based on the full four sessions, except for class I, where the normal class teacher was seen teaching a different class for two of the visits. Class I figures are based on two lessons only, therefore.

In general experienced teachers showed higher on-task and lower misbehaviour scores in this individual pupil survey, but in class E the student experienced less misbehaviour and achieved more on-task pupil behaviour.

Table 11.6 Average on-task and deviance index scores for experienced and student teachers

| Class | On-task scores | | | Deviance | | |
	Experienced	Student	Student difference	Experienced	Student	Student difference
A	71	71	none	3	7	higher
B	91	65	lower	0	7	higher
C	87	76	lower	0	5	higher
D	81	75	lower	2	1	lower
E	64	76	higher	3	1	lower
F	75	72	lower	1	6	higher
G	57	63	higher	6	10	higher
H	77	69	lower	4	9	higher
I	72	60	lower	3	13	higher
J	53	62	higher	10	12	higher

Observers' field notes and analysis of initial events collected in both student and experienced teachers' lessons helped explain and illuminate some of the data collected using quantitative methods. Observers' notes, for example, showed that noise levels tended to rise in students' lessons whenever the class teacher left the vicinity, and not all students reasserted the level they wished to have when on their own. Often it was a single group of children round one table who began to make more noise, hence the greater frequency of misbehaviour involving two to four or more than five pupils and the students' more frequent use of group reprimand or order to cease misbehaviour. Some students used the class teacher, who had often told pupils to behave in her absence, as an invisible surrogate authority. The following were all noted in various lessons given by one student:

> Richard, stop talking and get on with your work . . . Richard, remember what Mrs Jenkins [class teacher] said.

> [Looking up suddenly at noise.] Er, remember what Mrs Jenkins said. [Pupils fall silent.]

> This class is being so silly. Mrs Jenkins will not be pleased when I tell her.

Students were very conscious they were on another's territory. One student, when asked about an event involving two children who regularly misbehaved, said in interview after the lesson:

> They [the two children] are a constant problem. It's hard, because I don't want to split them up. Well, personally I'd probably split them up, but because it's Sally's classroom, she doesn't split them up very often.

Whereas in secondary schools students are frequently left to teach alone, in primary schools the class teacher is often near by, or even in the room. This awareness of the likely proximity of the class's normal teacher was thought to be inhibiting by some students, underlining in their own eyes and those of the pupils their novitiate status. Towards the end of one lesson the student told the class to put their work away. As she did so two pupils left the classroom. The class teacher had entered the room and another pupil told her about the two early leavers, whereupon the class teacher instructed her to go and recall them, asking them publicly, on their return, where they had been. The student explained she had told pupils they could leave when they had finished. The class teacher apologised. Afterwards in interview the student said:

> Well, I'd said they could go, but . . . it's really hard, because Janet [the class teacher] is such a forceful person and when she says (something), it's hard for me to do anything.

Students were not always overawed by the class teacher's style and way of doing things. Some could act quite independently. There were occasions when we saw both student and teacher, in different contexts, dealing with children who had become 'target' pupils, that is, those in receipt of more reprimands, either because they appeared to misbehave more frequently, or because they had become typified by the teacher as illustrative of a whole genus of misbehaving pupils. One such pupil was Roger, who attracted the frequent attention of both student and class teacher. Two events illustrate this. In the first Roger asked if he could go to the toilet just after playtime, and the class teacher said, 'You seem to think break time's for you to play and class time's for you to go to the toilet.' In the second event she suddenly looked up from the group she was with and called across the class, 'Roger, you shouldn't have pens in your hand, you should have a book in your hand . . . Put the pens down!' Roger complied. In interview the class teacher said about the first event:

> His mother's a bit odd. She came to see me and said, 'He gets embarrassed about going to the toilet during a break time,' and could I let him go when-ever he wants to. But you just wonder how often he's just swinging the lead.

On the pens incident, she said:

> He was just messing around, basically, trying to avoid getting down to his work – you get to know which children to double-check – and he was busy just having a chat and just fiddling with his pens . . . so it's just a point of letting him know you've noticed and remind him to get down to it.

The student teacher also had difficulties with Roger but actually achieved a higher on-task level in the lessons observed than the class teacher. On one occasion she reprimanded him for doing too many lines of writing when she had just congratulated another child for writing four extra lines. However, she often adopted a more positive strategy with him, reinforcing good behaviour when it occurred. On one occasion she said to the class:

> Everybody should be handling their work in to me, and then sitting down at a nice tidy table with their reading books out . . . (A minute later) . . . I can only see two children sitting down and reading, and that's Alan and Roger.

Soon afterwards she needed two children to fetch a piece of equipment, which was regarded as a privilege, and nominated Roger because he had been a good boy for reading his book as he had been asked. In interview she said:

> He [Roger] likes to be noticed. I think he likes playing around . . . All of them love going off to get things . . . they all like helping and because they [Roger and Alan] had been sitting reading I chose them to go and get it.

Misbehaving children were often seen by the class teacher as the joint responsibility of herself and the student. Amanda was a girl who was often reprimanded by the class teacher. Once she became so exasperated she shouted:

Amanda, where is your maths book? Don't you dare tell me you can't find it . . . I gave you your maths book . . . you go and find it quickly, young lady . . . (prodding her) . . . You've lost your playtime and your dinner time. You've just been idle, Amanda.

When the student teacher came she had similar problems to the class teacher:

Student   What did you think of the cavemen?
Amanda   It was boring. (Slight laughter from class.)
(later in lesson)
Student   Amanda, go and sit over there by the door!
Pupil   She's being stupid.
Amanda   I promise I won't be.
Student   I'll send you out if you're stupid, like I did yesterday.
Amanda   I don't care.
Pupil (to student)   You should split them up, they're being stupid.
Student   Amanda!
Pupil   They keep on being stupid.
Student   Amanda, if I tell you again you're going out.

The class teacher came in and later told the student to make sure Amanda was always seated next to her desk so she could keep an eye on her. In this instance, however, it was the pupils' running commentary on the student's lame attempts to control a disruptive child which reinforced the novitiate label. The class teacher took the line of offering to share responsibility away from the hearing of the class, but some primary age children are not so well socialised and offer their advice publicly.

Inevitably student teachers felt themselves under the tutelage of their class teacher supervisors, especially as these were second-year students on their first full teaching practice. Though many took on the procedures and ways of working of their mentors, the more independent-minded were not afraid of fashioning their own methods, even if these were different from usual practice, and in some cases what the students did seemed to be accompanied by lower deviance or higher involvement in the task, though in most instances the reverse was the case.

Study 3   Attitude change during teaching practice

Some of the research into student teachers' attitudes has suggested that their attitudes change and become less 'liberal' or 'child-centred' during teaching practice or in the early years of teaching (Wragg 1982), as if the realities of classroom life somehow hone down the novice's idealism. The close identification of students, usually nearer in age to the pupils they teach than the class's regular teacher, was pointed out in the 'first encounters' study earlier in this chapter. In order to see whether some of the students studied in the present research underwent such changes we took a sample of eighty-two trainees and showed them immediately before and immediately after teaching practice three of the photographs used in the research with children and experienced teachers in other studies during the Leverhulme Primary Project. In each case they were asked to complete two response schedules, firstly a freehand response to the pictures, asking what they would do in the same circumstances, and secondly responses to eighteen strategy statements, six for each picture, on a five-point Likert scale, ranging from 'strongly agree' to 'strongly disagree' with the mid-point, 3, labelled 'neither agree nor disagree'.

In the freehand accounts the students were asked, 'What, if anything, would you do?' and 'Why would you do it?' It was explained that, if the student chose to take no action, the 'Why?' question response should be used to explain why no action was taken. The freehand accounts were completed first so that the attitude statements in the second schedule would not affect the replies. In the second schedule six statements of attitude were given, all direct quotations from our interviews with experienced teachers, representing different strategies, namely delay, ignore, manipulate and engage in low, moderate or severe confrontation.

A total of sixty-four students completed both pre- and post-tests, and tables 11.7, 11.8 and 11.9 show the correlated t tests and degree of significance for

Table 11.7 Means and correlated t tests of sixty-four students' attitude scores before and after teaching practice for photograph 1 (two children seen pushing each other)

Statement	Category	Mean score before	after	t value
A I would simply move one of the children to another table	Confront (moderate)	2.28	2.36	−0.46 n.s.
B I would leave it until the end of the lesson then ask them to stay behind and talk to them about their behaviour	Delay	3.13	3.00	+0.88 n.s.
C I would pretend that I had not seen what was happening and hope they would eventually settle down to their work	Ignore	4.61	4.67	−0.73 n.s.
D I would go over to their table, look at their work and talk about how they could extend what they had already done	Manipulate	2.45	2.56	−0.87 n.s.
E I would punish them by making them stay behind when the bell went to finish the work they should have done during the lesson	Confront (severe)	3.09	2.88	1.44 n.s.
F I would sit down at the table with them and talk to them quietly about their behaviour	Confront (low)	1.84	2.22	−3.72 ***

each set of six statements. Students who did not complete both sets were dropped from the sample. In each case, since 'strongly agree' was coded 1 and 'strongly disagree' was coded 5, the higher the mean the higher the *disagreement* with the statement. A negative t value shows higher *disagreement* after teaching practice, and a positive t value higher *agreement* with the statement after teaching practice. Since no direction of difference was

Table 11.8 Means and correlated t tests of sixty-four students' attitude scores before and after teaching practice for photograph 2 (children rushing into classroom after playtime)

		Mean score		
Statement	Category	before	after	t value
A I would not say anything about it at the time, but just before lunchtime I would mention that I did not like the way they had entered after break and that I would expect them to enter in an orderly manner after lunch	Delay	3.30	3.64	−2.14*
B I would get the children together and talk to them quietly about the way they had entered the room. I would point out the reasons why they should not enter classrooms in that way, stressing the danger of someone getting hurt	Confront (low)	1.81	2.13	−2.87**
C I would not say anything about the way they had entered the room but I would immediately change the start of my lesson plan. I would get all the children together, around me, and do a 'quietening down' activity in which everyone would participate.	Manipulate	3.34	3.52	−1.37 n.s.
D I would raise my voice and tell them to stop and stand absolutely still. I would then tell them that such behaviour was disgraceful, that they should not enter my classroom in that manner, that they should sit down and get on with their work in silence and that I did not expect to see them ever entering the classroom in that way again	Confront (severe)	3.63	3.31	2.17*
E I would not make a fuss about this incident. I would simply tell the children to sit down and get on with their work	Ignore	4.11	4.36	−2.65**
F I would send the children outside, make them line up, wait until they were silent and then tell them to enter the classroom again in an orderly manner	Confront (moderate)	2.16	1.91	1.95 n.s.

hypothesised, a two-tailed t test was used to test the null hypothesis, that is, the assumption that there would be no change in attitude after teaching practice. In each of the tables the asterisk system is used to indicate the 0.05, 0.01 and 0.001 level of significance and n.s. means not significant.

What is interesting here is the direction of movement. The most consistent categories of strategy are 'ignore', where in each picture the scores show greater *disagreement* after teaching practice, and 'severe confrontation', where the scores show greater *agreement* in each case after teaching practice. The greatest significant changes occur in the category 'low confrontation', where students reveal they would be less inclined at the end of teaching practice to give a child a talking-to. The rank order shows that a low to

Table 11.9 Means and correlated t tests of sixty-four students' attitude scores before and after teaching practice for photograph 3 (girl calls teacher 'old cow')

	Statement	Category	Mean score before	Mean score after	t value
A	I would deal with the situation then and there. I would raise my voice and reprimand her for being so rude. I would then give her a punishment – something she did not like doing which would put her in her place	Confront (severe)	3.78	3.62	0.94 n.s.
B	I would pretend that I had not heard what she had said. I would avoid a confrontation by simply telling her to sit down and get on with her work	Ignore	4.03	4.17	-1.08n.s.
C	I would immediately tell the others to on with their work, and take her to one side. I would talk to her about scribbling on other people's books *and* about the language she had used. I would tell her that I did not want to hear her using such language again	Confront (moderate)	1.98	2.03	–0.40n.s.
D	I would see her later, at playtime, and talk to her about the comment she had made and why she had made it	Delay	2.37	2.35	0.11 n.s.
E	I would tell the girl to sit down with the group at the table she was standing next to. I would talk to her calmly and quietly about why she had used such language and what she meant by it. I would hope to deflate her aggression and neutralise the abuse by asking such questions	Confront (low)	2.73	2.62	0.87 n.s.
F	I would tell her to bring her work to my desk and then look through it for something I could comment positively on	Manipulate	3.32	3.22	0.74 n.s.

moderate degree of confrontation is the most preferred approach, and ignoring the behaviour the least favoured. Such movement as there is over the teaching practice is largely in the direction of students supporting more severe degrees of confrontation than was thought likely before the practice.

Freehand comments written before responses to the structured attitude statements further illuminate these shifts. All written responses were read independently by two members of the research team who then merged their analyses by agreement and selected illustrative quotations. One very striking change was that there were more strategies after teaching practice than before. The second photograph, showing children bursting into the classroom, elicited most responses, followed by the third photograph, where the girl calls the teacher 'old cow'. Table 11.10 shows this increase clearly.

Table 11.10 Mean number of strategies for each situation given before and after teaching practice

	Mean number of strategies	
Photograph	before	after
1 Two pupils pushing each other	3.0	3.5
2 Children rushing into room	5.2	5.8
3 Girl calls teacher 'old cow'	4.3	4.8

The medium confrontation strategy involving warning or threat doubled from 16 per cent of responses before teaching practice to 32 per cent afterwards. The post-teaching practice replies were usually more specific and detailed, both in strategies and in reasons, as these extracts from one student's response to the two children misbehaving in photograph 1 reveal:

Strategy before teaching practice   I would go across to the two children and remind them that I had already asked them to settle down. I would quietly point out that they were wasting my time and that I would waste theirs if they caused me to speak to them again.

Reason   I would approach them rather than shout, because I would not wish to draw attention to them. I feel that, without an audience, they would feel defeated. I would give them a final chance with a threat because I wouldn't want to deal out a punishment unless I was pushed to it.

Strategy after teaching practice   I would get up and go over to the two children, bend down so that I would be at their height level and very quietly remind them that this was the second time I had asked them to behave. I would say that if I needed to speak to them again they would be separated and stay behind at playtime to work.

Reason   I would do this to (1) not draw vast attention to them by shouting in front of the whole class, (2) let them know that I did not intend to stop the other children from working whilst I saw to them, (3) warn them of the consequences of continued disruptive behaviour and carry out my intended threats if necessary.

The use of body language (stooping to child height), the threat to separate, rather than 'waste their time', and awareness of the impact of a disciplinary act by the teacher on other pupils, are amongst several additional dimensions to this student's and others' responses after teaching practice. With photograph 1 there was little change in other categories of response like 'explain/ discuss behaviour with pupils' (57 per cent mentioned it before, 59 per cent after) and 'separate pupils' (59 per cent before, 57 per cent after).

In the case of the second photograph students had, in almost every case, encountered the incidence of children rushing into a room after break. Requiring children to repeat their entry in a more orderly manner went up from 58 per cent of respondents before teaching practice to 71 per cent afterwards, though 'explaining/discussing' was even more frequently cited (66 per cent before, 76 per cent after). After bruising first encounters early in the term students had often needed to become firmer at the very beginning of lessons, an awareness this post-practice response reveals:

> (I would) take the class back outside the classroom, tell them how I expect children to behave on entering a classroom, before making the class re-enter the classroom according to the code of conduct just established . . . I would do this in order to make the class realise that I am not prepared to accept a poor standard of behaviour in the classroom. This allows myself as a new teacher to establish my own set of rules, possibly with the aid of the pupils themselves.

Three categories of response showed notable increases after teaching practice. The first was to stop the children before they were all in, the second to state that the behaviour was unacceptable, the third was to shout or raise the voice. Comments like these were much more frequent after teaching practice than before:

> (I'd) say, 'Stop where you are!' wait for silence, tell them that their behaviour was unacceptable and point out the dangers of it . . . because of the danger hazard they were causing by pushing and shoving. I would have to stop them before they came into the classroom.

> (I'd) ask them what they thought of the way they'd entered the classroom (if necessary ask the more boisterous individuals), stress points of safety (tripping up, etc.) . . . ask them how they *should* come into classrooms.

The personal threat to the teacher's authority of the girl in photograph 3 calling the teacher 'old cow' evoked a range of responses, but 65 per cent of teachers before and 74 per cent after teaching practice mentioned the need to discuss, or ask the girl to explain, her behaviour, some addressing the insulting language, others the scribbling on books, often both, but sometimes it was not clear which misbehaviour would be discussed. Before teaching practice 48 per cent said they would want to see her alone, but this rose to 63 per cent afterwards. More students wanted an apology, either to the teacher or to fellow pupils, after teaching practice than before, though only ten students mentioned it at all. Reference to higher authority was one of the four categories to decline, as 17 per cent mentioned bringing in another teacher, the head or the child's parents before teaching practice, but only 11 per cent afterwards. Giving extra work, asking the girl to reflect on what she had done, waiting for her to behave well so that praise could be administered, and trying to discount her motives, all increased in frequency after teaching practice. About ten per cent of students suggested some kind of humiliation, and this number did not change over the period of teaching practice.

These three studies of student teachers give fascinating insights into the professional socialisation of teachers as well as the development of their views and practices in class management. The 'first encounters' study showed how good intentions could evaporate under the pressure of actual teaching; how students did not have in support those collective moral exhortations that characterised the beginning of the school year for experienced teachers; how content, rather than negotiating rules and relationships, would dominate early lessons; and how early in the teaching practice classes and individuals might test the limits when rules were not clear. The second study, of students on teaching practice, revealed how most pupil misbehaviour consisted of excessive noise rather than severe deviance, and the third study of the responses to photographs showed how students after teaching practice became more detailed in their responses to misbehaviour, but also tougher, less likely to ignore inappropriate behaviour, more likely to take on and confront those who misbehaved.

Their final position was not unlike the responses of experienced teachers, but the apparent increased toughness was still overlaid with elements of concern for the individual, a desire to empathise, to reason rather than dictate and discuss instead of always command. It was not the vague, sometimes ill-focused good intentions of the period of liberality that precedes teaching practice, but it had certainly not become hard, cynical or indifferent, simply more specific, pragmatic and a little closer to the practice of experienced teachers.

Chapter 12

Training skilful teachers

The research described in this book has considerable implications for the training of both student and experienced teachers. From the very first chapter the case has been put that there is no single omni-purpose good teacher stereotype. There are different ways of being effective in different circumstances. This lack of singularity, however, does not mean that nothing can be done to help teachers become more proficient. Quite the reverse. If there were a single stereotype of skilful teaching, the 'norm' of the nineteenth-century 'normal schools', all one would have to do would be to learn it off by heart. It is because there are numerous ways to help children learn that the challenge to train teachers intelligently, and for teachers themselves to improve the quality of their own practices, is all the more important.

In chapter 3 the study of first encounters showed how deftly some teachers could set up rules and relationships that soon led to harmonious working, even with young children being socialised into the ways of classrooms for the very first time in their lives. Chapters 4 and 5 reported the analysis of several hundred lesson observations and interviews that revealed how most classroom misbehaviour consisted of noisy chatter or illicit movement. More important, however, this study showed how certain teachers working in the most difficult circumstances were able to establish a positive climate for learning. Chapter 6 described some of the deft strategies developed by supply teachers, well experienced in managing first encounters and working in strange and novel surroundings.

The views of pupils reported in chapter 7 pose numerous questions for novice or experienced teachers. Children prefer teachers to be slightly strict, explain things clearly, use rewards and punishments in a fair-minded manner, and have a sense of humour. To what extent, therefore, should teachers strive to meet this paragon ideal? After all, some teachers do not find humour, for example, easy to generate or manage and would be ill at ease if they felt they had to be unnaturally jolly. Children's perceptions of teachers' responses to classroom misbehaviour were shown to be very closely related to what actually happened in the classrooms where we observed, more so than the idealised responses of some teachers to the same photographed situations.

The studies of teachers' questioning, explaining and subject knowledge reported in chapters 8, 9 and 10 also raise important training issues. That so many managerial questions are asked, alongside so few higher order questions requiring a response beyond mere information recall, is something that should be addressed whenever teaching is scrutinised, whether this is in training or during appraisal. There is no firm research evidence that asking more higher order questions produces more or better learning, but that does not mean that teachers should not query their own balance between different types of question, especially if they find they ask few that challenge pupils to think more deeply. Similarly, explaining is the skill most highly regarded by pupils. It lies right at the heart of professional competence, requiring teachers to choose the appropriate language register, practical work, illustrative examples, analogies, key concepts. This too should be set at the centre of any analysis of classroom proficiency. Subject knowledge demands on primary teachers are formidable in the late twentieth and early twenty-first centuries, but our evidence of teachers' lack of confidence in key subjects, like science and technology, suggests that massive training initiatives to equip primary teachers with improved subject and pedagogic knowledge are long overdue. Such training must be well conceived to recognise our finding from the use of science videos that teachers can easily learn more examples of principles, but that full understanding of the principles themselves is more elusive.

Proposals to improve the quality of the school-based elements of teacher training should be informed by many of the chapters in this book, especially chapter 11, where we studied student teachers and their supervising class teachers. Students frequently received little help in the management of their first encounters with pupils. It was pointed out in chapter 11 that schools make a massive collective effort to establish sound behaviour management principles in the first week in September, but that by the time students arrive this collective drive is much more low-key. Many students identify closely with their pupils and sometimes wish to establish a different relationship from the one they inherit. They will need much more help in negotiating this, especially if their early attempts encounter resistance or even hostility. If students do not analyse the situation in which they find themselves, they sometimes, in their attempts to establish a relaxed relationship, find themselves carping and demanding silence all day, filling out the very stereotype they sought to avoid. Yet teachers and supervising tutors sometimes give students a relatively long period in which things may 'settle down', when the early phase of first encounters is often the one that needs most reflection and analysis.

Policy and practice for the dynamic school

Given the clear evidence, not only in this study, but also in the research literature generally, that there is no single good teacher stereotype, there is no case for saying that all teachers and students in a school should teach in like manner. Yet the case studies reported in chapter 5 showed that even two teachers in virtually adjacent classrooms in the same school could have vastly different levels of pupil involvement in the task and misbehaviour. Duke (1978) found that, in schools where behaviour was good, there was clarity amongst the staff about what was required and what roles and conventions would be adopted. The principal focus of the research in the Leverhulme Primary Project was on the classroom, but there are implications in what we found for the whole school, especially for the school that wants to be dynamic and changing, rather than static.

In one school where we observed the classes were in general industrious and well behaved, even though the school was situated in an area with severe social problems. In the school prospectus there were written aspirations which were, so far as we could see, carried out in practice and endorsed by the majority of teachers:

> Children are taught to be caring and considerate to others. Good manners and self-discipline are taught and reinforced when necessary. Our children come here to be educated and we will not permit bad behaviour by one child to disrupt the progress of others . . . If a child does not respond to school discipline, which is rare, or the work is not satisfactory, then parents will be invited into school to discuss and remedy the situation . . . We believe in discipline, especially self-discipline. Our children are taught to think for themselves and accept the responsibilities we give to them.

Most lessons seen in this school over a four-week period were orderly and children worked assiduously. There was no feeling of repression or heavy-handedness. One or two teachers were not as able to carry through the policies the school espoused, but at least they knew what these were and so could work towards them, even if they still fell short of the high demands being made. What is more, the policy applied to playground and dining hall, not just classrooms.

The same can be said about the development of individual teachers' professional skills. The requirement that all teachers should be appraised and that their appraisal should be based, in part at least, on direct observation of their classroom teaching means that not only class management, but also questioning, explaining, subject knowledge, lesson preparation and planning, as well as topics we did not study in the present research, like pupil assessment, should be reviewed as a whole-school process, not just by each teacher in isolation. Similarly when student teachers come to a school for occasional or block teaching practice they should become part of a process of professional self-scrutiny which seems natural and sustained rather than sculptured and sporadic.

The Leverhulme Primary Project was not only a research but also a development project, and that is why we have based all the accompanying workbooks, on class management (Wragg 1993), group work (Dunne and

Bennett 1990), questioning (Brown and Wragg 1993), explaining (Wragg and Brown 1993) and all the other topics in the workbook series, on practical activities which allow either trainee or experienced teachers, or both, first to reflect on practice and then to try and improve it. For example, if pupils are as knowledgeable and insightful about teaching as was suggested in chapter 7, then perhaps there should be much more discussion with them about teaching and learning.

Schmuck and Schmuck (1975) describe how the teacher can sensitise children working in groups to the processes involved, and capitalise on their natural insights to make them partners in learning, rather than merely the recipients of teaching. When classes are badly behaved it should be possible for pupils and teachers to analyse together why relationships are poor. Sadly, those teachers with ineffective class management are the very ones who are least likely to be able to do this, and it may need another person to join them, an external tutor, trusted colleague or deputy head, with all the threat that offers to the teacher's sense of personal and professional competence. Experiments involving children in talking about what have often been teachers' professional secrets may be preferable to the traditional tendency to leave students or experienced teachers who are having discipline problems to flounder on with little support. One of the successful strategies we encountered was the sensible use of 'circle time', when pupils and teacher sit and talk about behaviour problems, ground rules, learning difficulties, or whatever else is legitimately on such an agenda. It was a process spoken well of by both teachers and pupils in interview, and, provided it does not become overdone and self-indulgent, can offer a proper forum for reflection and improvement of both teaching and learning.

In many teacher appraisal schemes, school-based in-service programmes, and even initial teacher training courses, there is still too little attention paid to such important basic classroom skills as questioning and explaining. Yet there have been a number of studies which offer a great deal of information about these skills, even if the evidence does not point unequivocally to the use of any single style. Furthermore, they are skills which lend themselves especially to discussion and practice in training. Students or teachers can note down the written and oral questions asked by teachers they observe or by their fellow students. They can plan and discuss key questions for groups they are teaching, analyse transcripts of lessons to work out the kind of thought or action being elicited by different sorts of question or by sequences.

Though many experienced teachers have often given considerable thought to their questioning, others have fallen into a routine of asking almost entirely management and data recall questions, which may be unexacting for many of their pupils. Slower-learning children are perfectly capable of responding to higher order questions, especially if the teacher sequences them carefully. This was shown by some of the teachers described in chapters 8 and 9 and was the subject of research by the late Hilda Taba at San

Francisco State College. She produced teaching modules (Simon and Boyer 1968) showing how social studies teachers could ask questions that moved up from simple recall to grouping, labelling, predicting, making inferences and establishing generalisations. Sadly she died just as her work was beginning to grasp the imagination of a number of teachers and trainers.

In view of the very large number of questions that many teachers ask, it is important that they reflect on the context and the nature of the topic during which questioning takes place, the demands questions place on pupils, the appropriateness of the language of questions to the individual or group concerned and the effect of questions on subsequent learning and related activities. It is quite straightforward to set up training programmes, either for beginners or for experienced teachers, to let them explain certain concepts, principles or events to each other or to a group of children, and then analyse an audio or video recording of the explanation. This can be combined with a simple test of recall or interviews with individual pupils to see what they have understood from the explanation. In addition, it is a good safe environment in which people can reflect on the kind of explanation they have given, and the extent to which it was helped by diagrams, pictures, questions from the teacher or pupils, examples and illustrations.

Questions and explanations are in turn related to the nature of the tasks which children undertake in their classroom, whether these are whole-class activities or assignments for individuals and small groups, and whether they are given by the teacher, chosen by the pupil or negotiated by both. The high inverse correlation we obtained between task involvement and deviance of -0.56 reported in chapter 4 suggests that there is a strong relationship between a high degree of involvement in the task and low levels of misbehaviour. Another fruitful source of reflection and action, therefore, by groups of teachers and associated trainees in a school is to scrutinise the nature of the tasks being set. It requires immense professional skill to create, or elicit from pupils, tasks which are not only appropriate to the age, intelligence and previous experience of the child and the field being studied, but which extend the imagination and stimulate thought and action. Much of human learning may require repeats and rehearsals of what has gone before, and may also perhaps need to be unintimidating and reassuring, but if too much is in that category which makes but modest demands on the learner, then classroom life becomes tedious and fails to fire enthusiasm.

Teachers in training can profitably analyse the tasks set by experienced teachers or by fellow students, and this is another activity which can be set up during a training course without a great deal of difficulty. It is also one which has an immediate and positive pay-off. When novices and experienced teachers work together to analyse process in this way then all may benefit. The students discover how they might better structure pupils' learning, the teachers put their own or a student's practice under the microscope and modify it for the better in the light of what they learn from the analysis, and not least the pupils may in future, hopefully, be the recipients of more stimulating assignments from teachers, or may themselves develop a bigger stake in what they do if they are party to the consultation process, as they should be. Much has been written about teachers' need to reflect (Schoen 1983), but reflection without action can be sterile. Faced with numerous changes in society, the dynamic school makes judicious alterations to practice, based on shrewd reflection. Dynamic practitioners, in turn, review and reflect on their own classroom practices, and work hard to improve them. Without dynamic practitioners there can be no dynamic school.

Indeed, in a dynamic school the dividing line between initial training and in-service professional development becomes almost non-existent, as the interests and aspirations of the two groups should coalesce. If student teachers did not exist, then one very effective way of stimulating experienced teachers to improve their own classroom practice would be to invent them. Yet relatively few primary teachers have been trained properly to analyse their own teaching in a systematic way, or to study the practice of others. It is regrettable that teaching has so fully absorbed the time and energy of practitioners themselves that they have rarely, in some cases never, had the opportunity to watch and reflect on the practices of others at work.

Although we saw a small number of teachers who were less competent than their colleagues, we were in general very impressed by the professional skills of many of the teachers we saw. One is sometimes privileged, as a witness to classroom life, to see the skill which the best practitioners possess. Some of the teachers who most excited the imagination were amongst the most reluctant to talk about their professional expertise. Indeed, after the research was over I urged one teacher, whose pupils showed the highest learning gains of anyone in the sample when we studied the teaching of topics like 'insects', to write up his experiences for others to read what he did and how he set about his teaching. He declined on the grounds that it was nothing special and colleagues might think he was boasting. It seems difficult to imagine surgeons who develop new surgical techniques taking the same view. There is much more of an obligation in some professions to spread expertise first to immediate colleagues and then to a wider professional and lay constituency. Hence the importance of whole-school awareness and practice on these matters.

Another valuable contribution to the enhancement of teaching proficiency within a school can be made if teachers are freed from some of their duties, not merely to observe each other's presentation or organisational skills, but to look at the outcome of these. One of the most valuable ways to do this is to embark on a study of individual pupils. The advantage of individual pupil studies, however superficial, is that they force the observer to concentrate on one pupil and disregard other distractions. When one observes a lesson with no particular focus, the eye wanders naturally to whatever catches its attention, and this may be a piece of bad behaviour, a noise, laughter, a movement, the teacher doing something significant or an outsider entering the room.

Studies of individual pupils reveal that many of them work on unperturbed through all kinds of distraction. Even in lessons where there was considerable disruption there would often be twenty pupils out of thirty who played no part in it, and much of this we were able to document. Some pupils would happily devote well over 90 per cent of their time to their work, others would have developed strategies of perambulating to little purpose, spending large amounts of time fiddling with pencils or rulers, and in the end have devoted but a fraction of their time to the task in hand. Any school that sought to maximise the amount of time spent on the task, achieving this in a benign manner, would be spending time and energy wisely.

Nurturing and enhancing professional competence

In the Leverhulme Primary Project we concentrated on the management of pupils' behaviour and work, on teachers' professional skills like questioning and explaining, and on their subject knowledge. The question of teacher competence raises several important matters, and indeed sometimes arouses strong feelings. Not the least of these is the one raised first in chapter 1, whether these skills should be learned in part or as a whole. The extreme part-learning stance is taken by some supporters of competency-based teacher education who believe that the teaching can be atomised into hundreds of discrete mini-acts which can be systematically learned and appraised, and the extreme holist stance is adopted by those who contend that teaching is an art, and that to seek to segment it is to destroy it. This view is expressed in striking form in Goethe's early poem *Die Freuden*, which tells how he pursues a dragonfly and dismembers it to discover its beauty, only to be left with a crumpled heap of lifeless parts in his hand.

My own belief, for what it is worth, is that if one tries to break down teaching to the atomic level, it not only becomes silly, but makes the student or teacher self-conscious. I once saw a micro-teaching session where the supervisor was analysing a video recording with a student and telling her to smile more, as he would be looking out for this feature in the re-teach lesson. There was indeed a greater incidence of what was arguably 'smiling' in the second lesson, but it carried as much conviction as a party political broadcast. To smile with sincerity, people need to feel genuinely pleased. It is probably better to say to the student, 'Why not listen more carefully to the pupils' answers, they are often very interesting?' Ensuing smiles, if they occur, may be more spontaneous.

On the other hand, it is wrong to expect that if the general development of the person is sound, then all the skills of teaching will emerge of their own accord. There is now a useful literature on teaching skills. There are reflections and exercises one can undertake in a positive attempt to improve the

practice of some aspect of teaching. We have concentrated on class management, questioning and explaining as key skill areas, but this is not to imply
either that there is nothing else, or that we have exhausted these aspects.

In training one can concentrate on a particular aspect of teaching whilst not
excluding others. Thus, the emphasis in one training session may be on
explaining. A teacher may be videotaped explaining something to a group of
children and then the video may be played back and analysed. It would be
foolish indeed to restrict one's attention only to the act of explaining. It might,
for example, rule out the use of questions because that was next week's topic,
which would be an absurd stance to adopt. During the explanation, no doubt,
questions will occur, and quite possibly the pupils if they are bored will
misbehave, which will in turn raise matters to do with class management. The
aim in such a training session should, therefore, be to give prominence to one
aspect of teaching skill and proper attention to such others as naturally occur.
In that way the art of teaching can be nurtured, and such science as exists from
empirical studies can be fed in if thought to be germane.

Nor should the study and development of classroom skills be seen as in
opposition to other forms of training. Some emphasis on specific skills in an
initial training course, in school-based in-service programmes of professional
development, in the training of mentors or appraisers, does not replace other
forms of reflection and practice, but rather should work in harmony with
them. My own inclination has increasingly been to move much more towards
an inductive approach to reflection and the teaching of educational theory.
When students or teachers study classrooms with a set of assignments, things
to look for, questions to ask heads and fellow teachers, teaching ideas to try
out, pupils to talk to, and so on, they collect in a slightly hit-or-miss way an
enormous amount of valuable empirical data. A good theory course can start
by trying to make sense of what students report, and then elicit key constructs
which may or may not be endorsed in the traditional literature. In this respect,
I am not so much on the side of Erasmus and those classical humanists who
believed that instruction should precede experience, but more in accord with
the empiricists like Comenius who argued that we should study the heaven,
the earth, oaks and beeches before books.

In the early stages of an initial or post-experience training course,
therefore, the emphasis can be on collecting sense data, experiences, impressions, with the trainers and teachers using their own knowledge to structure
these in such a way that they are valuable and fruitful rather than pointless or
random. Subsequently, debriefings can ensue which will usually produce a
great deal in common with established precepts about pupil learning or
failure to learn, motivation, language, social and cultural background, home
and school, curriculum, teaching strategies, learning styles, choice, child
development, school organisation. Subsequent courses which cover theory
and practice in a more systematic way will, if all has gone well, find their
studies and reflections more closely related to practice, and will thereby

engage commitment much more firmly than has sometimes been the case in the past.

Furthermore, the theory behind the practice will receive much more rigorous scrutiny. Generations of trainee primary teachers in the 1930s, 1940s and even 1950s and beyond were told firmly by many teacher trainers that children should not be taught to read until they were 6. This was based on statements by such as Morphett and Washburne (1931) that children were not ready to read until they had obtained a mental age of 6 years 6 months. It was bunk, and students engaged in the sort of inductive experience-led early training I have described above would have reported countless examples to show it was not true. With an inductive approach bad theory is likely to be seen off.

There are numerous ways of conceiving teaching skills. Our research leads me to conclude that such aspects as class management can be seen as 'threshold', 'trigger' or 'enabling' skills, since, without competence in them, the other skills, like questioning and explaining, cannot operate, nor can teachers put their subject knowledge and life experience at the disposal of their pupils. Professional competence is intelligent thought translated into intelligent action. In deciding how to teach class management it may, therefore, be worth thinking about initial levels of proficiency, which will enable novices to be operational and permit them to exercise their other skills, and higher levels towards which experienced practitioners can strive.

In class management, for example, a notion like 'organise the handing out and collection of materials' might be a fairly basic matter, involving a teacher thinking about how this can best be organised. Indeed, children themselves could work it out. On the other hand, 'judging the right language register, appropriate response to and suitable activities for a pupil bewildered by a new mathematical or scientific concept' clearly exerts a much higher level of intellectual and practical demand.

At Exeter University (Harvard and Dunne 1992) primary trainees assess themselves and are assessed on a set of nine dimensions. These include direct instruction, monitoring, management of order, planning and preparation. In each case, there are eight levels through which teachers can progress, level 1 being what is expected of beginners and level 8 being the mark of a competent practitioner. Some examples are:

Level 1

1 Distribute provided materials; check children's responses.
2 Attempt to operate some procedures for orderly activity.
3 Plan basis resources for children working on a given activity.
4 Give some account of own performance.
5 Check clarity of explanation by appropriate questions; convey enthusiasm with appropriate verbal and non-verbal behaviour.
6 Use planned and unplanned opportunities to hold conversations with

children in order to establish their perspectives; be sensitive to problems of teacher intrusion.

7 Continue with attempts to operate in an established formula of rules and procedures.

Level 5

1 Provide a programme of guided practice in core areas of the curriculum to suit the range of attainments in the class; choose appropriately matched and sequenced practice exercises.

2 Experiment with planned conversational teaching on particular aspects of the curriculum.

3 Plan a short programme of work to engage a variety of identified skills and intellectual processes and demonstrate attention to transition between activities.

4 Offer justifiable explanations of children's response to work; use explanations in practicable ways to plan the next phase of work; show understanding of the diversity of pupils' attainments.

Level 8

1 Make explanations efficient and concise: choose examples for their power in the subject.

2 Sustain a broad programme of diagnostic teaching.

3 Achieve a situation in which order is endemic to the work system.

4 Plan for efficiency in the use of time and resources with clear reference to the careful management of the teacher's time.

The problem with a hierarchical view is that, by the time one reaches the demands of the highest level, the requirements are such that even the most gifted teachers may pale, and all of us feel guilty that we do not attain them. Nonetheless, such a mapping exercise does at least clarify what people might aspire to, and the Exeter model is offered as an example, not as a paragon ideal to be copied. It is far more effective if people as a group work out a set of precepts to which they feel committed personally and professionally.

In 1963 the American researcher Ned Flanders wrote of his disappointment at the lack of congruence between theory and practice and the relatively low value accorded to the act of teaching itself:

> To be understood, concepts in education must be efficiently conceptualised to gain insight. With most present practices, the gorge between theory and practice grows deeper and wider, excavated by the very individuals who are pledged to fill it.

Since that time there has been a move towards recognising the importance of teaching skill. Our principal intention in the project was both to investigate teaching skills via the research described in the book, and also to influence practice, not only through the training books on class management, group work, questioning and explaining, but to help, along with others working in this field, to shift the balance of training courses for new and experienced teachers more in the direction of developing skilful teaching.

It is sometimes assumed that anyone can train teachers, hence the proposal from time to time that all one need to do is to place students for longer periods in a school and then the teachers will automatically teach them how to teach, or that one invites a good practitioner out of school to talk to students, or that experienced teachers simply need to keep on teaching and they will automatically improve with age. There is a craft to training teachers which it takes time to acquire, and both teachers and teacher trainers, however experienced, can learn a great deal about teaching skills and how to support others who are developing the art and science of skilful teaching. If teaching children is one of the most important responsibilities a society can ask some of its members to undertake, then the challenge to nurture and enhance the professional skills of each new generation of teachers for the vastly complex world of the twenty-first century, and sharpen the proficiency of teachers already in post, must be an equally valuable assignment.

Bibliography

Adams, R. S. and Biddle, B. J. (1970) *Realities of Teaching*, New York: Holt, Rinehart & Winston.

Alexander, R., Rose, J. and Woodhead, C. (1992) *Curriculum Organisation and Classroom Practice in Primary Schools*: a discussion paper, Department of Education and Science.

Anderson, H. H. (1939) 'The Measurement of Domination and of Socially Integrative Behaviour in Teachers' Contacts with Children', *Child Development*, 10:73–89.

Anderson, L. M., Evertson, C. M. and Emmer, E. T. (1980) 'Dimension in Classroom Management Derived from Recent Research', *Journal of Curriculum Studies*, 12:343–56.

Argyle, M. (1967) *The Psychology of Interpersonal Behaviour*, Harmondsworth: Penguin.

Ausubel, D. P., Novak, J. D. and Hanesian, H. (1978) *Educational Psychology: A Cognitive View*, New York: Holt, Rinehart & Winston.

Balding, J. (1990) *Young People in 1989*, Schools Health Education Unit, Exeter University.

Ball, S. (1981) *Beachside Comprehensive*, Cambridge: Cambridge University Press.

Bantock, G. H. (1965) *Freedom and Authority in Education*, London: Faber.

Barnes, D. H. (1971) 'Language and Learning in the Classroom', *Journal of Curriculum Studies*, 3, 1:27–38.

Barnes, D. and Todd, F. (1977) *Communication and Learning in Small Groups*, London: Routledge & Kegan Paul.

Bellack, A. A., Hyman, R. T., Smith, F. L. and Kliebard, H. M. (1966) *The Language of the Classroom*, New York: Teachers College Press.

Bennett, S. N. (1976) *Teaching Styles and Pupil Progress*, London: Open Books.

Bennett, S. N. and Carré, C. G. (1993) *Learning To Teach*, London: Routledge.

—— and Dunne, E. (1992) *Managing Classroom Groups*, Hemel Hempstead: Simon & Schuster.

——, Desforges, C. W., Cockburn, A. and Wilkinson, B. (1984) *The Quality of Pupil Learning Experiences*, London: Erlbaum.

Biddle, B. J. and Ellena, W. J. (eds) (1964) *Contemporary Research on Teacher Effectiveness*, New York: Holt, Rinehart & Winston.

Bloom, B. S. (1956) *Taxonomy of Educational Objectives*, New York: Longman.

Blurton Jones, N. (1972) *Ethological Studies of Child Behaviour*, Cambridge: Cambridge University Press.

Brammer, L. M. (1985) 'Client-centred Counselling' in Husen, T. and Postlethwaite, T. N. (eds) *International Encyclopedia of Education*, 2:765–7, Oxford: Pergamon.

Brophy, J. (1981) 'Teacher Praise: A Functional Analysis', *Review of Educational Research*, 51:5–32.
—— (1987) Educating Teachers about Managing Classrooms. Occasional Paper No. 115, Institute for Research on Teaching, Michigan State University, East Lancing, Mich.
Brophy, J. E. and Evertson, C. M. (1976) *Learning from Teaching: A Developmental Perspective*, Boston: Allyn & Bacon.
Brown, G. A. (1978) *Lecturing and Explaining*, London: Methuen.
—— and Armstrong, S. (1984) 'Explaining and Explanations' in Wragg, E. C. (ed.) *Classroom Teaching Skills*, London: Croom Helm.
—— and Edmondson, R. (1984) 'Asking Questions' in Wragg, E.C. (ed.) *Classroom Teaching Skills*, London: Croom Helm.
—— and Wragg, E. C. (1993) *Questioning*, London: Routledge.
Buckley, N. K. (1977) 'An Ethnographic Study of an Elementary School Teacher's Establishment and Maintenance of Group Norms', PhD dissertation, University of Houston.
Charles, C. M. (1981) *Building Classroom Discipline from Models to Practice*, New York: Longman.
Cohen, L. and Manion, L. (1981) *Perspectives on Classrooms and Schools*, London: Holt, Rinehart & Winston.
Crawford, J. and Gage, N. L. (1977) 'Development of a Research-based Teacher Education Program', *California Journal of Teacher Education*, 4:105–23.
Crowhurst, S. J. (1988) 'Explaining in the Primary Classroom', PhD thesis, Exeter University.
Delamont, S. (1976) *Interaction in the Classroom*, London: Methuen.
Denham, C. and Lieberman, A. (eds) (1980) *Time to Learn*, Washington: National Institute of Education.
DES (1978) *Mixed Ability Work in Comprehensive Schools,* London: HMSO.
—— (1991) HMI Survey of Competencies in Teacher Education, London: DES.
Deutsch, M. (1960) *Minority Groups and Class Status*, Society for Applied Anthropology, Monograph No. 2.
Diamond, C. T. P. (1991) *Teacher Education as Transformation*, Milton Keynes: Open University Press.
Docking, J. W. (1980) *Control and Discipline in Schools*, London: Harper & Row.
Dodl, N. R. (1973) *The Florida Catalog of Teacher Competencies*, Florida Department of Education, Talahassee.
Domas, S. J. and Tiedeman, D. V. (1950) 'Teacher Competence: an Annotated Bibliography', *Journal of Experimental Education*, 19: 101–218.
Doyle, W. (1978) 'Paradigms for Research into Teacher Effectiveness' in Shulman, L. S. (ed.) *Review of Research in Education*, 5, Itasca, Illinois: Peacock.
Duke, D. L. (1978) 'How the Adults in your Schools can cause Student Discipline Problems – and What To Do About It', *American School Board Journal*, 165, 6:29–30.
—— (ed.) (1979) *Classroom Management: the Seventy eighth Yearbook (Part 2) of the National Society for the Study of Education*, Chicago: NSSE.
Dunkin, M. J. and Biddle, B. J. (1974) *The Study of Teaching*, New York: Holt, Rinehart & Winston.
Dunne, E. and Bennett, S. N. (1990) *Talking and Learning in Groups*, Basingstoke: Macmillan Education.
Edwards, A. D. and Furlong, V. J. (1978) *The Language of Teaching*, London: Heinemann.
Eisenhart, M. (1977) 'Maintaining Control: Teacher Competence in the Classroom'. Paper presented at the 76th Annual Meeting of the American Anthropological

Association, Houston, Texas, December.

Eltis, K. J. (1978) 'The Ascription of Attitudes to Pupils by Teachers and Student Teachers', PhD thesis, Macquarie University, Sydney.

Elton Report (1989) *Discipline in Schools: Report of the Committee of Enquiry*, London: DES and the Welsh Office, GBDS.

Emmer, E. T. (1985) 'Management in the Classroom: Elementary Grades' in Husen, T. and Postlethwaite, T. N. (eds) *International Encyclopedia of Education*, 6:3179–88, Oxford: Pergamon.

—— Sanford, J. P., Evertson, C. M., Clements, B. S., and Martin, J. (1981) *The Classroom Management Improvement Study: An Experiment in Elementary School Classrooms*. R and D report No. 6050. Austin Research and Development Centre for Teaching Education, University of Texas.

Ennis, R. H. (1969) *Logic in Teaching*, Englewood Cliffs, NJ: Prentice-Hall.

Evans, K. M. (1962) *Sociometry and Education*, London: Routledge.

Evertson, C. M. and Anderson, L. M. (1978) *Correlates of Effective Teaching*, University of Texas, Austin.

—— and Emmer, E. T. (1982) 'Effective management at the beginning of the year in junior high classes', *Journal of Educational Psychology*, 74, 4:485–98.

Feagans, L. and Farran, D. C. (eds) (1981) *The Language of Children Reared in Poverty*, New York: Academic Press.

Fink, C. H. (1976) 'Social Studies Student Teachers – What Do They Really Learn?' Paper presented at the Annual Meeting of the National Council for the Social Studies, Washington, November.

Flanagan, J. C. (1949) 'Critical Requirements: a New Approach to Employee Evaluation', *Personnel Psychology*, 2:419–25

Flanders, N. A. (1960) *Interaction Analysis in the Classroom: a Manual for Observers*, University of Michigan, Ann Arbor.

—— (1963) 'Intent, Action and Feedback: a Preparation for Teaching', *Journal of Teacher Education*, 14:251–60.

Francis, P. (1975) *Beyond Control?* London: Allen & Unwin.

Freiberg, H. J. (1983) 'Consistency: the Key to Classroom Management', *Journal of Education for Teaching*, 9, 1:1–15.

Gage, N. L. (1978) *The Scientific Basis of the Art of Teaching*, New York: Teachers College Press.

—— (1985) *Hard Gains in the Soft Sciences*, Bloomington, Ind.: Phi Delta Kappa.

Gage, N. L., Belgard, M., Rosenshine, B., Unruh, W. R., Dell, D., Hiller, J. H., Carrol, J. B. and Glaser, R. (1972) Chapter 9 of I. Westbury and A. Bellack (eds), *Research into Classroom Processes*, New York: Teachers College Press.

Gall, M. D. (1970) 'The Use of Questions in Teaching', *Review of Educational Research*, 40:707–21.

Galton, M. J. (ed.) (1978) *British Mirrors: a Collection of Classroom Observation Systems*, University of Leicester.

—— Simon, B. and Croll, P. (1980) *Inside the Primary Classroom*, London: Routledge & Kegan Paul.

Giaconia, R. M. and Hedges, L. V. (1985) 'Synthesis of Teaching Effectiveness Research' in Husen, T. and Postlethwaite, T. N. (eds) *The International Encyclopedia of Education*, 9:5101–20, Oxford: Pergamon.

Glass, G. V. (1978) 'Integrating Findings: the Meta-analysis of Research' in L. S. Schulman (ed.) *Review of Research in Education*, 5, Itasca, Illinois: Peacock.

——, Coulter, D., Hartley, S., Hearold, S., Kahl, S., Kalk, J. and Sherretz, L. (1977) *Teacher 'Indirectness' and Pupil Achievement*, Boulder: University of Colorado.

Glasser, W. (1969) *Schools without Failure*, New York: Harper & Row.

Gnagey, W. J. (1975) *Maintaining Discipline in Classroom Instruction*, London: Macmillan.

Goffman, E. (1971) *The Presentation of Self in Everyday Life*, Harmondsworth: Penguin.

Guetzkow, H., Kelly, E. L. and McKeachie, W. J. (1954) 'An Experimental Comparison of Recitation, Discussion and Tutorial Methods in College Teaching', *Journal of Educational Psychology*, 45:193–209.

Hamilton, D. (1975) 'Handling Innovation in the Classroom: Two Case Studies' in Reid, W. A. and Walker, D. F. (eds) *Case Studies in Curriculum Change*, London: Routledge.

Hargreaves, A. (1978) 'The Significance of Classroom Coping Strategies' in L. Barton and R. Meighan (eds), *Sociological Interpretations of Schooling and Classrooms: a Reappraisal*, Nafferton, Driffield: Studies in Education.

Hargreaves, D. H. (1967) *Social Relations in a Secondary School*, London: Routledge.

——, Hester, S. K. and Mellor, F. J. (1975) *Deviance in Classrooms*, London: Routledge & Kegan Paul.

—— (1977) 'The Process of Typification in the Classroom: Models and Methods', *British Journal of Educational Psychology*, 47:274–84

Harvard, G. and Dunne, E. (1992) 'The Role of the Mentor in Developing Teacher Competence', *Westminster Studies in Education*, 15, Abingdon: Carfax.

Haynes, H. C. (1935) 'The Relationship of Teacher Instruction, Teacher Exposition and Type of School to Types of Question', PhD dissertation, Baltimore, Md: Peabody College for Teachers.

Heath, R. W. and Nielson, M. A. (1974) 'The Research Basis for Performance-based Teacher Education', *Review of Educational Research*, 44, 4:463–84.

Highfield, M. E. and Pinsent, A. (1952) *A Survey of Rewards and Punishments in Schools: a Report*, London: NFER Newnes Educational.

HMI (DES 1987) *Quality in Schools: the Initial Training of Teachers, an HMI Survey*, London: HMSO.

Hollis, A. W. (1935) 'The Personal Relationship in Teaching', MA thesis, Birmingham University.

Houston, W. R. (1985) 'Competency-based Teacher Education', in Husen, T. and Postlethwaite, T. N. (eds) *International Encyclopedia of Education*, 2:898–906, Oxford: Pergamon.

Hyman, R. T. (1974) *Teaching: Vantage Points for Study*, New York: Lippincott Press.

ILEA, Research and Statistics Branch (1989) *Teacher Absence and Cover Arrangements*, RS 1231/89, London: ILEA.

Jackson, P. W. (1962) 'The Way Teaching Is', *NEA Journal*, 54:10–13.

—— (1968) *Life in Classrooms*, New York: Holt, Rinehart & Winston.

Johnson, M. and Brooks, H. (1979) 'Conceptualizing Classroom Management' in Duke, D. L. (ed.), *Classroom Management*, NSSE Yearbook 78, 2, Chicago: University of Chicago Press.

Kerry, T. (1984) 'Analysing the Cognitive Demand Made by Classroom Tasks in Mixed-ability Classes' in Wragg, E. C. (ed.) *Classroom Teaching Skills*, London: Croom Helm.

King, R. A. (1978) *All Things Bright and Beautiful?* Chichester: Wiley.

—— (1980) Analysis and Aggregates – Method and Meanings Perspectives 1, School of Education, University of Exeter, 38–43.

Knapp, M. C. (1980) *Essentials of Non-verbal Communication*, New York: Holt, Rinehart & Winston.

Kounin, J. S. (1970) *Discipline and Group Management in Classrooms*, New York: Holt, Rinehart & Winston.

—— and Gump, P. V. (1958) 'The Ripple Effect in Discipline', *Elementary School Journal*, 35:158–62.

Kulik, J. A., Kulik, C-L. C. and Cohen, P. A. (1979) 'A Meta-analysis of Outcome Studies of Keller's Personalized System of Instruction', *American Psychology*, 34: 307–18.

Lacey, C. (1970) *Hightown Grammar*, Manchester: Manchester University Press.

Lewin, K. (1943) 'Psychology and the Process of Group Living', *Journal of Social Psychology*, 17:113–31.

——, Lippitt, R. and White, R. K. (1939) 'Patterns of Aggressive Behaviour in Experimentally Created "Social Climates"', *Journal of Social Psychology*, 10:271–99.

Little, J. W. (1990) 'The Mentor Phenomenon and the Social Organisation of Teaching', *Review of Research in Education*, 16.

Loveys, M. (1988) 'Supplying the Demand? Contract, Mobility and Institutional Location in the Changing World of the Supply Teacher' in Ozga, J. (ed.) *Schoolwork*, Milton Keynes: Open University Press.

Lowenstein, L. G. (1975) *Violent and Disruptive Behaviour in Schools*, Hemel Hempsted: National Association of Schoolmasters.

McKeachie, W. J. (1963) 'Research on Teaching at the College and University Level' in N. L. Gage (ed.) *Handbook of Research on Teaching*, Chicago: Rand McNally.

McNamara, D. (1981) 'Attention, Time-on-task and Children's Learning: Research or Ideology?' *Journal of Education for Teaching*, 7:284–97.

Marland, M. (1975) *The Craft of the Classroom*, London: Heinemann.

Marsh, H. W. (1985) 'Student Ratings of Teaching' in Husen, T. and Postle-thwaite (eds) *International Encyclopedia of Education*, 8:4867–73, Oxford: Pergamon.

Maslow, A. H. (1970) *Motivation and Personality*, 2nd edition, New York: Harper & Row.

Medley, D. M. (1977) *Teacher Competence and Teacher Effectiveness*, Washington: American Association of Colleges for Teacher Education.

—— and Mitzel, H. E. (1963) 'Measuring Classroom Behaviour by Systematic Observation' in N. L. Gage (ed.) *Handbook of Research on Teaching*, Chicago: Rand McNally.

Meighan, R. (1977) 'The Pupil as Client: the Learner's Experience of Schooling', *Educational Review*, 29:123–35.

Morphett, M. V. and Washburne, C. (1931) 'When Should Children Begin to Read?' *Elementary School Journal*, 31:496–503.

Mortimore, P. (1988) *School Matters*, London: Open Books.

Nash, R. (1973) *Classrooms Observed*, London: Routledge.

—— (1976) *Teacher Expectations and Pupil Learning*, London: Routledge.

Neill, A. S. (1962) *Summerhill*, London: Victor Gollancz.

Partington, J. A. and Hinchcliffe, G. (1979) 'Some Aspects of Classroom Management', *British Journal of Teacher Education*, 5, 3:231–41.

Peters, R. S. (1966) *Ethics and Education*, London: Allen & Unwin.

Plowden Report (DES 1967) *Children and their Primary Schools*, Report of the Central Advisory Council for Education, London: HMSO.

Preece, P. F. W. (1979) 'Student Teacher Anxiety and Class Control Problems on Teaching Practice', *British Educational Research Journal*, 5, 1:13–19.

Redfield, D. L. and Rousseau, E. W. (1981) 'A Meta-analysis of Experimental

Research on Teacher Questioning Behaviour', *Review of Educational Research*, 51:237–45.

Rich, R. W. (1933) *The Training of Teachers in England and Wales during the Nineteenth Century*, Cambridge: Cambridge University Press.

Robertson, J. (1981) *Effective Classroom Control*, London: Hodder & Stoughton.

Rogers, C. R. (1970) *On Being a Person*, Boston: Houghton Mifflin.

Rosenshine, B. (1976) 'Classroom Instruction', in Gage, N. L. (ed.) *The Psychology of Teaching Methods*, Chicago: University of Chicago Press.

—— and Furst, N. (1973) 'The Use of Direct Observation to study Teaching', in Travers R. W. (ed.), *Second Handbook of Research on Teaching*, Chicago: Rand McNally, 122–83.

Rowe, M. B. (1972) 'Wait-time and Rewards as Instructional Variables'. Paper presented at the National Association for Research in Science Teaching, Chicago, April.

—— (1978) *Teaching Science as Continuous Enquiry*, New York: McGraw-Hill.

Rutter, M. *et al.* (1979) *15,000 Hours: Secondary Schools and their Effects on Children*, London: Open Books.

Ryle, G. (1949) *The Concept of Mind*, London: Hutchinson.

Sadker, M. and Sadker, D. (1982) 'Questioning Skills' in Cooper, J. M. (ed.) *Classroom Teaching Skills* (2nd edition), Toronto: D. C. Heath.

Samph, T. (1976) 'Observer Effects on Teacher Verbal Behaviour', *Journal of Educational Psychology*, 68, 6:736–41.

Schoen, D. (1983) *The Reflective Practitioner*, New York: Basic Books.

Schmuck, R. A. and Schmuck, P. A. (1975) *Group Processes in the Classroom*, Dubuque, Iowa: William C. Brown Co.

Simon, A. and Boyer, E. G. (eds) (1968) *Mirrors for Behavior*, 5, Philadelphia: Research for Better Schools.

Skinner, B. F. (1954) 'The Science of Learning and the Art of Teaching', *Harvard Educational Review*, 24:86–97.

Smith, B. O. and Meux, M. (1970) *A Study of the Logic of Teaching*, Urbane: University of Illinois Press.

Soar, R. S. (1973) *Follow-through Classroom Process Measurement and Pupil Growth*, Gainesville: Florida Educational Research and Development Council.

Stallings, J. A. and Mohlman, G. G. (1985) 'Observation Techniques' in Husen, T. and Postlethwaite, T. N. (eds) *International Encyclopedia of Education*, 6:3640–5, Oxford: Pergamon.

Stebbins, R. A. (1981) 'Classroom Ethnography and the Definition of the Situation' in Barton L. and Walker S. (eds), *Schools, Teachers and Teaching*, Barcombe, Sussex: Falmer Press.

Stenhouse, L. (1975) *An Introduction to Curriculum Research and Development*, London: Heinemann.

Stevens, R. (1912) 'The Question as a Measure of Efficiency in Teaching', *Teachers College Contributions to Education*, 48, Columbia, New York.

Stubbs, M. (1976) *Language, Schools and Classroom*, London: Methuen.

Swift, L. F. (1961) 'Explanation', in Smith B. O. and Ennis R. H. (eds) *Language and Concepts in Education*, 179–94, Chicago: Rand McNally.

Taba, H. (1966) Teaching Strategies and Cognitive Functioning in Elementary School Children, USOE Cooperative Research Project No. 1574, San Fransisco: San Fransisco State College.

——, Durkin, M. C., Fraenkel, J. R. and McNaughton, A. H. (1971) *A Teacher's Handbook to Elementary Social Studies*, 2nd edition, Reading, Mass.: Addison-Wesley.

Tickle, L. (1987) *Learning Teaching, Teaching Teaching . . . A Study of Partnership in Teacher Education*, London: Falmer Press.

Tisher, R. P. (1970) 'The Nature of Verbal Discourse in Classrooms and Association between Verbal Discourse and Pupil Understanding in Science' in Campbell, W. J. (ed.) *Scholars in Context*, Sidney: Wiley.

Tobin, K. (1983) 'The Influence of Wait-time on Classroom Learning', *European Journal of Science Education*, 5, 1:35–48.

Trotter, A. and Wragg, E. C. (1990) 'A Study of Supply Teachers', *Research Papers in Education*, 5, 3:251–76.

Turney, C. (ed.) (1973) Sydney Microskills Series 1, University of Sydney, Australia.

Weber, M. (1964) *The Theory of Social and Economic Organization*, New York: Free Press.

Weinstein, R. S. (1983) 'Student Perceptions of Elementary Schooling', *Elementary Schools Journal*, 83:288–312.

Wheldall, K. and Glynn, T. (1989) *Effective Classroom Learning: a Behavioural Interactionist Approach to Teaching*, Oxford: Basil Blackwell.

Wickman, E. K. (1928) *Children's Behavior and Teachers' Attitudes*, New York: Commonwealth Fund.

Wilkinson, A. (1975) *Language and Education*, London: Oxford University Press.

—— et al. (1980) *Assessing Language Development*, Oxford: Oxford University Press.

Winne, P. H. (1979) 'Experiments Relating Teachers' Use of Higher Cognitive Questions to Student Achievement', *Review of Educational Research*, 49:13–50.

Woods, P. (1979) *The Divided School*, London: Routledge.

Wragg, E. C. (1972) 'An Analysis of the Verbal Classroom Interaction between Graduate Student Teachers and Children', PhD thesis, Exeter University.

—— (1976) *Classroom Interaction,* Milton Keynes: Open University Press.

—— (1981) *Class Management and Control*, Basingstoke: Macmillan.

—— (1982) *Review of Research in Teacher Education*, Windsor: NFER–Nelson.

—— (1984) (ed.) *Classroom Teaching Skills*, London: Croom Helm.

—— (1988) *The Wragged Edge*, Stoke on Trent: Trentham Books.

—— (1990) *Riches from Wragg*, Stoke on Trent: Trentham Books.

—— (1991) *Mad Curriculum Disease*, Stoke on Trent: Trentham Books.

—— (1993) *An Introduction to Classroom Observation*, London: Routledge.

—— (1993) *Class Management*, London: Routledge.

—— and Brown, G. A. (1993) *Explaining*, London: Routledge.

—— and Dooley, P. A. (1984) 'Class Management During Teaching Practice' in Wragg, E. C. (ed.) *Classroom Teaching Skills*, London: Croom Helm.

—— and Wood, E. K. (1984) 'Teachers' First Encounters with their Classes' in Wragg, E. C. (ed.) *Classroom Teaching Skills*, London: Croom Helm.

——, Bennett, S. N., Carré, C. G. (1989) 'Primary Teachers and the National Curriculum', *Research Papers in Education*, 4, 3: 17–45. Windsor: NFER–Nelson.

Index